Praise for Peter Navarro

"[A] loyal, patriotic servant to our great President."

—**Mark Levin**

"A hero of mine, Peter Navarro…more than anybody else set the tone for our policy in dealing with China…. He was the single most effective and competent member of the entire Trump team."

—**Dick Morris**, *Dick Morris Democracy*

"I don't think anyone knows better what was happening inside the Trump White House, knowing all the players and almost all the conversations, than Peter Navarro."

—**Sean Duffy**

"One of the most important people that served in the Trump administration and was loyal to the President to the very end."

—**Charlie Kirk**, Turning Point USA

"The author of the original book exposing China…which was one of the best books I've ever read, I've been a fan of Peter Navarro for a very long time. He's been my hero, he's also been right there on voter integrity, on the scam and the fraud that went on."

—**John Fredericks**, *The John Fredericks Show*

"Part of the reason that President Trump was so successful on economic issues was because he had a brilliant economic adviser, Dr Peter Navarro."

—**Jeff Katz** on WRVA Radio, 11-11-21

"Someone who served with distinction in the Trump administration [who] really was able to…make a very positive impact…. You are a treasure."

—**Jeff Crouere**, *Real America's Voice*, 11-8-21

"He is consistently one of the guests most raved about when he comes on the show! And I'll tell you what, he's a ball of lightning."

—**Chris Stigall**, *The Chris Stigall Show*

"Smart guy and a tough guy, I love the way he rolls up his sleeves."

—**Bernie** of *Bernie & Sid* on 77 WABC Radio, "New York's News & Talk Station"

"The man that was facing off against Fauci! Peter Navarro."

—*The Trevor Carey Show*, 10-27-21

"One of my favorite people [and] one of the strongest fighters when it comes to being able to say that they actually did something to try to reverse the debacle of the 2020 election, to try to correct the errors that were taking place."

—*The JD Rucker Show*, 10-28-21

"He's awesome, wow…. I thought we were going to have a little marshmallow roast and he brought a flamethrower, I love it."

—**Clay** Travis and **Buck Sexton**

TAKING BACK
TRUMP'S
AMERICA

Also by Peter Navarro

The Coming China Wars: Where They Will Be Fought,
How They Can Be Won

Death By China: Confronting the Dragon – A Global Call to Action

Crouching Tiger: What China's Militarism Means for the World

In Trump Time: A Journal of America's Plague Year

Taking Back
TRUMP'S
AMERICA

*Why We Lost the White House
and How We'll Win It Back*

Peter Navarro

BOMBARDIER
BOOKS

Published by Bombardier Books
An Imprint of Post Hill Press

Taking Back Trump's America:
Why We Lost the White House and How We'll Win It Back
© 2022 by Peter Navarro
All Rights Reserved

ISBN: 978-1-63758-678-5
ISBN (eBook): 978-1-63758-679-2

Post Hill Press
New York • Nashville
posthillpress.com

Published in the United States of America
3 4 5 6 7 8 9 10

To the best president in modern American history, Donald John Trump. Read this book in the warm and clear light of a Mar-a-Lago day, Boss, take its lessons to heart, and you'll be even better the next time. And by the way, don't shoot the messenger. This is both my debt to history and my hope for the future.

Contents

Introduction

The mission of this book is to provide a strategic blueprint for taking back Donald Trump's America. These two of the most famous quotations in history perfectly encapsulate this book's central theme:

> *What's past is prologue.*
>
> —*The Tempest*, William Shakespeare

> *Those who cannot remember the past are condemned to repeat it.*
>
> —George Santayana, *The Life of Reason*

Here, if we are to win back the White House in 2024, we must prove Shakespeare to be as wrong as Santayana is right.

Our 2020 presidential election past must *not* be our 2024 prologue. Yet, if we in the Trump movement fail to remember the mistakes and key strategic failures of the 2020 campaign and first Trump term, we will indeed be condemned to repeat them.

We must not stumble a second time. With the Biden regime failing in virtually every dimension, we urgently need to take back our country under the red, white, and blue banner of Trumpism and Populist Economic Nationalism.

So as my old boss used to say at the beginning of every journey: "Let's Go!"

PART ONE

The Beginning and Beginning of the End

ONE

A Restive Lion Wintering in Mar-a-Lago

Elections have consequences. Stolen elections have catastrophic consequences.

—Stephen K. Bannon

Just why exactly was it that you might not have voted for Donald Trump in 2020?

Was it because of the strongest economy in modern history that Trump created, with record low unemployment, nary a whiff of inflation, and rising real wages, particularly for blue-collar and black and brown Americans?

Or was it because Trump cracked down on Communist China's economic aggression, forced an uneasy peace upon North Korea and Iran, and kept Vladimir Putin tightly pinned down in a strategic box?

Or maybe it was Trump's securing of our southern border and global supply chains while he rebuilt America's manufacturing and defense industrial base?

Or maybe, just maybe, it was those damnable tweets.

If so, how's that working out?

Clearly, not very well, as under the Joe Biden regime, everything that can go wrong seemingly is going wrong.

On the economic front, the Biden White House is grappling with a virulent stagflation, the likes of which we have not seen since the 1970s.[1] Amidst slow growth and recession, inflation has soared even as real wages have fallen.[2] While Wall Street hedges its bets and Corporate America raises prices, Main Street and blue-collar America are bearing the entire economic burden.

Not coincidentally, on our southern border, millions of illegal aliens have blown by what once was a well-functioning border wall and a solid cadre of Customs and Border Patrol agents.[3] That border is now in complete disarray as drug cartels and child traffickers transport huddled masses from around the world to our country.[4]

Never mind that it is black and brown and blue-collar Americans who now find themselves suffering from higher unemployment and stagnant wages from this invasion. Never mind that American schoolchildren are being forced to sit in ever more crowded classrooms as diseases like tuberculosis, chickenpox, and measles once thought to be under control now make a comeback in Joe Biden's Woke America.[5]

Yet, as bad as our economy and southern border are, it may be worse on the foreign policy front—and certainly more dangerous.

- A Biden-bungled Afghanistan has become a breeding ground and sanctuary for all manner of Death to America Radical Islamists;[6]
- Iran is once again fomenting state-sponsored terrorism even as the missiles once again fly in the skies over North Korea on their way perhaps one day as far as Seattle, Chicago, and New York;
- Communist China's dictator Xi Jinping has renewed his march for global domination from Africa and Latin America to the Taiwan Strait;
- A revanchist Vladimir Putin has accelerated his bid to recapture the old countries of the Soviet Union, including a battered and bleeding Ukraine;[7] and
- Xi and Putin themselves have formed an unholy alliance to mutually reinforce their imperialist and revanchist claims.

Meanwhile, with the days of Trump energy independence for America long gone, frantic calls from the Oval Office and State Department beg hostiles like Venezuela for oil even as the fracking wells of North

Dakota, Pennsylvania, and Texas remain under siege from a Let Them Eat Solar, Green Raw Deal Left.[8]

Then, there is this irony: far more people have died under the Biden regime from a virus spawned by the Chinese Communist Party than under Donald Trump's watch.[9] Wasn't Trump supposed to be the incompetent one with blood on his hands?

Faced with this bleak landscape, many Americans who voted for Joe Biden are suffering from a terminal case of buyer's remorse. According to poll after poll, if the election were held today, Trump would beat Biden handily.[10] Meanwhile, more than a third of American voters want the 2020 election overturned.[11] Yes, overturned!

None of this American angst should come as a surprise. During the 2020 election, I and others repeatedly warned of the dangers of turning the keys of the White House over to a puppet of the radical Democrats and to a man with clearly diminished mental capacity. Yet far too many Americans voted *against* an incumbent president who, simply based on this stellar record, does indeed qualify for consideration as one of the greatest presidents in American history, certainly on the economy and even perhaps on foreign policy.

So *how* exactly did this abomination happen? Just *why* is a true lion now taking his restive winters in Florida at Mar-a-Lago even as a forgetful pack mule for globalism and corporate corruption sits behind the Resolute Desk in Washington, DC?

Read on, dear reader, and all shall be revealed.

TWO

Five Strategic Failures & the Fall of the White House of Trump

Valentine's Day without my wife. My scheduled meeting with the president does not occur. His advisors are focused more on preventing him from doing what his instincts are telling him to do on tariffs than on fixing America's unfair trade problems.

—Peter Navarro, Journal Entry, February 14th, 2017

If you were to ask me what above all is Donald J. Trump's Achilles' heel, I would tell you in a nanosecond that it is Bad Personnel choices. This is a man—a figure rightly larger-than-life—who ran hard on a transformational platform of Populist Economic Nationalism on behalf of the working class.

Yet, barely after the votes were counted, President-Elect Trump would begin to surround himself with a confederacy of globalists, Never-Trump Republicans, wild-eyed Freedom Caucus nut jobs, While-and self-absorbed Wall Street transactionalists who had neither an understanding of, nor empathy for, the Trump Deplorables and those Trump Democrat blue-collar and black and brown workers who had propelled the president to his stunning and historic 2016 victory.

It would be precisely these Bad Personnel who would come to plant so many poisonous Bad Policy Trees during the Trump administration. The fruit of these poisonous trees would be Five Strategic Failures that would inexorably lead to Bad Politics, and ultimately the Fall of the White House of Trump. In effect, these Five Strategic Failures would make the 2020 presidential race close enough for Joe Biden and the Democrats to steal.

Strategic Failure #1 was, hands down, the most consequential and unforgivable. This was the failure to make Communist China the single most important issue of the 2020 campaign.

This failure would turn out to be one of the greatest missed opportunities in presidential campaign history. Indeed, running against Communist China would have effectively hit two dangerous Dragons with one very lethal campaign message.

Not only was Middle America *already* boiling mad at a mercantilist and predatory China for stealing American jobs, offshoring our factories, and killing us with deadly opioids like fentanyl. America's heartland was primed, locked, and loaded to become even more angry at an authoritarian and brutal country that was clearly responsible for a pandemic that, in real time, was turning the American Dream into a made-deadly-in-China nightmare.

Strategic Failure #2 was the failure of the president to first govern, and then run in 2020, as an unreconstructed and firebrand Populist Economic Nationalist. This failure was far from *his* fault.

Over his four years in office, many members of the president's economic, trade, and national security teams simply forgot, when critical policy decisions were being made, just what had gotten him into the Oval Office to begin with.

In their globalist-tinged amnesia, these advisors forgot how, in 2016, it was the Populist Economic Nationalism of "Buy American, Hire American," "Build That Wall," and "America First" that Candidate Trump had used as a cudgel to first vanquish sixteen Republican rivals in a primary election. This Trumpian Economic Nationalism then resonated and rolled like a Red Republican Tide across the American heartland and helped crumble the Democrat's vaunted Blue Wall states of Wisconsin, Michigan, and Pennsylvania.

It would be these three key battleground states that would help propel President Trump to his stunning victory in 2016. In 2020, however, many key players within the West Wing and on the Trump campaign would forget what we had stood for in 2016—or simply had no allegiance to the Trump agenda to begin with.

Strategic Failure #3 was the surprising and abject failure of the Trump campaign itself. To be brutally frank here, this was perhaps the most grossly mismanaged presidential campaign in modern history.

It was a campaign that went from a beautifully executed 2016 Steve Bannon masterpiece with twenty people on Trump Force One barnstorming flyover country to the ugliest kind of 2020 Air Force One equivalent of Hillary Clinton's beyond bloated Hindenburg of a campaign.

This was also a campaign that failed to see obvious trouble on the horizon in key Republican strongholds like Arizona and Georgia even as it failed to mount even a semblance of an effective offense—much less defense—against a rival who ran as little more than a middle-of-the-road chimera, cipher, and mirage in a basement.

The construction of this doomed campaign Hindenburg may be laid squarely at the doorstep of the anything but dynamic duo of the Geek Freak Brad Parscale (putatively, the campaign manager) and the Clown Prince himself, Trump son-in-law Jared Kushner (the real campaign manager). These "dumb and dumber" political geniuses—Jeff Daniels and Jim Carrey should play them in the movie version—squandered hundreds of millions of dollars on ridiculous baubles like Super Bowl ads and a massively bloated payroll.

The ultimate tragedy here was this: in that critical month of June, when the skies of American cities were black with arsonist smoke and his fortunes looked bleakest, President Trump had a chance to bring back the master strategist Bannon and put him at the helm of the campaign. The story of why that did *not* happen is one of the most compelling in this book.

Strategic Failure #4 tracks directly to the incompetence of two key Bad Personnel advisors, Treasury Secretary Steve Mnuchin and White House Chief of Staff Mark Meadows. In this particular disaster, the Boss entrusted Mnuchin and Meadows to successfully bring home a massive Phase IV Stimulus and Relief Bill prior to Election Day. Such legislation would have provided big checks in the mail to tens of millions of distressed American households and thereby given a big electoral boost to the president who had mailed those checks.

To be crystal clear here, these two "we know better than the president" Grundoons—Mnuchin and Meadows—had repeated directions from the commander in chief himself to consummate a beautiful, Make America Great Again $2 trillion package that would have helped bring our manufacturing base and supply chains home. Yet, in a glaring failure of the chain of command, both Mnuchin and Meadows let their own agendas, ideologies, and incompetence get in the way of successfully maneuvering Democrat Speaker of the House Nancy Pelosi and Senate Minority Leader Chuck Schumer into a pre-election deal.

As for Strategic Failure #5, it was the surprising inability of the White House Communications Team to fight back against the information warfare of large cadres of Never-Trump newspapers, networks, and journalists. This Orange Man Bad, Never-Trump media would run fake news circles around us, thereby dominating the all-important "daily news cycle," and ultimately leave the Boss to bellow, howl, and lash out on an almost daily basis, even as both his job approval and favorability ratings sank.

* * *

Here is the punchline and a key theme of this book: if President Trump had avoided just a few of these Five Strategic Failures, he would have won the 2020 Election in a landslide. The obvious question, of course, is just how and why did these Strategic Failures happen? The answer to this question necessarily begins in the West Wing itself.

THREE

An Insider's Look at a West Wing Dumpster

It's not the battles we lose that bother me, it's the ones we don't suit up for.

—Toby Ziegler, *The West Wing*[12]

To lay the predicate for our discussion of the Five Strategic Failures that would lead to the Fall of the White House of Trump, how about you and I take a little Aaron Sorkin "life imitates art" tour of where much of the action will occur. In the spirit of that old sports stadium maxim, "You can't tell the players without a program," I will also offer you a brief look at some of the Trump administration's key players as they take up residence in their West Wing haunts—or foxholes, as it will turn out to be.

Truth be told, the West Wing, glamorous though it may have seemed on the Martin Sheen TV series, is pretty much a dump. President Trump may or may not have once described it as such during a golf game; but there are humorously conflicting accounts of that particular alleged Trump double bogey in the press.[13]

The notable exceptions to the dumpster critique are the magnificent Oval Office, the history-drenched and regal Roosevelt Room, and the only slightly less splendid Cabinet Room in which the president's chair is slightly taller than all others. There is also the chief of staff's office if for no other reason than its comfortable size, high ceilings, and back door patio and pool.

Part of the reason why the West Wing is a such a dump is because it is so folded in upon itself. One journalist wryly dubbed it "a rabbit warren of cramped offices that seem inadequate for the powerful people who occupy them."[14] True that.

Everything small and claustrophobic about the West Wing architecture follows from the overly pragmatic goal of its 1933 renovator, New York architect Eric Gugler. That myopic goal was to simply maximize the West Wing office space.

Gugler, in his unwitting homage to the Dilbert cubicle, obviously never put himself in the shoes—or behind the desks—of the actual office occupants. Nor did Gugler ever consider in his West Wing designs the Eastern philosophy of feng shui, which involves harmonizing one's own living and working environment—an oversight which may account for the *lack* of harmony that has so very often existed over the course of the multiple administrations.

These dumpster qualities notwithstanding, I still must say it never got old walking over to the West Wing from my perch in the Eisenhower Executive Office Building for a meeting in the Roosevelt Room or the Oval Office or to grab a very decent meal in the albeit drab and equally cramped Navy Mess dining room. So walk with me now as we take a tour of the office foxholes as they were initially set up for what soon would become a polarizing war amongst all the president's men—and occasional women.

Where Situations Are Born

As you enter under the awning into the West Wing's basement, you can walk to the right to the fabled and largely windowless Situation Room—really a maze of rooms and hermetically sealed communications nodes located on the southwest corner of the building.

The Situation Room was created by President John F. Kennedy's National Security Council Director McGeorge Bundy after the 1961 Bay of Pigs Cuban invasion fiasco; and, for you Trivial Pursuit or *Jeopardy* buffs, you should know that it literally sits on the footprint of an old bowling alley. Together with an adjacent briefing room, this "Sit Room," as it is called, functions simultaneously as an intelligence support dispenser, a global communications hub, and the ultimate in crisis management theaters.

In the Sit Room, presidents and senior staff over the years have done everything from celebrating the capture of Saddam Hussein and the killing of Osama bin Laden to bungling the Iranian hostage crisis and managing the chaos after the attempted assassination of Ronald Reagan.

The Sit Room is also the Cadillac of the White House "SCIFs"— the Sensitive Compartmented Information Facilities which seal off any eavesdroppers and are strategically placed throughout the West Wing and Eisenhower Building.[15] And one of the fun things I learned early on about the Sit Room during one particular emergency is that you can ask the staff to hunt to ground just about anybody in the world on the phone, typically within minutes. I *loved* being able to do that.

Where Trade Actions Came to Die

On the opposite northwest corner of the basement are the offices of the staff secretary, who manages the paper flow throughout the White House—from the signings of presidential orders to the circulation of documents among staff and across the various agencies. It would be here where Rob Porter, a man with a perfect resume and perfect connections—Harvard, Oxford, classmate of Jared Kushner,[16] close associate of Reince Priebus—would set up an extremely efficient Never-Trump bureaucratic operation to delay, deter, and derail the president's trade agenda.

On this basement floor, in the center of the building, there were also the offices of Homeland Security Advisor Tom Bossert, and the executive secretary and chief of staff of the national security council, Lieutenant General Keith Kellogg. Among the West Wing senior staff, the youthful Bossert and grizzled veteran Kellogg were two of my most admired and respected colleagues.

Bossert's favorite expression was "lead with intelligence." He always kept his chin up and his head down, and when the hurricanes hit Houston, Florida, and Puerto Rico, all within twenty-five days,[17] Bossert would shine like the noonday Caribbean sun in the eyes of said hurricanes.

As for Kellogg, he literally *was* a grizzled veteran. He won the Silver Star for gallantry in Vietnam and also served with distinction in 1990 during Operations Desert Shield and Desert Storm.

Kellogg's favorite expression was: "If I'm not included on the take-off, I won't participate in the landing." So when Kellogg's boss H. R. McMaster would refuse to allow Kellogg to formally participate in any one of a number of policy debates—a poster child was McMaster's globalist bid to increase troop strength in Afghanistan—Kellogg would refuse to publicly join any chorus of support after the fact.

Unlike McMaster, Kellogg was a true Trump believer on the need for trade reform. Dating back to his post-army days as a corporate executive for Oracle and the Cubic Corporation, Kellogg had witnessed firsthand the unfair trade practices Communist China and others had heaped on America's heartland.

Most importantly, Kellogg was that rare breed of military man who totally understood this core Trump principle: never sacrifice America's trade policy and the factories of Ohio or Michigan or Pennsylvania on the altar of national security goals. This was a principle that McMaster in his early days, Secretary of State Rex Tillerson up to his final days, and the Pentagon's Jim Mattis in his obtuseness, would continually violate.

When Mike Flynn was fired in the first few weeks of the administration after being falsely ensnared by the FBI in a phony Russia Hoax, Kellogg would serve an ever so brief seven days as the interim NSC director. Keith was also one of the leading candidates for the permanent job, and the choice of McMaster rather than Kellogg to replace Flynn would turn out to be one of the biggest Bad Personnel mistakes of the administration.

That mistake would lead not only to more of America's workers being laid off from the factory floors of the Midwest. It would result in more American soldiers being killed, maimed, or wounded in the desert battlefields of the Middle East. The haste in hiring the globalist McMaster would indeed lay waste to the Trump agenda.

The First Floor House of Cards

As to where McMaster would hang his hat in the West Wing, let's walk now up the narrow staircase from the basement to the first floor. This is the floor where much of the administration's *House of Cards cum Game of Thrones* drama would play out, and McMaster's office on the northwest corner of the building would prove to be one of the busiest and most pivotal in pushing a foreign policy and trade agenda totally out of step with that of the president.

From his privileged perch, McMaster would often publicly contradict the president, effectively litigating issues through the press rather than privately in the Oval Office. A prime example was McMaster's insistence that the US would pay for South Korea's missile defense even as the president was asserting the opposite.[18]

As for the National Security Council itself, it was established by the National Security Act of 1947[19] and put under the umbrella of the White House in 1949.[20] In these early Cold War days, the NSC's primary mission was to add heft to the State Department's attempt to contain a rising Soviet Union.

Over time, the NSC has morphed into one of the most powerful bureaucracies in government, with broad authority to integrate foreign and defense policies and to coordinate the air force, army, marine corps, and navy, along with other national security nodes like the Central Intelligence Agency.

The real power of the NSC lies in its sheer size. Its staff hovers around 400—up from only 40 during the Clinton presidency—and this compares to less than 50 for the National Economic Council, Domestic Policy Council, or Council of Economic Advisers.[21]

As was the common practice of new NSC directors, before his firing, Mike Flynn had intended to zero out the NSC's staff of career bureaucrats detailed from various agencies like the Departments of State and Defense. Flynn would then quickly build that staff back up in the president's America First, no nation-building, end to endless wars image.

Instead, in the chaos that followed Flynn's abrupt departure, McMaster would engage in no such purge. This would prove to be a huge setback for the Trump agenda as it left McMaster in charge of a bureaucracy absolutely riddled with Obama Loyalists and Never-Trumpers.

Not without irony, the only people McMaster would wind up firing would be several top NSC staff with loyalties to Trump nationalism. They included, most prominently, Derek Harvey, Rich Higgins, and Ezra Cohen-Watnick.[22]

The Priebus Daze

Just down the hall from McMaster's office and on the opposite southwest corner of the first floor was the spacious suite and reception area of Chief of Staff Reince Priebus. It would be from this particular neck of the West Wing woods where Reince would create his own particular brand of chaos while perfecting one of his most endearing habits—the art of walking out the back door of his office to the presidential pool where he would take cell phone calls bouncing on the diving board in a pinstripe suit.

What would ultimately drown Priebus was not falling off that diving board, but rather a number of would-be chiefs of staff, including one in an office literally two doors away. This was the office of Trump son-in-law, political novice, and Rasputin in training, Jared Kushner.

Along with National Economic Council Director Gary Cohn, Kushner would constantly undermine Priebus's authority by going around, through, or over Priebus to get right to the president. The practical effect was to create a weak and hydra-headed chief of staff.

The V.P. and Bushie of Operations

Between the suites of Priebus and McMaster was Vice President Mike Pence's West Wing office. While this office was modest in size, the VP had a much more palatial setup in the Eisenhower Executive Office Building. As VPOTUS would shuttle back and forth, I would bump into him frequently; and he would always lift my spirits with a smile and a handshake and a good word—and as you shall see, at least on one occasion, he even personally intervened to make sure Gary Cohn and Treasury Secretary Steve Mnuchin did not succeed in their demands to have me fired.

In the middle of the first floor, with nary a window in sight, there was the dark lair of the deputy chief of staff for operations, Joe Hagin. To me, the Darth Vader Hagin represented a microcosm of everything that was wrong with the initial staffing of the White House. This was because Hagin was the proverbial double whammy—both a former blue blood George W. Bushie AND a loyal soldier for Priebus's anti-Trump Republican National Committee.

A soft and billowy marshmallow of a bureaucrat with all of the humor of Dick Cheney, Hagin had wormed his way into the halls of power with a frat boy BA from Kenyon College. He got his start by helping George H. W. Bush during his failed presidential bid in 1979 and then leveraged that stint into working as Bush's personal assistant when he was vice president. After serving as George W. Bush's deputy campaign manager during the 2000 presidential run, Hagin then latched on to the operations job for most of the Bush presidency.

That people like Hagin would wind up in positions of power within the Trump administration always boggled my mind, and during both the Priebus Daze and Kelly Interregnum, Hagin would use his not inconsiderable powers to subtly thwart the more transformational aspects of the Trump agenda. Most notably, this included trade and immigration policy reforms that were anathema to the Bushies and Republican National Committee crowd.

For example, Hagin could block the hiring of staff that he viewed as Trump subversives by pleading, as he often misleadingly did, a lack of budget. It was all so much Bushie BS—he was swimming in discretionary cash.

Never In My Wildest Dreams

Rounding out the first floor of the West Wing, there was the Oval Office, which we will talk much more about later, and the Roosevelt Room, where I lost many a battle in the trade wars. There were also the offices of the press secretary where Priebus ally and former RNC communications director Sean Spicer would preside over a decidedly not so merry band of support staff.

The collective foul mood and low morale in the press shop was the direct result of having to constantly shovel the angry manure Spicer would fertilize the downstairs press room with during what would soon become his infamously contentious and counterproductive daily briefings.

As for the Roosevelt Room itself, it sits windowless in almost the exact center of the West Wing's first floor. Named for both Teddy and Franklin Delano Roosevelt, it is the room that originally housed Teddy's West Wing office.

By the way, the Roosevelt Room is also the place Franklin Delano used to call the "fish room" because he kept his aquariums there. In an ever so subtle thumbing of his nose at FDR and his liberalism, President

Richard Nixon would rechristen the Roosevelt room in honor of both FDR *and* Teddy.

In the battleground of the Roosevelt Room, I would often be the only person in a group of fifteen or more senior staff and cabinet secretaries who agreed with the president's trade agenda. When the president himself was in the meeting, the two of us would have to fight the likes of Tillerson, Cohn, Mattis, McMaster, Mnuchin, and Secretary of Agriculture Sonny Perdue on issues ranging from the imposition of steel tariffs to the termination of the NAFTA trade deal.

Most commonly, particularly in the early days of the administration, that globalist majority would carry the day in the Roosevelt room. They would simply wear the president down by coming at him from all angles. I simply didn't have the firepower to give him the support he needed.

The first time this happened, I was flabbergasted. Never did I imagine in my wildest nightmares that the strongest opposition to the president's trade agenda would come from *inside* the White House perimeter. However, as these fifth-columnist attacks by the president's closest advisors happened time and time again, I came to understand that there is a not-so-fine line between loyalty to the president versus loyalty to the president's agenda, and it was a line that far too many of POTUS's senior staff and cabinet officials were willing to cross.

It is indeed a slippery slope to believe that to be loyal to a president, you must be disloyal to his agenda. But that is the slope far too many people in the Trump administration chose to toboggan down at breakneck speed.

A Globalist Dog of War

While the first floor of the West Wing was ground zero in the battle for the heart and mind of the president, the second floor of the West Wing was no less contentious. On one side of the building was Gary Cohn's National Economic Council suite of offices. It was housed alongside a number of smaller suites for the president's daughter Ivanka Trump, the administration's most pugnacious media surrogate Kellyanne Conway, and one of the most nimble of bureaucratic infighters, the political seductress otherwise known as Dina Powell.

Cohn was pure Goldman Sachs testosterone, prone to putting his leg up on a chair like a dog. He would actually comically try that shtick right in the Oval Office during our infamous "fiery exchange" on day sixty-six of the administration—stay tuned for that account in all its slapstick comedy glory.

On the other side of the wall from Cohn's foxholes, and light-years away from Cohn in both demeanor and ideology, was the president's speechwriter and senior policy advisor, the thirty-something wunderkind Stephen Miller. By day one of the administration, the supremely devotional and introverted Miller had already made the perhaps forgivable but huge mistake of actually doing his duty—which in the run-up to Inauguration Day had been mostly to draft the president's speech.

Through such devotion, Miller would take his eye off the power ball and wind up losing much of his turf to Cohn's National Economic Council. In the first fifty days of the administration, I would personally suffer from Miller's singular focus on his speechwriting while he ignored the ugly politics and turf battles swirling around him. By the time Miller woke up, it was too late, and Miller would later come to deeply regret this miscalculation.

Legal Eagles and Legislative Affairs

Rounding out the key offices on the second floor of the West Wing were those of the White House Legal Counsel, with Don McGahn at the helm, and the Office of Legislative Affairs, run by the oil and water dueling duo of Rick Dearborn and Marc Short.

McGahn is perhaps most famous for his quite successful efforts to eliminate any restrictions on campaign financing. McGahn thereby opened the door to the massive infusions of corporate cash into America's elections that followed in the wake of the 2010 *Citizens United* Supreme Court decision.[23]

While McGahn's old law firm's website describes him as one of the "architect(s) of the campaign finance revolution,"[24] his detractors on the Common Cause side of the money aisle think of him as a Swamp Creature counter-revolutionary who opened the floodgates of Washington to even more dark special interest money.[25] (Just for the record, I think Common Cause had it right.)

I would very quickly and quite unwittingly get blindsided by Don McGahn because I naively assumed his office would enthusiastically embrace the trade-related executive orders and presidential memoranda I had developed during the presidential transition and had ready for signing on the first business day of the administration. These presidential actions, which in hindsight were clearly alien to McGahn's ideology, had been carefully vetted for what's called "form and legality" by a walled-off compartment of the Obama Justice Department specifically assigned to the Trump transition team for such matters. However, McGahn viewed my orders like they were the plague, and along with Staff Secretary Rob Porter, Gary Cohn, and Reince Priebus, McGahn would be part of the institutional tonnage that would crush those Trumpian presidential actions faster than a Chinese tank running over a Tiananmen Square protester.

It would also be McGahn's office that would let slip a poorly crafted and sparsely vetted immigrant ban executive order just one week into the administration. This order sought to temporarily suspend the entry of refugees and the re-entry of green card holders into the US from some of the worst incubators of Islamic extremism on the planet, including Iran, Libya, Somalia, and Yemen.[26] However, the flawed order would get embarrassingly hung up in the courts for months.

This rookie mistake by the White House's legal team had the practical and paralytic effect of making it far more difficult to get even the simplest executive order through the review process. It was a mistake that would haunt my own efforts to move executive orders through the review process for months—although in hindsight, I now strongly suspect McGahn might have made that alleged mistake on purpose to sabotage both Bannon's efforts and the Boss's actions.

As for the Office of Legislative Affairs just down the hall from McGahn, the décor for this bank of cubicles should have been early *Titanic*. It was here where the foolish idea to start the legislative agenda with the "repeal and replacement" of Obamacare was blessed. Priebus and Leg Affairs would, however, fail abysmally to deliver the requisite votes on Capitol Hill, and this crushing early Obamacare defeat would prove to be a millstone around the necks of both a Republican Congress wracked by infighting and a White House wondering what freight train just hit it.

At least part of this failure stemmed from the lack of anyone within Leg Affairs with the ability to actually cross the aisle and woo Democrats. The even bigger problem, however, was the inherent friction and blurred lines of authority between Rick Dearborn and Marc Short.

Dearborn was the former chief of staff to Alabama Republican senator Jeff Sessions. Sessions had been the very first Senator to endorse Candidate Trump, and that endorsement had come at a very critical time in the campaign. During that campaign, Dearborn would prove to be an indispensable soldier and an unimpeachable Trump loyalist and his cream would rise to the top in his role as executive director of the transition team.

In recognition of his service, Dearborn had originally been promised complete control of the Office of Legislative Affairs in his role as a White House deputy chief of staff. However, in yet another move to establish the primacy of the Republican National Committee over the Trump loyalists, Priebus had brought in Marc Short, fresh off campaign trail for Vice President Mike Pence.

Short was not just an RNC RINO blue blood. He was also a Koch network dark conservative money conduit who had as little affinity for the Trump trade agenda as the Koch brothers themselves. While Short would technically report to Dearborn, Priebus made sure that technicality was ignored, and Short was then free to rule the Leg Affairs roust.[27] This would indeed turn out to be a train wreck for the Trump agenda.

And so, within the West Wing, the foxholes were manned and womaned on day one. The battle lines were clearly drawn, and the epic struggle that would be billed by the media without any appropriate nuance as a match between the globalist and nationalist wings of the Trump administration was about to unfold.

PART TWO

Prelude to a
Post-Mortem

FOUR

The Coming China Wars Gets My Trump Ball Rolling

This is not some natural disaster. It is politician-made disaster. It is the consequence of a leadership class that worships globalism over Americanism.

—Candidate Donald J. Trump, Jobs Plan Speech, June 16, 2016[1]

One of the most surreal mornings I ever spent was in early June of 2016. I had taken the eight-minute walk down the hill from my home in Laguna Beach to one of the most beautiful stretches of sand on the planet, Victoria Beach.

This stunning half mile of sandy heaven overlooking the Pacific Ocean was my hallowed ground from where I would launch my paddle board and cruise out among the seals and dolphins. And on a clear day, sometimes I would just sit in the warm sand and gaze at Catalina Island just over thirty miles of cold clear water away.

On this particular day, however, there would be nary a glimpse of Santa Catalina. It was crisp and overcast with the infamous "June Gloom" clouds that afflict Southern California annually. The surreal nature of the morning began when my cell phone rang with a call from Stephen Miller, who had already hooked his rising star to Candidate Trump as his number one (and only) official speechwriter.

For weeks, I had been working *unofficially* with Stephen on a major policy address Candidate Trump was scheduled to give on June 16 at a steel recycling facility outside of Pittsburgh. Stephen was calling to go over some of the final text of that speech, and as I sat down in the sand hoping that my cell phone reception would hold, the key thing that kept popping into my mind was how close I was to power—yet, in tiny Laguna Beach, so far away.

Parsing the China Price

My journey to Victoria Beach—and eventually to the Trump White House—had begun years earlier in 2003 in an MBA classroom at the University of California-Irvine. It was at UCI where I would spend more than twenty-five years of my professional life teaching macroeconomics and public policy primarily to fully employed MBA students.

These students would dutifully report for their MBA duty on weekends and evenings, and this was a schedule ideally suited to my own sensibilities and biorhythms as it allowed me to get my analytics and writing done in the clear light of day—with more than a few breaks for some sunshine and exercise.

It was in 2003 when I began to notice two peculiar trends begin to emerge. First, a significant number of my *fully employed* students were losing their jobs. This was particularly strange given the strength of the Orange County job market, perennially one of the most robust and resilient in the country.

The second disturbing trend was that even those students who *were* employed were no longer getting the same kind of generous tuition support from their corporate employers. This was no small thing as it is at least $100,000 to get that MBA degree.

Clearly, something was afoot—and perhaps very rotten—in the MBA market; and with my curiosity piqued, I set about investigating just what might be going wrong. Very quickly, all roads began leading to Beijing.

What I discovered was a phenomenon known as the "China Price," which was the ability of Communist Chinese producers to offer products in the global marketplace at prices astonishingly low—often 50 percent below that of competitors and sometimes, equally curiously, at prices well below the cost of production. With the China Price as the tip of their spears, these Chinese Communist producers were grabbing huge chunks of global market share, particularly here in the United States—and thereby beginning to put Americans like my MBA students out of work.

It was no coincidence that the effects of Communist China's attack on world markets began to surface in 2003. This was shortly after China joined the World Trade Organization in December of 2001.

While I tell that particular "Pirate China joins the WTO" story in great detail in my 2011 *Death by China* film and companion book, I had as yet, in 2003, not put that particular plot point together. Instead, the prevailing conventional wisdom at the time—and null hypothesis as we say in the trade—was that Communist China's competitive advantage was derived simply from a seemingly endless source of cheap labor. Skeptic that I was, I thought there might be something else going on.

So it was that I set about analyzing the China Price phenomenon in typical MBA professor fashion. For a full year, I conscripted my cadres of MBA students to do a deep dive on just how the Communist Chinese were winning the global market wars. In the course of that year, over two hundred of my students would be involved in both developing company-specific case studies and doing deep-dive statistical analytics. The result was a seminal "production cost analysis" published in the academic journal *China Perspectives*.

The top line findings from this seminal study presaged my framing of Communist China's economic aggression in the White House as China's "Seven Deadly Mercantilist Sins." These findings pointedly noted the role of unfair trade practices such as currency manipulation, counterfeiting, and illegal export subsidies in China's assault on American and global markets.

Here is how I wrote the research up for publication in *China Perspectives*—and note my ever-so-small "boxers versus briefs" attempt at humor, even in an academic journal. Sometimes, I just can't help myself:

Chinese manufacturers have the capability to significantly undercut prices offered by foreign competitors over a wide range of products. Today, as a result of the "China price," China has captured over 70%

of the world's market share for DVDs and toys, more than 50% for bikes, cameras, shoes and telephones, and more than one-third for air conditioners, colour televisions, computer monitors, luggage and microwave ovens. It has also established dominant market positions in everything from furniture, refrigerators and washing machines to jeans and underwear (yes, boxers and briefs).

This article examines the eight major economic drivers of the China price and provides estimates of their relative contributions to China's manufacturing competitive advantage. Lower labour costs account for 39% of the China price advantage…. The remainder…is **driven by elements challenged as unfair trade practices by foreign competitors.** *These include export subsides, which account for 17% of the advantage, an undervalued currency (11%), counterfeiting and piracy (9%), and lax environmental and worker health and safety regulatory regimes (5%).*[2] *[emphasis added]*

It would be this seminal research that would give rise to my first book and what would turn out eventually to be a Communist China trilogy. These prescient works would include *The Coming China Wars* (2006), the aforementioned *Death By China* (2011), and *Crouching Tiger: What China's Militarism Means For The World* (2015).

The Coming China Wars would be my first bestseller, and it would lay bare both China's economic aggression as well as its tendency to sell to the American consumer literally millions of products that could harm or kill you or your pets. More importantly in terms of this opus, it would be The Coming China Wars that would be responsible for me winding up in the Trump White House.

In 2011, Citizen Trump would place *The Coming China Wars* in his top ten favorite books about China. That kindness would, in turn, catalyze a correspondence between me and the president through his executive assistant Rhona Graff. And when the Boss announced his candidacy for president in 2016, in part on a Tough on China platform, *I was all in.*

And so it was that I now found myself sitting in the warm sand on Victoria Beach talking to Candidate Trump's one and only speechwriter about what would become arguably the best speech—at least on economics and trade—of the president's career.

Prelude to a Post-Mortem

Pure Deplorables Poetry

The Pittsburgh "Jobs Plan" speech as it was dubbed began like this:

> *We are thirty miles from Steel City [and] the legacy of Pennsylvania steelworkers lives in the bridges, railways and skyscrapers that make up our great American landscape. But our workers' loyalty was repaid with betrayal.*
>
> *Our politicians have aggressively pursued a policy of globalization—moving our jobs, our wealth and our factories to Mexico and overseas. Globalization has made the financial elite who donate to politicians very wealthy. But it has left millions of our workers with nothing but poverty and heartache.*
>
> *When subsidized foreign steel is dumped into our markets, threatening our factories, the politicians do nothing. For years, they watched on the sidelines as our jobs vanished and our communities were plunged into depression-level unemployment. Many of these areas have still never recovered.*
>
> *Our politicians took away from the people their means of making a living and supporting their families. Skilled craftsmen and tradespeople and factory workers have seen the jobs they loved shipped thousands of miles away. Many Pennsylvania towns once thriving and humming are now in a state of despair.*
>
> *This wave of globalization has wiped out our middle class. It doesn't have to be this way. We can turn it all around—and we can turn it around fast.*[3]

At least to my high mind and perhaps low brow tastes, this is pure Deplorables poetry. Note the Make American Great Again or "MAGA" play on words where American steel "make(s) up our great American landscape." Note, too, the sharp angle of attack on unfair trade with its references to "subsidized foreign steel…dumped into our markets" while the "politicians do nothing."

This Jobs Plan speech also debuts the enduring blue-collar theme of "American Carnage," an anti-globalization theme that is as far from Norman Rockwell as Cleveland is from Beijing. Intones Trump, from "thriving and humming" towns, we have descended into a "state of despair" as globalization "has wiped out our middle class."

Of course, it's the politicians who are really to blame because they took away our "means of making a living and supporting [our] families."

27

Promises Candidate Trump: "It doesn't have to be this way." "We"—note the "we"!—"We can turn it all around, and we can turn it around fast."

Abe Lincoln wrote the Gettysburg address in 269 words. Donald Trump's beautiful introduction to his Jobs Plan speech, which perfectly captures the essence of Trumpism, is but 206 words.

Complain now all you want that Trump is certainly no Abe Lincoln—and I will agree. But this speech was sheer political and policy poetry, and I got to be a part of it sitting in the Southern California sand listening to the good vibrations surf pound the shoreline as I spoke with Stephen Miller on the phone.

Now here is my second favorite part of that speech. It's barely longer than a haiku. Note its tight cadence:

> *The inner cities will remain poor.*
> *The factories will remain closed.*
> *The borders will remain open.*
> *The special interests will remain firmly in control.*[4]

That's as pure a political call to action as it gets. Time for a change. Throw the rascals (and Crooked Hillary) out! She is a puppet of the special interests. I, Donald John Trump, am your MAGA huckleberry.

Next in the speech quickly comes a core Populist Economic Nationalist principle: to make America great again, we must make American manufacturing great again. Says Candidate Trump:

> *America became the world's dominant economy by becoming the world's dominant producer. The wealth this created was shared broadly, creating the biggest middle class the world had ever known.*
>
> *But then America changed its policy from promoting development in America, to promoting development in other nations. We allowed foreign countries to subsidize their goods, devalue their currencies, violate their agreements, and cheat in every way imaginable.*
>
> *Trillions of our dollars and millions of our jobs flowed overseas as a result.* [5]

Again, that's pure MAGA magic. If you want your blue-collar job and your white picket fence back, then America must once again become the "dominant economy" and "dominant producer." The only way that happens is if a *President* Donald Trump cracks down on the unfair trade practices of foreign countries like China that "subsidize their goods, devalue their currencies, violate their agreements, and cheat in every way imaginable."

Promises Made, Promises (Sort of) Kept

This historic 2016 Jobs Plan speech ends with seven critical promises to the American people, and here, I can say that President Trump at least *sort of* kept every one of those promises. But that was the problem—and would be part of the strategic failures—in 2020. President Trump only "sort of" kept all of those promises.

Promise #1 was to withdraw the United States from the Trans-Pacific Partnership, the TPP. We did this literally on the first business day in office with me standing to the Boss's side in the Oval Office, and there is an iconic newswire photo capturing this epic moment in American economic nationalist history.[6]

What I love about this iconic photo—one of the few pictures that hangs in my new office as I am not a sentimental man—is that it is a study in my own survivability. Little did I know at the time that of the ten senior staff ringed around POTUS at his Resolute Desk, the only two of us in the picture who would survive the entire administration would be me and my fellow Jobs Plan speech writer Stephen Miller. Gone either in the short or long run would be Reince Priebus, Kellyanne Conway, Hope Hicks, Don McGahn, Steve Bannon, Rob Porter, Andrew Bremberg, and Stephanie Grisham.

And by the way, it was a very good thing we withdrew from the TPP because the entire architecture of that job-killing, sovereignty-sapping abomination was designed to ship off our auto and auto parts industries to Vietnam and Japan—all in the hopes of gaining some kind of ill-defined geopolitical advantage over a rising, predatory, and increasingly militaristic Chinese Communist beast.

Beijing's Ambassador of Sleaze

Promise #2 was to "appoint the toughest and smartest trade negotiators to fight on behalf of American workers." While I would like to think that I might fit that bill, I can't think of a single other person in the administration who consistently met that high standard.

Instead, Bad Personnel like Gary Cohn, Larry Kudlow, and Steve Mnuchin fought fiercely on behalf of Wall Street capital. Wilbur Ross was at best an uncertain trumpet. And almost everybody else in the rest of the Trump cabinet as well as our diplomatic corps traveled on the globalist side of the offshoring street—Ag Secretary Sonny Perdue, King Rex at State, and the ambassador to China Terry Branstad were particularly notable disasters.

By the way, there are a lot of examples I could offer to corroborate the claim of POTUS that he is a "genius," but the appointment of Branstad, a former sleazebag governor from the farm state of Iowa, to be ambassador to Communist China certainly would not be one of them.

Any damn fool knew going into a tough negotiation with China that the one place the ChiComs could, and certainly would, exert maximum political pressure on America would be in our farm states. This is because Communist China buys *massive* quantities of everything from soybeans, wheat, and sorghum to poultry and beef—and therefore buys considerable political leverage.

As such a damn fool myself, I knew damn well—and POTUS should have too—that as soon as we started applying any kind of tariff pressure, the Beasts of Beijing would slap retaliatory tariffs on American farmers. And they would also screw with our farmers by doing other things like leaving shipments of soybeans and fresh produce like cherries to rot on the docks of Shanghai—a nasty little tactic known in unfair trade circles as a "nontariff barrier."

So looking at this particular chessboard, the last person you would want to send to Beijing as the ambassador would be someone like Branstad who would always be whining about the pressure on the farmers in his home state—a state, by the way, which is arguably *the* politically most important of the farm states.

And it wasn't just whining with Branstad. He was constantly screwing with the cable traffic flow from China and trying to insert himself into the trade negotiations with the Communists in ways that often weakened Ambassador Robert E. Lighthizer's position as Chief Negotiator.

By the way, the other thing that REALLY pissed me off about Branstad was his Deep Swamp unregistered foreign agent of a son Eric. After briefly working for Secretary Wilbur Ross at the Department of Commerce, this Branstad spawn would set up his own consulting firm to leverage daddy's position as ambassador and thereby cash in on the China trade. At one point, young Branstad would even play a critical role lobbying POTUS to needlessly pull a critical punch thrown at the scofflaw Chinese spy company ZTE—much more about that later.

A Micromanager Mucks It All Up

Promise #3 to "identify every violation of trade agreements" and "end these abuses" was one of my greatest disappointments as I worked personally on writing the executive order to keep that promise. The order was, in fact, published on April 29, 2017 and directed Secretary of Commerce Wilbur Ross to get the job done.[7] At the helm of a hapless bureaucracy he had no real idea how to run, Wilbur instead just fell flat on his face.

I was not surprised in the least. Little in Ross's extensive Lone Ranger vulturing experience as Wall Street's "King of Bankruptcy" prepared Wilbur to also be the King of Bureaucracy, and his tendency towards micromanagement made him his own worst enemy.

I remember one time when we had an executive order on what was literally its twentieth and final iteration. After what should have been a simple *pro forma* approval from someone down the bureaucratic chain at Commerce, I got back handwritten copy edits from Wilbur—that's right, copy edits—on a smudged copy of the order sent by fax.

My first thought was: "Who uses frigging fax machines anymore?" My second was: "This is crazy. If Wilbur is wasting his time doing stuff like this, just imagine what he is NOT doing."

The Elmer Fudd of Bankruptcy

The first time I met Wilbur was at Candidate Trump's suggestion. It was at the 2016 Republican National Convention in Cleveland on July 19, 2016, and it was a fun and very heady time in my life.

At the very last redeye flight minute, I had been dispatched to the convention by the campaign to handle some of the media hits. With all of the hotels fully booked by that point, I grabbed a very cool Airbnb apartment just north of the airport.

The next day, I met Wilbur at noon in a big hallway of one of the convention buildings, and we sat on a bench *sans* any refreshments and just talked about what we might do together. My first impression of him was that of the old Looney Tunes character Elmer Fudd, albeit with an IQ at least one hundred points higher.

Truth be told here, Wilbur just comes off a bit goofy with that deliberate monotone of his and occasional impish smile that plays so well on business networks like *Bloomberg* and CNBC but often falls flat when he takes that show on the road to CNN or MSNBC or *Fox and Friends*.

At any rate, the story Wilbur told me that day was as priceless as it was instructive. In the early 2000s, as the unfair trade practices and massive dumping of countries like Communist China began catching up to the US steel industry with a vengeance and more than thirty US steel companies went bankrupt, in swooped Wilbur the Bankruptcy King to snap up American icons like Bethlehem Steel.[8]

Wilbur would wind up flipping these companies for a profit in the hundreds of millions of dollars, but not before he personally lobbied President George W. Bush for steel tariffs that would prop up the industry. These Bush tariffs would thereby turn the "distressed assets" he had just acquired into moneymaking machines ripe for a quick sale at a tariff price premium.

Wilbur was quite matter-of-fact about how he had his lobbying way with W. Bush in the Oval; and that is the point here: Wilbur not only saw an opportunity to buy distressed assets at a steep discount; he baldly and boldly manipulated the political process to make sure that the value of those assets would spike even higher than the market might otherwise yield.

The bigger takeaway of this story is this: Wilbur spent his entire life running the corporate equivalent of a small Seal Team that made him rich enough for the Palm Beach life. Yet, when he got to Washington, DC, he was poorly equipped to manage a bureaucracy like the Department of Commerce with its more than forty thousand employees, and our trade policy would suffer mightily.

A NAFTA Tariff Sellout

Promise #4 was to renegotiate NAFTA. Check *that* box, although it took over three years to close the deal.

To my deepest regret, it would take the gutting of our steel and aluminum tariffs by United States Trade Representative Bob Lighthizer to get the new United States-Mexico-Canada Agreement (USMCA) to the finish line. The primary problem with getting to "yes" on the USMCA was with the hardliner Canadians—their hidden agenda was to keep NAFTA just the way it was because, at least for them, NAFTA was like legalized highway robbery of American auto workers, steel producers, loggers, dairy farmers, and the American economy writ large.

Lighthizer's sacrifice of the steel and aluminum tariffs to get to a NAFTA "yes" would, however, turn out to be a very bad MAGA trade-off that would inflict great cost and pain in Blue Wall country. It likely cost us swing blue-collar votes in several key battleground states where the alleged Biden victory was very narrow.

Neville Mnuchin Ignores the Chain of Command

Now, if you have read any of my books or research articles on Communist China, you may guess that my biggest disappointment with President Trump's Jobs Plan list of promises was our failure to follow through in a timely way with Promise #5. This was for the Boss "to instruct my Treasury Secretary to label China a currency manipulator."

It's not that the Boss didn't order Treasury Secretary Steve Mnuchin to do this numerous times. It's just that Steve always refused. This was a classic example of Mnuchin disobeying the chain of command to advance his own Wall Street agenda.

It would take until August 5, 2019, and at least twenty knock-down, drag-out fights in the Oval between me and the Munchkin for Stevie to finally label China a currency manipulator.[9] But even then, it was a case of "so what?" Mnuchin would NEVER use the full powers of the Treasury Department to actually make this designation meaningful.

If, instead, we had immediately labeled China a currency manipulator on that same day in January of 2017 that we had withdrawn from the Trans-Pacific Partnership—and I had written a very clear and crisp executive order instructing Mnuchin to do so—we would have struck right at the heart of one of the worst abuses of Communist China. Moreover, and this kind of subtlety was always lost on both Mnuchin and, later in the administration, Larry Kudlow, designating China a currency manipulator, with all the powers such a designation entailed, would have given us an invaluable bargaining chip for the China trade negotiations.

As for Promises #6 and #7, these laid out our strategy to bring trade cases against China to stop its "unfair subsidy behavior" and "use every lawful presidential power," including Section 301 of the Trade Act of 1974.

Besides Promise #1, getting out of the Trans-Pacific Partnership, these were the two promises where we really shined. But boy, as I have shown you, did we leave a lot of good things that would have helped us in 2020 both on the table and the cutting room floor. As to why this was so, let's continue this walk down memory lane as it provides a lot of the appropriate context for our ultimate strategic failures.

FIVE

A Two-Day Big Apple Popover Turns Into a Five-Year Tour

Gilligan: Hiya, Professor. What are you doing?

Professor Roy Hinkley: I'm making notes for a book. It's to be a chronicle of our adventures on the island...I think it's a book people will want to buy, don't you?

Gilligan: Sure, I'll buy one. I'm dying to find out what happens to us.

Gilligan's Island, 1964

So just before noon on September 16, 2016, I get into the back of a black SUV and sit behind the Boss. It will be my first face-to-face meeting with him—but I don't quite see his face yet.

He's talking on his cell phone first to Rupert Murdoch. "How we doing Rupert? How are we doing? What are you hearing?"

And then as the SUV begins bobbing and weaving on our way out to LaGuardia Airport to board Trump Force One, he's talking rapid-fire to Roger Ailes: "How are the polls looking Roger? I think they are looking good. I'm feeling good."

Then Donald John Trump ends the call and looks back at me. I'm speechless as he tries to figure out who the hell I am. Then, he puts two and two and *The Coming China Wars* together, and he hits me with a big welcome-aboard smile.

Yes, welcome to the Big Apple you Laguna Beach rube. And welcome to the big time.

And the big time it was. But in a peculiarly small way.

It was twenty people on an airplane. One hundred more in the Trump Tower War Room, working seven days a week. A few money guys upstairs raising about half of what Hillary would spend.[10] And all the free press the mainstream media could give this never-before-seen roadshow. That was the ethos, strategy, and organizational culture of the come-from-behind, close the deal Trump 2016 campaign, and I was about to become an integral part of it.

Death By China Does Manhattan

Two days earlier, I had flown at my own expense from Orange County, California to New York City with only the suit on my back and a laptop bag on my shoulder. It was supposed to be a quick, two-day, no luggage tour of the Trump for President headquarters. Little did I know at the time that this would be the beginning of the end of my days as an academic in sunny SoCal and, like Gilligan, the beginning of five long years on the island of Trump.

Months earlier, I had become one of the first to predict Candidate Trump would win the presidency and the first economist to endorse him—Harvard PhD, circa 1986, if you are interested in my bona fides. I made that startling Trump-will-crush-it prediction based on years of research as well as some intimate boots-on-the-ground knowledge.

Four years earlier during the 2012 presidential campaign between Mitt Romney and Barack Obama, I had toured the heartland of America with my *Death By China* film trying to raise political awareness on both sides of the aisle of the importance of unfair trade in the decline of the US industrial base.

During that barnstorming tour, I saw firsthand some of the more than fifty thousand American factories that had been shut down because of bad trade deals like NAFTA and unfair trade practices like currency manipulation, intellectual property theft, and sweatshop labor. I had also spoken with hundreds of laid off workers about their own personal descents into socioeconomic hell—the bankruptcies and foreclosures; the divorces and increased drug use; the abject despair, alcoholism, and depression.

While neither Barack Obama nor Mitt Romney would ultimately make trade reform the centerpiece of their 2012 campaigns as I had hoped and strived for, Candidate Trump brought trade abuses front and center stage in 2016. He saw early on that his path to victory ran through the political swing states hardest hit by import competition—Michigan, Ohio, and Pennsylvania most certainly but also other key states like North Carolina, Wisconsin, and even dirt poor, hardscrabble Maine.

Donald J. Trump—DJT as those closest to him call the man—had indeed seen the problem of unfair trade early on. As far back as the 1980s, then Real Estate Tycoon Trump had complained bitterly about how Japan was having its way with American workers while President Ronald Reagan played the free trade dupe—and a running joke between DJT and me was whether it was he or I who first saw the trade abuse problem.

For the record, it was DJT, and he beat me by more than a decade and country mile. This classic DJT quote from a 1988 appearance on *The Oprah Winfrey Show* perfectly foreshadowed Candidate Trump's anti-globalist, fair and reciprocal trade platform.

> [W]e let Japan come in and dump everything right into our markets. It's not free trade. If you ever go to Japan right now and try to sell something, forget about it Oprah. Just forget about it. It's almost impossible. They don't have laws against it. They just make it impossible. They come over here. They sell their cars. Their VCRs. They knock the hell out of our companies. And hey, I have tremendous respect for the Japanese people. I mean you can respect somebody that's beating the hell out of you. But they are beating the hell out of this country.[11]

Just substitute the word China for Japan in DJT's 1988 quote, and you basically have both the cornerstone of the Trump 2016 trade platform and the linchpin of DJT's stump speech.

The New York Kazillionaires Club

On my first full day in New York city, I spent the morning at the campaign headquarters at Trump Tower. There, I got a tour of the 14th floor War Room, and met some of the key players face to face—Jason Miller, director of communications; Bryan Lanza, Jason Miller's deputy in charge of the TV surrogates; the policy at least semi-wonks in the personas of Dan Kowalski and John Mashburn; Dave Bossie, the former head of Citizen's United and the campaign's deputy campaign manager; Brad Parscale, the computer geek; a very gruff and growly Stephen K. Bannon; and, of course, at the top of my list of folks I wanted to meet in person, the Candidate's speech writer Stephen Miller, who had recruited me for the visit.

Duly welcomed, I then walked down Fifth Avenue to the regal digs of the Economic Club of New York. There, I watched with no small awe and amusement as Candidate Trump shocked the crowd of mostly arrogant, hostile, and skeptical kazillionaires with fiery, in-your-Wall-Street-face, fair trade luncheon remarks that riffed off many of the passages and promises in the Pittsburgh Jobs Plan speech. Said DJT to his New York skeptics:

> *If China does not stop its illegal activities, including its theft of American trade secrets and intellectual property, I will apply countervailing duties until China ceases and desists.*
>
> *Just the single action of enforcing intellectual property rules alone would add millions of new American jobs.... We are going to stop the outflow of jobs from our country, and open a new highway of jobs back into our country.*[12]

Of course, these fighting words in the belly of the Wall Street beast were breathtaking in their scope. At this inspiring time, however, I had no idea of the sturm and drang and inside attacks that would be coming—and many for me. Instead, in my ignorant bliss, Candidate Trump's rhetoric was simply heady stuff.

The Florida Poor Boys Club

It was even headier stuff when I hopped on the Trump campaign plane the next day and headed down to Florida for one of the Candidate's signature rallies. As we approached the arena, those unfortunate enough not to have gotten tickets ringed the venue—there would be twice as many supporters outside as in.

At the rally itself—really more of an admixture between a 1960s love-in and a gospel choir revival in the Bible Belt—the excitement was beyond palpable. On the floor of the arena, as I mingled in my suit and tie and rubbed elbows with the T-shirted crowd, I watched the Candidate weave countless improvisations into a bare bones teleprompter speech for more than an hour. He would leave this merry band of what Hillary Clinton would later haplessly dub as "Deplorables" with great hope. Their economic misery would soon end with a wave of Trumpian tax, trade, immigration, and regulatory reforms—and no more endless war adventures either, thank you very much.

On the plane ride back to the Big Apple, I saw the chess board perfectly—DJT was going to win if only he continued to carry that same Populist Economic Nationalist message. When Stephen Miller asked me to stay in New York and help develop a more detailed economic plan for the campaign, that's exactly what I did, and the very next day, I set up shop on the 14th floor of Trump Tower in its famous War Room. Like Gilligan, a two-day trip would turn into a five-year tour before the Trump mast.

The Fastest Elevator in the Western World

The Trump 2016 War Room really consisted of two discrete and separate areas spread across one floor of Trump Tower, which stands between 56th and 57th streets on Manhattan's Fifth Avenue. As to which floor that War Room *actually* was on, that is a matter of some amusement.

To get to the War Room, you indeed had to push the elevator button for the 14th floor, and then it was the fastest elevator ride in Manhattan. This was not because the elevator was particularly fast. Rather, it was simply because the 14th floor in Trump Tower is actually the fifth floor. That is, once you get to the fourth floor, the next floor up is labeled the 14th.

So what's up with that? Of course, it was a typical marketing gambit from Developer Trump. The Boss simply inflated the floor numbers on the theory that higher floors would command higher rents.

Who knows if this shell game actually worked. But it does provide at least a little sneak peek into the mind of one of the great geniuses in real estate.

And by the way, you could walk down a filthy, darkened stairway to the fourth floor right to where DJT's old show *The Apprentice* used to be filmed. Truth be told here, the set looked like a proverbial dung hole. This stark visual made me all the more impressed with Donald

John Trump because it made it abundantly clear that it was the force of Trump's personality alone that had truly turned that sow's ear of an *Apprentice* set into pure ratings silk.

At any rate, half the War Room floor was like a mini football field. It featured stacks of big screen TVs tuned in to all the various cable news channels across one big wall, a beehive of desks crammed mostly with young, eager-beaver worker bees, and a few glass enclosure offices housing campaign littlewigs like Jason Miller and Hope Hicks.

On the other side of the floor from the worker bee hive was a honeycomb of much smaller offices along with a very small kitchen and some conference rooms. It was this side of the War Room where the bigwigs hung out—the aforementioned Bannon, Bossie, and Stephen Miller along with a little throne for the Clown Prince himself, Trump son-in-law Jared Kushner, and a spacious but rarely occupied suite for Kellyanne Conway.

Me and Malcolm X

On my first official day at work, I staked out a Malcolm X-type spot in the far back of the worker bee War Room where I could see all of the TVs along with everybody else in the room and anybody who might arrive. Note for the record: Malcolm X always did the same thing whenever he went out into a restaurant, but a lot of good that did *him*.

At any rate, I would quickly set up a workstation and makeshift stand-up desk constructed out of empty printer paper boxes and initially worked on my small and clunky laptop. Eventually, my big full screen Apple computer would arrive by pony UPS express, and that would help me dramatically improve my productivity.

During my sixteen- to eighteen-hour work days in the War Room, I would crank out op-ed articles, position papers typically written with Wilbur Ross, and other assorted campaign missives designed to message what would become my own mantra for the Trump campaign—my "four points of the growth compass" construct.

For much of the eight years of the Obama-Biden administration from my perch in Laguna Beach as a TV commentator, I had publicly chastised Obama and his idiot advisors like Larry Summers, often on Fox business shows like *Varney & Co.* and *Making Money with Charles Payne* and CNBC's *Squawk Box*. My major beef was the inability of the

Obama-Bidenites to distinguish between a *cyclical* downturn of the business cycle amenable to Keynesian stimulus—which they favored—versus the very real *structural* problems with the American economy that I saw as primarily associated with America's globalist trade policies.

The Trump prescription I helped craft as the president's top economic advisor targeted four key structural changes that we believed would strengthen and expand American manufacturing and reboot productivity and rising wages. That four points of the compass growth prescription and mantra was simply tax cuts, deregulation, energy independence, and fair—as opposed to simply free—trade. And yes, these structural changes—along with a big boost in defense spending—would indeed propel the Trump economy to unparalleled prosperity, at least right up until the point that the pandemic from Communist China hit.

A Free Man in Paris

The beauty of working in Trump Tower was that I had no boss. Steve Bannon was doing his strategy thing and seemed to have no real interest in either what I was up to or in talking to me. I think at the time he saw me as some ivory tower Harvard don lacking his nuts-and-bolts experience from across the river at the Harvard Business School, and therefore he assumed that I would be useless for any real campaign.

Dave Bossie had no seeming interest in policy and was simply engrossed in the nuts and bolts of running the campaign.

As for Steve Mnuchin—the man who would become treasury secretary and my soon-to-be undisputed bête noire in the White House—I had very little contact with him during the campaign other than to frequently go on TV to clean up the messes Stevie would make with confusing statements on Candidate Trump's proposed tax policies. I do, however, remember one of the most prescient conversations I ever had at Trump Tower in the bigwig wing of the building.

An angry Bossie had called me down to his office to talk about the latest screw up on tax policy—it had something to do with the arcane concept known as "carried interest." When he called me down to the office to ask me what had happened, I said it was Mnuchin again popping his mouth off to the press. I then added, "God help us if Mnuchin winds up as treasury secretary." To which Bossie replied, "That will never happen." After which Bannon said, "And we are screwed if it does." And screwed we would be.

As for Kellyanne Conway, I rarely saw her, although I am sure she was working her butt off—she always did. And Stephen Miller was either too busy with Candidate Trump flying around the country or too much of a hermit when he was back at the mothership to take much of an interest in what I was doing. While he had recruited me great enthusiasm, once I arrived, he simply left me alone to do my thing.

That was all well and good with me because it left me the freedom to become a Trump policy entrepreneur filling a very real void within the Trump campaign. While the Boss himself knew exactly what he was doing, most of the folks working for him were young and green and didn't really have a clue about Populist Economic Nationalism and Trumpism and how these powerful ideas might help get Trump elected. That was my role during the campaign—to figure these things out and help broadcast that message.

To that end, as one of the most experienced media surrogates and one with a good rapport with many of the TV anchors spread across the cable news diaspora, I would frequently drop in to the New York studios of CNN or MSNBC or CNBC and especially Fox, often to debate my Clinton counterparts like Austan Goolsbee or Jared Bernstein or simply joust with Never-Trump anchors like MSNBC's Joy Reid and Stephanie Ruhle.

Here, it didn't hurt that the Boss was always watching, often with great approval. In fact, one of the funny lessons I would learn in working with Donald Trump was that sometimes it was easier to talk to him on TV than actually go visit him in his office. For whatever reason, if he saw you on TV say something, he often took it more seriously.

From Worker Bees to Termites in the House

The Trump Tower War Room of 2016 would turn out to be of no small consequence for the 2020 campaign. This is because many of the worker bees in 2016 would wind up in key roles in the Trump White House, and later on in the Trump 2020 campaign. While some of these worker bees would make outstanding contributions to the administration, far too many would wind up as Never-Trump termites in the White House of Trump.

On the positive side of the ledger, there were policy and political studs like Alex Gray and Andy Surabian. Alex I would come to dub the Mozart of foreign policy. In his late twenties, bespeckled, a bit soft in the gut, and as tall as a power forward, Gray not only understood the politics, geopolitics, and dangers of a rising Communist China, he had the academic training and skill set to clearly and crisply communicate his concerns.

I note with some mentor's satisfaction here that our cowritten crescendo piece right before election day was a beautiful article in *Foreign Policy*. After laying waste to Hillary Clinton's China appeasement policies in the introduction to the article, we then laid out a peace through strength Trump vision to "rewrite America's relationship with Asia."[13] That article would become an important part of the architecture of our Tough on China policies.

As to how young Alex had found his way to the Trump Tower War Room, he had reached out to me to express his interest, and I had dutifully landed him a plum little spot on the Asia desk—which consisted of him and him alone.

Alex would go on to be my chief deputy in the White House, and we would do great work together, particularly when it came to strengthening and expanding our defense industrial base. To this day, our Pentagon report and companion executive order on that mission remains the definitive work in Washington on the subject.

As for Andy Surabian, he was the *de facto* head of our boiler room ninjas—the guys tasked to monitor all negative press and immediately hit back when any slime came our way. And Andy was—and is—tough as nails.

In fact, Andy was so tough he never hesitated to chew my head off if I screwed up on TV. His favorite phrase in these circumstances was: "Well, that was not good." And Andy would levy his scathing critiques despite the fact that he was young enough to be my grandson.

Joining Andy on the ninja team were warriors like Steven Cheung, Brad Rateike, and Clay Shoemaker. All of these ninjas would make it to the White House, but each would be quickly exiled across the street from the West Wing by the RNC RINO Sean Spicer to the Eisenhower Executive Office Building. There, these neutered ninjas would languish until picked off one by one by the second chief of staff, John Kelly. Kelly was yet more fruit from the Bad Personnel tree—the dour general was as Never-Trump as they come.

Wasted By Thinking Below the Waist

At the top of the list of those on the negative side of the Trump ledger was the aforementioned press secretary Jason Miller. Full disclosure here: I like Jason and the tactical thing here would be to just leave him alone to stew in his own misery.

Yet, if I am going to tell the whole truth and nothing but the truth about my Trump experience, I simply cannot ignore an individual who, even as he did an excellent job helping us win the 2016 campaign, would do enormous and lasting damage to President Trump that would ripple forward to the 2020 campaign. So here is how that tawdry little tale goes, and it starts with the best I can say about Jason: By nature, temperament, and intelligence, Jason Miller is a tactical master of the art of political messaging. To put this another way, Jason is to politics what a day trader is to investing.

What I mean by that is that Jason has no real concept of overall long-term strategy. Yet, when the dung hit the fan, as it so often did on a daily basis during the 2016 campaign, there was no one better than Jason—other than the Boss—at counterpunching back in the press.

The best example I can give you of Jason's lack of strategic political cal acumen and a longer-term political horizon is the comical advice he gave to Steve Bannon in the summer of 2020. After Steve's *War Room: Pandemic* had become the number one podcast in politics, Jason advised Steve to drop the word "Pandemic" from the show's title under the ridiculous assumption that the pandemic would soon be over.

Unfortunately, Jason's personal life was a mess during the campaign. Some below the waist thinking would not only get him into very real personal trouble. It would prove very costly to the president himself and the Trump administration.

In Jason's case, both his wife and a campaign worker became pregnant by him[14] all in the same week—and both would give birth some nine months later. The ensuing scandal would break shortly *after* Election Day *and* after Jason had been announced as the new press secretary for the Trump White House.

Here is Jason's obligatory "I need to spend more time with my family" exit from the Trump administration statement in the *Huffington Post*. It's the kind of CYA drivel that invariably accompanies every political sex scandal:

> *Jason Miller, who was named President-elect Donald Trump's White House communications director just two days ago, announced Saturday he will not be taking a job in the incoming administration. The 41-year-old aide, who served as Sen. Ted Cruz's (R-Texas) communications adviser before joining Trump's campaign, said he needed to spend more time with his family. He also noted he and his wife are expecting their second child.*[15]

What pissed me off about the whole thing was not just how stupid Jason had been and how cruel Jason had treated the campaign worker. I had worked side-by-side with her, she was a tough and elegant Cuban-American and one of our best surrogates, and she would have had a great future in the Trump White House.

No, what really pissed me off was how the whole sad and sordid affair opened the door to what would be a succession of weak and incompetent press secretaries and a constantly bumbling and fumbling press shop that would time and time again fail the president.

Indeed, like a bad Molière play, as Jason Miller stumbled off the stage out one door juggling two newborn babies from two separate women, Sean Spicer strutted in another door and immediately began making us look like idiots as early as Inauguration Day.

A Mooch Meets the Pillsbury Dough Boy

My favorite Sean Spicer story revolves around the day I walked into his office pitching some Tough on China message. As ever-the-free-trader Sean was rebuffing me, I couldn't help notice the salad on one side of him, and the French fries on the other. That was quintessential Sean. This Pillsbury Doughboy could never make up his mind, and his tenure was anything but healthy for the Boss.

In fact, Spicer's overzealous claim of the "the largest audience to ever witness an inauguration"[16] would only be topped for comedy in the press shop by the ten minutes of fame and infamy of the shortest lasting director of White House communications in presidential history, Anthony Scaramucci.

Truth be told—please do not tell the Boss—I really liked "The Mooch." Anthony went to my alma mater, Tufts University, and shared some of the same professors I had so it was fun to talk to him about that. The Mooch actually had great talent as a communicator, and in all likelihood, he would have cleaned the press shop up if only he hadn't put his foot in his mouth so quickly. Instead, Anthony became just one more of a rather large number of Trump loyalists who got so screwed over by Never-Trumpers within the West Wing that he would eventually turn bitterly on the president.

I put Omarosa Manigault, Cliff Sims, and Stephanie Grisham in that same Trump loyalist scorned category. While "The Mooch" got reamed by Reince Priebus, both Omarosa and Cliff Sims would get screwed by John Kelly while Stephanie Grisham would get raked every which way but loose by Trump's fourth chief of staff, Mark Meadows.

I know that last Grisham fact quite directly because Stephanie cried at least figuratively on my shoulder several times about her ill-treatment by Meadows. It was indeed ill-treatment because Grisham never did anything to trigger the wrath of the hapless Meadows.

Grisham never did anything, that is, other than to stand in the way of his replacing her with two people handpicked by Meadows, Alyssa Farah and Kayleigh McEnany. Of course, those last two press corps peaches would, each in their own way, dump all over the president come the January 6 violence on Capitol Hill. To be clear, each would throw the Boss under the bus to salvage their own media careers on cable news. Boy, did I see a lot of that kind of kowtowing going on at the end—Kudlow, Grisham, Mulvaney, Farah, McEnany. Just pathetic.

I want to emphasize here again that all of these cases of Trump loyalists scorned were self-inflicted wounds by incompetent chiefs of staff that would cost the president. The Mooch would constantly hound Trump during the campaign as he offered himself up time and time again as a more than willing useful idiot for CNN and its Trump-bashing. For their scornful parts, Omarosa, Sims, and Grisham would write tell-all trash books ravaging the president and/or First Lady. It was all so unnecessary.

SIX

The November 9thers Cometh and an RNC Original Sin

On Tuesday, November 8, "Donald Trump elected president" graphics and gizmos were ready, just in case, but few expected to use them. "We went into the night knowing there was a chance Trump could win," PBS "NewsHour" anchor Judy Woodruff said. "But all the smart people said it was not going to happen." It wasn't just pollsters, pundits and political whizzes who were assuming Hillary Clinton would cruise to victory—it was Republican bigwigs and Trump campaign staffers, too.

—CNN Business[17]

Not me. Nope. I never doubted DJT would win. Not even when the Billy Bush "grab them by the pussy" scandal hit Trump Tower like a neutron bomb and sent whiners like Reince Priebus and Mike Pence into their respective closets to clutch their pearls.

Nope. Never a doubt. I had been in the trenches with the Boss, I knew the mood of the country, I was intimately familiar with the political terrain of the Blue Wall battleground states, and I was sure we were going to take more than enough blue-collar, AFL-CIO Democrats away from haughty Hillary to smash that Midwest Blue Wall with the force and magic of Thor's hammer.

So it was that on Election Day, I worked right up until sunset in the Trump Tower War Room. Then, against my better judgment—fancy restaurants are just not my thing—I hoofed it over to some upscale bistro across the street from Central Park to meet Wilbur Ross and his wife Hilary along with Andy Puzder and real estate mogul *cum* long-time Trump confidante Richard LeFrak for dinner.

For the first thirty minutes, I had to listen to these folks bitch and moan about how we had lost the election. Their problem was they had been drinking the Kool-Aid served up by the corporate media that had Trump losing in a landslide.

After listening to these defeatists *ad nauseam*, I finally told everyone around the table to knock it off. Trump *was* going to win what would be a tight race. Then, I went outside to take a call from Toby Taylor, a producer at CNBC who wanted me to appear early the next morning on *Squawk Box* before the stock market opened—but only if Trump won.

"Sure," I said above the din of the street noise and with a harsh cold wind at my back, "Count me in, and I'll bet you one hundred bucks that the Boss will have the election in the bag by then." While Toby wouldn't take my bet, she did take my booking, and so I was set for 6 a.m. the next day.

From the dinner, I hoofed it a little more—I always walked in New York City or took the subway and rarely used a taxi. My destination was the Hilton Midtown Hotel on Avenue of the Americas where the Trump campaign had set up either for the biggest surprise victory party in presidential history or for drowning our sorrows in a cheap liquor defeat. Of course, surprise would win the day—and that night.

Dow 25,000 Equals Navarro on the Bench

The next morning, my appearance on CNBC would be a forecasting *tour de force*—if I do say so myself. For just as Michael Jordan played one of his best games beaten down by the flu, I would have one of my best TV appearances a little after 6 a.m. on November 9 sleep deprived, exhausted, and beyond groggy after a fitful few hours tossing in my bed.

Unfortunately, my best CNBC appearance would also be fodder for one of the worst pieces of luck I would ever experience. This is because that single appearance would play a major role in my initial and extreme marginalization as a power player within the Trump White House. Here's the back story: For almost ten years, I had been a CNBC contributor from my perch in Laguna Beach. My specialty following the publication of my bestselling 2001 investment book *If It's Raining in Brazil, Buy Starbucks*, was to forecast movements of the stock and bond markets based on emerging trends in the US and global macroeconomies.

Explaining the title of the *Raining in Brazil* book in some way explains the niche I had carved out on the cable news financial networks. To wit: If rain falls in Brazil to break a drought, the coffee crop will be more plentiful. Coffee beans will therefore be cheaper on world markets, the profit margins for Starbucks will be wider, and, on this expectation of higher profits, investors will bid up the price of Starbucks stock with news of the rain. So if it rains in Brazil, buy Starbucks!

In that *Brazil* book, I also described many other such "macro waves" to underscore the importance of factoring exogenous shocks like nuclear power plant disasters, tsunamis, and, dare I say, stunning election outcomes into the investment calculus.

For example, and these are the kinds of macabre things I would think about, when the Chernobyl disaster hit, it triggered a sell signal for companies like General Mills. This is because the Russian and Ukrainian wheat crops would take a hit and drive up grain prices.

By the same token, a tsunami in Thailand might disrupt the global supply chain for everything from computer chips to auto parts. Accordingly, it might be time to sell short the auto sector after such an event.

Armed with this kind of unique analytics, I had indeed carved out a nice little side career in television. I saw these appearances both as a public service as well as a platform to plug my books, and from that perspective, I never expected to be paid for any of my appearances. Then, a funny thing happened to me on the way to my bank.

When Fox launched its Fox Business network in October 2007, CNBC freaked out, and as a preemptive measure, it began signing contributors left and right and offering them lucrative deals. I was one of the lucky ones to be wooed, and thus began my acquaintance, and eventual friendship, with at least a few of CNBC's Trump faithful like *Squawk Box*'s Joe Kernen, one of the very best in journalism and financial analysis (along with Rick Santelli and Jim Cramer) CNBC has to offer.

At any rate, when I walked bleary-eyed onto the *Squawk Box* set after having a little bit of makeup thrown on my face and my hair combed, I sat down at the big round table where Joe and his foil and sometimes nemesis Andrew Ross Sorkin were sitting. At this time, the futures for all three major averages—the S&P 500, Dow Jones Industrial Average, and NASDAQ—were all heading dead red down on what appeared to be a wave of mass panic and horror on Wall Street about a Trump presidency.

Trouble not, I thought to myself. I've got this. And more importantly, Donald Trump has got this. So here's how the interview went—and as the interview went on, the futures steadily moved up. And up. And up. And the market would finish strong that day and never look back, at least for the next three years before the coming of a pandemic from Communist China.

Let's just look at the chessboard. Everybody out there. The world is literally watching this show. Do you go short, long or into cash?

Let me simply make the long argument. I see Dow 25,000 within the first term of the Trump administration. How do we get there from here? If you look at the policies Mr. Trump will enact in the first hundred days starting with day one, let me just walk you through that.

The first is cutting taxes for all Americans and, most importantly, from a growth point of view, cutting the corporate tax from 35 percent down to 15 percent. If you simply do that, you get a 30 percent increase in net earnings for corporations which is very, very bullish.

The second thing which Mr. Trump can do administratively is put a moratorium on all new regulations that don't threaten public health and safety. We have a $1 trillion regulatory burden now...he will order, at the agency level, a review of regulations trying to reduce that burden. That's a pure Reagan supply-side effect that will lower costs and move things forward.

The third thing is stopping the war on oil, natural gas, shale, [and] clean coal. If we lower our energy prices, that will make our corporations more competitive globally. If we lower our electricity costs, that will put more money in our consumers' pockets for savings and investment growth....

If you move to the trade issue, there are tremendous amounts of executive powers Mr. Trump has. He has said all along, as [have] all of his surrogates, that Trump is a free trader. He seeks nothing more than to rebalance this economy by increasing our exports at the margin and decreasing our imports; and we lose a point [of GDP

growth] a year—let's face it—we lose a point of growth a year to that.
So we will proceed in a stable manner with great trading partners,
and that will be good for the economy....

And so if you just look at the chessboard...everything points
towards the direction of growth; and that is good for the markets
because growth brings up corporate earnings, it brings up stock prices.
So if you are out there today, just look at the chessboard. This is...a
very bullish thing for the markets and Dow twenty-five thousand is
going to be like the Reagan years, and it is a good thing.[18]

So yes, I had it exactly right. The Dow would reach twenty-five thousand on the wings of Donald Trump's four points of the growth compass. That historic day would come just fourteen months later on January 4, 2018.[19]

Of course, the funniest part of the interview was the part where the laconic and not easily impressed Joe Kernen points out quite correctly that twenty-five thousand on the Dow, no matter how outlandish it might've sounded right at that point, really didn't represent that big of a deal as it translated to only about an 8 percent gain per year over four years of a Trump administration.[20]

Yep, you got me there Joe, but I did not want to sound too crazy by reaching for thirty thousand.

Unfortunately, "crazy" was exactly what Trump campaign strategist Stephen K. Bannon thought I was when he saw me that morning delivering my forecast.

For that reason, as good as that forecast was and as good my performance was that day—I still rank it as the best appearance I've ever made on television—it would prove to have a consequence so dramatic that I wouldn't understand it until years later.

Brother Bannon Gives Me the Hook

The short rendition of this consequence was that my CNBC star turn would lead to Steve Bannon pulling me from ALL television appearances until after Inauguration Day. This would put me out of sight and therefore out of the president's mind and thereby help lead to my marginalization at the White House.

The longer version goes like this: Later in the day, I was told by Jason Miller in no uncertain terms that the word had come down from on high that all of our surrogates—not just me—would be taken off television. This was, as it would turn out, a complete lie—I was the only target. Yet, I wouldn't uncover this big lie until five years later after I left the White House.

This big reveal happened one cold winter day when Steve and I were hashing out some strategy around his conference table at his Breitbart Embassy headquarters in Washington, DC. Steve sheepishly let it slip that it had been he who had ordered me off TV and acknowledged the mistake and its unfortunate consequences.

Said Steve: "I saw this crazy guy from the campaign go out on CNBC and make this wild prediction about 25,000 on the Dow, and I needed to put an immediate stop to that. As a guy from the other side of the river at the Harvard Business school, they always teach us that nobody can forecast the stock market, and I certainly did not want to raise outlandish expectations at this point." So "get Navarro off the air" went down the chain and Jason Miller delivered the bad news.

Of course, in Trump Land, my removal from the airways would turn out to be a stake to the heart of my nascent career as a possible high-ranking White House official. No good forecast goes unpunished.

Here is how the rest of my fall from power and grace all played out, and it began with a visit to Jared Kushner's office a few blocks from Trump Tower at his 666 Fifth Avenue digs.

An RNC Coup at Trump Tower

After my CNBC gig, I went back to my apartment to grab a little shuteye and then some very late breakfast before heading back to Trump Tower to see what was shaking. What was shaking was an earthquake in the middle of my beloved War Room.

This earthquake came in the form of a large phalanx of what we Trump campaigners would come to call the "November 9thers." These were the Goths and Vandals who would arrive at Trump Tower to stake out their own positions of power and claim their own spoils of the Trump wars after having done *absolutely nothing* to help the president vanquish Crooked Hillary.

Heading this phalanx was one of the truly evil characters I would meet at this early stage of the Trump administration, a Cruella-like witch otherwise known as Katie Walsh. She was the chief deputy for the chairman of the RNC, to whom I have already introduced you, Reince Priebus.

While at the time I had no idea who Walsh was, she already had a target on my back courtesy of Reince. They both saw me as the dangerous trade policy guy who was most likely to push Donald Trump from the globalist RINO orthodoxy of open borders and free trade.

At any rate, this phalanx of RNC mercenaries would provide me with my first up-close-and-personal look at what Steve Bannon would dub the "Original Sin" of the administration. This was for then president-elect Trump to enter into an alliance with the traditional and establishment RINO wing of the Republican Party represented by the likes of Priebus at the RNC, Mitch McConnell, who by dint of the election had now graduated from minority leader of the Senate to the majority leader, and House Speaker Paul Ryan.

All of these RINOs firmly embraced three of the four points of my growth policy compass—tax cuts, deregulation, and an expansion of the petroleum sector in a way that would get us to energy independence. Yet, each of these DC movers and shakers was vehemently opposed to any kind of trade actions that would prevent their corporate donors from offshoring American jobs.

Of course, one of the key ways to scuttle the Trump trade agenda would be to take out yours truly—Trump's "trade guy." Yes—and I had no idea at the time—I was about to be in for a very rough time.

What a Handshake Deal in New York Is Worth

That rough time actually started quite smoothly on November 10— now two days out from Trump's upset victory. I had been summoned that afternoon by Jared Kushner for a meeting which I saw as an exit interview and opportunity to say goodbye. Jared, on the other hand, saw this meeting quite another way.

To be clear, at this point, I had a casual but very cordial relationship with Jared. We had talked a few times while I was at Trump Tower, and it had always been friendly. And, in typical Jared fashion, Kushner had always been quite complimentary about the contributions I had been making.

At any rate, when I got to Jared's office, he asked me what my plans were. I said I'd be heading back home to California to get ready to teach at UCI in the winter quarter, which would begin the first week of January.

He replied—I believe quite sincerely at the time—that the president-elect needed me, and he asked me what I would need to stick around. I had, of course, given some thought to this, although my leanings were to simply leave this life behind and get back to my beautiful wife and home and the stability of academic life. But, I told him, if there was one position where I thought I could make a big difference in the White House, it was that of director of the National Economic Council (NEC).

Along with the treasury secretary and the chairman of the Council of Economic Advisers within the White House, the NEC director helps coordinate economic (and by extension trade) policies within the administration. So that would be a perfect niche for me.

Jared apparently thought so too. When I put my offer on the table, he quickly replied: "Consider it done."

So we shook hands on the deal, and off I went back to Trump Tower oblivious to the first rule of New York City—a deal is never really done until it is done.

And this is where my "out of sight, out of the president-elect's mind" problem contributed to what would be a very painful unsealing of that deal. But it would take another month before I would be run over by a Goldman Sachs bus driven by one of the worst and most treacherous misfits of the entire Trump administration, Gary Cohn.

SEVEN

An Ambassador Strategy and Some Shuttle Diplomacy

A major split among senior White House officials over whether to effectively create a new tax on imported goods has stalled the broader tax overhaul effort on Capitol Hill, with Republicans looking to the Trump administration for leadership on an issue that has drawn fierce resistance, according to several officials with direct knowledge of the matter.

White House chief strategist Stephen Bannon, senior adviser Stephen Miller and National Trade Council director Peter Navarro have all voiced internal support for the creation of a border adjustment tax or something like it. They believe it would incentivize companies to keep jobs in the United States and raise the cost of items that are imported.

But Treasury Secretary Steven Mnuchin and National Economic Council Director Gary Cohn have raised concerns....

—The *Washington Post*, March 3, 2017[21]

Back at Trump Tower, seemingly secure in my position in the Trump White House, I began working in earnest on the transition. To that end—and already fully aware of the Ronald Reagan admonition that "personnel is policy"—I accelerated my work with one of the smartest guys I have ever met, Martin Silverstein.

Martin was a pure Trump trooper, and he had been tasked well prior to Election Day with finding solid Trump loyalists to fill the thousands of "Plum Book" positions in what might be an eventual Trump administration. As one of Martin's chief talent scouts, I would send him referral after referral, he would do his obligatory vetting, and over time, we assembled a large dossier of folks who could be plugged immediately into the Trump machine, perform at a high level, and provide no worries of any possible disloyalties.

So much for best laid plans. Once Reince Priebus, Katie Walsh, and an ever-expanding band of November 9thers seized control of the transition apparatus in New York, Martin Silverstein's mountain of Trump loyalist dossiers would find their way quite literally into the trash can.

That single act of disappearing hundreds of potentially high-ranking Trump officials who would have done yeoman's work in blowing up the Deep Administrative State and actually getting things done on behalf of the Trump agenda was arguably one of the worst actions taken by Priebus and Walsh.

As for Martin Silverstein himself, loyalist though he was, he would never be given a position in the Trump administration. It was not that Martin wasn't promised one—by none other than Jared Kushner. However, like me, Martin would simply get lost in the Original Sin shuffle.

By the way, the position Kushner promised Martin, and the only one Martin really wanted, was administrator of the United States Agency for International Development. As a former ambassador to Uruguay, Martin was perfectly suited for the USAID job. But it was a job that would go to a far less qualified candidate, albeit with far greater political connections[22]—yet another one of many big misses and messes when it came to the appointment process.

And speaking of big misses and messes, one appointment that the Boss absolutely hated was that of Jerome Powell for the Federal Reserve. That was strictly a Mnuchin play, with Stevie assuring POTUS that Powell would be a loyal pro-growth disciple. *Not!*

Powell's misdirected monetary policies would cost us at least a point of GDP growth in 2019 alone. So whenever I wanted to have a little bit of fun tormenting or triggering Mnuchin in the Oval, all I had to do was say, "How's that Jay Powell thing working out, Stevie?" God, was that fun.

A New Way of Containing Communist China

Besides working with Martin Silverstein on personnel, Alex Gray and I would conspire with Mike Flynn's assistant Matt Pottinger on an "ambassador strategy" we had strategically devised to diplomatically encircle Communist China. The core proposition was to place hardliners in key ambassador positions across Asia.

So on our recruitment board, we had, for example, China Hawk and renowned China scholar Mike Pillsbury going as the ambassador to China. Boy, would heads explode in Beijing on that pick alone.

We also had the indefatigable Captain James Fanell headed for Thailand. Jim had been pushed out of his post as chief of intelligence for the US Pacific Fleet because of his outspoken warnings about Communist China and would be an invaluable China Hawk asset in Bangkok.

Then there was former Pac Fleet commander and retired navy admiral Harry Harris. We had Harry down for either Singapore or South Korea where, by the way, he eventually landed.

Alex and I even had the bright idea to send Naval War College Professor Toshi Yoshihara to serve as the director of the American Institute in Taiwan. Fluent in Mandarin, Yoshihara had cowritten the definitive work on the rise of Chinese Communist naval power—*Red Star Over the Pacific*,[23] and I had gotten to know Toshi by interviewing him for my *Crouching Tiger* documentary series.

As director of the American Institute in Taiwan, Toshi would have served as the implicit ambassador to that bulwark of democracy—Taiwan has no formal American embassy. And yes, it would have been a beautiful thing having Toshi in Taipei just one hundred miles from Communist Chinese shores as the People's Liberation Army rattled its swords and battleships over and in the Taiwan Strait.

The last thing I should say about this ambassador strategy is really a confession about one of my most spectacular misses. This was, at least as it would turn out, the not-so-bright idea to nominate Professor Stefan Halper as the ambassador to Indonesia.

Halper would subsequently be exposed as an FBI operative who played a key role in helping to perpetrate the Russia Hoax. In the meantime, I make no apologies for thinking that Halper might be a great ambassador who would help us strike fear in the hearts of the ChiComs.

After all, Halper had written a bestselling and scathing critique of Communist China called *The Beijing Consensus*, taught at Cambridge, wrote deep think pieces under contract with the Pentagon, and projected not a whiff of scandal.

What I would learn with the Halper affair, however, is that sometimes in Washington, things just blow up in your face. In fact, the only thing worse than Halper was what happened with my efforts to turn a Kodak manufacturing plant into the premier producer of our essential medicines—but you will have to wait for another time and another book to get that particular story.

Flynn and the Boy Scout

As a third line of effort I would engage in during the transition at Trump Tower, I would dig in with Mike Flynn, Trump's choice for National Security Advisor.

I liked Mike from the outset. He had a no-nonsense, let's-take-the-hill kind of military sensibility that appealed to my own temperament. He also left no doubt that he saw Communist China at the top of the pyramid of existential threats to the United States. Not Russia. Not Iran. Surely not Cuba or Venezuela. Nope. China, China, China.

The other great appeal of Mike Flynn to me was his aforementioned and soon-to-be deputy Matt Pottinger. Pottinger was a fluent Mandarin speaker who had worked in China for nearly five years for the *Wall Street Journal* as a reporter. To his credit, young Matt had managed to get beaten up by some Chinese jackboots for his zealousness in uncovering inconvenient Beijing truths and thus had some considerable street cred.

In 2005, Pottinger enlisted in the marines and wound up serving in Afghanistan where he met Flynn. Now, he had hooked his wagon to the rising Flynn star, and he was schooling Flynn on the subtleties of Chinese mercantilism and the geopolitics of Chinese soft power weapons like its Belt and Road Initiative. Pottinger was as hawkish and clear-eyed about Communist China as I was.

I would be remiss in not adding here, however, that ultimately Pottinger was a big disappointment to me—as well as to the Boss. With his expertise as a *Wall Street Journal* reporter, Pottinger had mastered the art of the strategic leak. What Pottinger would do towards the end of the administration using that mastery was leak all sorts of information that portrayed Matt as a hero at the expense of POTUS, myself, and even of his own boss Robert O'Brien.

When the books—and yes it was more than one book—came out portraying Matt as a cross between Superman and the second coming of Christ juxtaposed against the devil of Trump and everybody else in the West Wing, we all knew exactly who the source of the leak was.

More than miffed, POTUS let O'Brien know in no uncertain terms how pissed off he was at Pottinger and wanted him out of the building. O'Brien pretty much felt the same way as did I.

Secret NAFTA Negotiations With the Mexicans

Still a third major mission I would focus upon during the transition would send me like a comet blazing across the trade negotiator sky. To wit:

A few days after the election, Wilbur Ross and I began some quiet and delicate negotiations with several high-level Mexican diplomats regarding the president-elect's ironclad promise to quickly renegotiate NAFTA—the North American Free Trade Agreement. Wilbur and I both liked the idea of beginning with the Mexican side for several reasons.

First, it was in Mexico where far too many American jobs had been offshored because of the unbalanced nature of the NAFTA agreement. Key aspects of NAFTA had also helped spark a wave of illegal immigration into the US. So the biggest problems with NAFTA were with the Mexico side.

The second reason why we liked to deal with the Mexicans first—and Wilbur knew this better than I did at this point—was that the Canadians are exceedingly difficult to negotiate with. In fact, I can safely say that of all the diplomats that I came into contact with across scores of countries, the only diplomats who were more treacherous and disingenuous than the Canadians were the Communist Chinese.

Our thinking was that if we could get a deal with Mexico, we could force the Canadians to accept that deal by making the very real, credible threat that we would simply withdraw from NAFTA entirely and sign a new bilateral agreement with Mexico. The Canadian economy would be crushed by any such withdrawal, particularly their auto and steel sectors which were heavily integrated into the US economy through NAFTA.

At any rate, Wilbur and I opened communications with two people who would turn out to be two favorites of mine that I would encounter during my White House years—Luis Videgaray, then secretary of finance and public credit of Mexico, and Narciso Campos, Videgaray's main deputy. It was a strictly one-way type of shuttle diplomacy as Narciso and Luis would always visit us at Wilbur's New York apartment.

Luis is that elegant, manicured Spaniard kind of a Mexican from the upper classes and a throwback to the days of gentility and good manners. With a PhD in economics from the Massachusetts Institute of Technology, Luis knew his way around macroeconomics and trade policy better than anyone I've ever met.

For his part, Narciso was as good a Robin to Luis's Batman as any deputy could be, and it would be with Narciso that I would spend long hours polishing the language on what eventually would become the Ross-Navarro version of a NAFTA deal and a memorandum of understanding.

So it was that throughout December of 2016, Luis and Narciso would fly up from Mexico to the Big Apple, and we would meet in Wilbur's Manhattan apartment. And Wilbur and I were a good team—a quintessential good cop–bad cop tandem. This was because Wilbur and I knew exactly what we wanted from the negotiation going in.

The key provision in any new NAFTA treaty had to be a dramatic increase in so-called "domestic content." The idea here is simple: anything manufactured in the new NAFTA zone would have to have a very substantial US, that is, "domestic," manufacturing content. Through this one mechanism alone, we would be able to control just how much production—from autos and auto parts to air conditioners, electronics, and fabricated steel—would take place north and south of the US border.

Besides being the primary draftsman on the American side of what would indeed become a memorandum of understanding—Narciso performed that draftsman duty on the Mexican side—my role was to hold a very hard line on just how far the Trump side would be willing to go.

Over the course of several meetings with the Mexican side, there were some very tense moments where Luis would furrow his brow, shake his head back and forth indicating his disagreement, and threaten to walk out. But we all knew it was an empty threat.

This is because the beauty of the whole negotiation—and the beauty of Donald Trump—is that the Mexicans knew damn well we were serious and would not hesitate to withdraw from the NAFTA agreement.

So it was that by the end of several weeks, Wilbur, Luis, Narciso, and myself had hammered out what the Boss might have called a "beautiful" MOU and handshake deal. And if you compare that original December 2016 memorandum to the architecture of the eventual successor to NAFTA—the United States-Mexico-Canada Agreement signed on November 30, 2018, at the G20 summit in Buenos Aires—Wilbur and I pretty much nailed it.

That said, that MOU would never see the light of day. One of the folks who would stick a fork in it would be the president's nominee for United States Trade Representative, Robert E. Lighthizer.

Lighthizer would review the document with nothing but scorn, telling both Wilbur and me about how we knew nothing about how real trade agreements were negotiated. What Bob himself didn't understand is how we could do things differently in the Trump administration if only we weren't constrained by the notions of how things were "supposed" to go.

In this case, it would have been quite easy to announce a tentative agreement with Mexico based on the original memorandum of understanding, force Canada to go along, and then let the lawyers—with Lighthizer in the lead—simply flesh it out with appropriate contract language suitable for congressional approval. But Bob couldn't quite wrap his head around that strategy, so we spent three more years before we got to the finish line.

The ChiComs Are Rational Until They Aren't

While working with Luis Videgaray and Narciso Campos on the NAFTA deal was a hell of a lot of fun while it lasted, it was a very different cup of oolong tea when it came to my first face-to-face meeting with the Chinese Communists.

In late December, Steve Bannon, Jared Kushner, and I would secretly meet with a contingent of ChiCom diplomats. This small group included Cui Tiankai, China's ambassador to the US, along with the former ambassador and current state councillor Yang Jiechi—a hard-liner George H. W. Bush had once dubbed "Tiger Yang."

Like the Mexicans, the Chinese were totally freaked out about what might be coming from the trade policies of Donald John Trump. And freaked out they damn well should have been, at least at that point, as it seemed like we were going to come at them hard.

I have one particularly enduring memory of that meeting, which was held in a large conference room at Kushner's triple-six Fifth Avenue building. That memory begins with my surprise at how so much of what the Chinese would say to us was carefully scripted. While Bannon, Kushner, and I had addressed these Communists without notes or props, their principal spokesman Tiger Yang would simply and politely read from his notes.

Tiger Yang did so, that is, right up to the point Jared Kushner made what he thought was an offhand remark about how under the Trump administration "there would be no games." For whatever reason, it was suddenly *game on* as this offhand remark would turn this Tiger on a dime from a bland apparatchik into a fire-breathing dragon. Suddenly, careful scripting went by the wayside as this "we will bury you Americans" Tiger *cum* Dragon went on a long and threatening rant.

As Yang did so, I looked down the table first at Kushner, who had turned even paler than usual, and then at Bannon, who had just the beginnings of a smile on his face and a twinkle in his eye. As Steve has said to me on more than one occasion: "The Chinese are the most rational people in the world. Until they aren't."

A BAT Out of Heaven

A final type of negotiation I would play a role in during that fateful transition period had to do with what was effectively a hot buttered croissant that two traditional free trade Republicans on Capitol Hill were paradoxically trying to serve up as a backdoor protectionist tariff to the newly elected president.

Follow me along here as the lost battle over the border adjustment tax (BAT) would prove to be one of the single most important missed opportunities, not just for the Trump administration, but for the country. Indeed, if Congress had passed such a border adjustment tax, it would have obviated the need for many of the other trade policies we would try to implement to reduce our trade deficit and bring our manufacturing jobs back on shore.

Just why would a BAT have been such a magic bullet? Stripped of rhetoric, a border adjustment tax is nothing more—or less—than a tariff mechanism designed to offset the unfair tax advantages that mercantilist countries around the world are using to subsidize their exports into American markets. This unfair tax advantage comes from a quite peculiar disparity within the World Trade Organization (WTO).

Under WTO rules, countries like Germany and China and Vietnam that rely heavily on a value-added tax or VAT for their revenues can use VAT rebates to heavily subsidize their exports to the United States. Yet, under WTO rules, American exporters are not allowed to use our *income* tax system to do the same. The patently unfair result for the American nation and American workers is an American trade deficit far larger than it would otherwise be and a substantially smaller and weaker American manufacturing base.

Like so many rules of the international road, this disparate treatment by the WTO is, of course, crazy. And, to their credit, two free trade Republicans in the House of Representatives—Kevin Brady of Texas, then chairman of the all-powerful House Ways and Means Committee, and Paul Ryan, then Speaker of the House—came up with the quite ingenious idea to use a BAT—a border adjustment tax—to offset the VAT tax export subsidies and thereby circumvent the WTO's mercantilist and predatory rules.

If Congress had simply enacted the Brady-Ryan BAT, it would have, with one single stroke of the pen, eliminated a significant amount of the unfair trade plaguing American workers. Indeed, it was an absolutely beautiful implicit tariff, and it was my strongest of advice to President Trump to jump all over it.

As to how I came to love the BAT, it would stem from my second round of shuttle diplomacy. Beginning in December, Wilbur and I began to meet secretly with Kevin Brady to plot and scheme about how to turn the border adjustment tax into law.

To that end, Brady dutifully made the pilgrimage up to the Big Apple and Wilbur's apartment. Brady did so after I had paved the way with my own trip to Washington to discuss the ins and outs of the BAT with Brady's tax policy advisor and the man who would eventually be appointed as chairman of the White House Council of Economic Advisers—Kevin Hassett.

I would meet Kevin, then with the American Enterprise Institute, in the basement of a nondescript Residence Inn in Foggy Bottom on a raw and windy December DC day. My first impression of Kevin was that he was the quintessential nerd who had difficulty explaining complex subjects like the border adjustment tax in plain terms.

In fact, it took Kevin three times explaining the BAT for me to finally wrap my head around what was going on—me, a Harvard PhD economist. Yet, when I grasped the simplicity and power of the BAT, I was immediately in.

After the meeting, with as much excitement and enthusiasm as I ever muster, I called Wilbur to let him know that we needed to jump all over the BAT. So Hassett quickly arranged a meeting between Wilbur, myself, and Kevin Brady, and we tried to move things along.

Ultimately, however, the BAT proposal would likewise fall prey to the Original Sin of the administration—the presence of too many Never-Trump personnel inside the perimeter. The obvious political problem here—I guess I buried the lede—was tremendous opposition to a border adjustment tax by American retailers hooked on cheap, subsidized Chinese and other foreign imports.

This retailer contingent included particularly politically powerful big-box retailers like Walmart and Target and Best Buy whose campaign contributions feathered many a nest on Capitol Hill regardless of political party. These retailers knew full well that any elimination of the export subsidies that countries like China and Germany and Vietnam were using to prey on America would mean that they would have to pay more for what they imported from those countries—and that would be a big hit on their bottom line.

Do I need to say out loud that these putatively American corporations do not give a damn about American workers and could care less about the need for a strong American manufacturing base? It is all about their green bottom line—not what's good for the red, white, and blue.

Now here is the quite predictable Bad Personnel plot twist: By Inauguration Day, this coterie of special retailer interests had recruited both Treasury Secretary Steve Mnuchin and the National Economic Council

Director Gary Cohn to oppose the border adjustment tax inside the White House. Both of these former Goldman Sachs Wall Street jackals would dutifully whisper bitter BAT nothings into President Trump's ear and thereby poison the well for any broader rational discussion of the BAT with a larger group of advisors.

This was one of the early great flaws of the Bad Policy process inside the White House. Once Never-Trumpers like Mnuchin and Cohn were allowed to work behind the scenes to sour the president on a proposal because of their quick and preferential access to the Boss, it was very difficult to undo those deeds and damage if and when the issue ever came up in a meeting of the full trade team in the Oval Office.

So it was in this case that, having drunk the Mnuchin-Cohn anti-BAT Kool-Aid, President Trump initially took a hard pass on the Brady-Ryan proposal. By the time POTUS got religion on the BAT—both Kevin Hassett and I and eventually Lighthizer would lobby the Boss on its virtues—it was too late. The legislative window of a lifetime—two high-ranking free trade Republicans pushing a HUGE implicit COR-RECTIVE tariff—slammed shut. Like so many doors during my four years in the White House, it would never be opened again.

EIGHT

What a Handshake Deal
Is Worth in Manhattan

Experience teaches you that the man who looks you straight in the eye, particularly if he adds a firm handshake, is hiding something.

—Clifton Fadiman, 1962

As we have discussed, during the transition I would help Martin Silverstein scout for Trumpian talent, plot and scheme with Mike Flynn, and conduct several rounds of shuttle diplomacy on issues as disparate as NAFTA, a border adjustment tax, and China's economic aggression. Yet, my primary job was to help draft close to a dozen executive orders and presidential memoranda.

These presidential actions were designed to fulfill the seven major promises in the Pittsburgh Jobs Plan speech while also advancing the Boss's two most simple rules: Buy American, Hire American. And here is the plain and simple truth:

If President Trump had simply signed all the actions on Inauguration Day that I had prepared during the transition, we would have dramatically changed the course of history.

While I have a PhD in economics rather than a law degree, I was not unprepared to draft these quintessentially legal documents. This is because early on in my economics career, I toiled extensively in the vineyard of electric utility regulation.

In this particular form of scholarship, it is quite necessary to cross-fertilize one's economics training with an understanding of the interface between law and economics. This cross-fertilization necessarily includes the ability to read and interpret case law.

Moreover, as an electric utility regulation scholar, I had published a number of articles in law journals, and I do think that if I hadn't found my way to the field of economics, the next likely landing spot might have been in the law. My point, of course, is that this was not my first legal rodeo.

Now here is the most important thing I can tell you about any executive order or presidential memorandum: the preamble must clearly establish the statutory authority from which the president is drawing his own power to take such a policy action. Having such solid statutory authority is, as we say in the trade, a necessary condition of any successful presidential action.

In this particular case, I would work primarily with Stephen Vaughn and Gil Kaplan, top DC lawyers from the white-shoe firm of King and Spalding, along with Andrew Bremberg. Both Stephen and Gil were nonpareil experts in trade policy, an absolute delight to work with, and I would play some small role in getting each top spots down the line in the Trump administration.

Stephen would wind up as general counsel for United States Trade Representative Robert Lighthizer. That was not my doing, but with a little maneuvering, I had been able to move out a career bureaucrat and get Stephen into the position of acting USTR until Lighthizer was confirmed on May 11, 2017.

As for Gil Kaplan, I would help him secure one of the most important positions at the Department of Commerce, that as under secretary for international trade. Gil thereby headed the elite unit at Commerce that oversees the slapping of antidumping and countervailing duties on trade cheats, from China and Vietnam to Turkey and, yes, "Oh Canada."

I can safely say here that at least for the first few months of the administration, my best contribution to advancing the Trump agenda was not on trade policy but rather by working below the radar helping to put at least a few pro-Trump folks like Robert O'Brien over at the

State Department and eventually Gil Kaplan at Commerce into positions of power. That I was able to quietly do, even if I didn't have a lot of power at the time myself.

Regarding Andrew Bremberg, his participation in the transition would prove to be a cautionary tale—at least for Stephen Miller. Bremberg had supported RINO Mitt Romney in the 2012 presidential election and Scott Walker in 2016 race, and Trumpism was anathema to the free trader Bremberg. Yet Miller would wind up giving Bremberg the plum job of director of the Domestic Policy Council.

Proving once again that no good deed goes unpunished, Bremberg himself would go on to form an unholy alliance with Gary Cohn and help Cohn strip Miller of much of the power he otherwise would have had in the White House. Effectively, the Bremberg-Cohn alliance would reduce Stephen Miller to the role of speechwriter rather than as the head of White House policy that Miller had envisioned.

Bremberg, by the way, would fight me tooth and nail on what would arguably be my greatest solo achievement in the administration. This was elimination of the international subsidies for Chinese mail packages into the United States that were authorized by the international Universal Postal Union headquartered in Bern, Switzerland. Here is how this resounding victory for America was reported in the Associated Press:

> Peter Navarro was dispatched from Washington with a U.S. delegation to help reform the Universal Postal Union at a time when e-commerce has vastly reshaped the postal business and private, non-postal operators like UPS, DHL, FedEx and others want to snare a larger market share. The administration had threatened leaving a group the United States helped create in 1874.
>
> The head of the 192-member body, Kenya's Bishar Hussein, warned a U.S. walkout would "completely shut down" the traditional system of shipping some types of mail. The extraordinary congress, called this week to respond to the U.S. threat, was only the third for a 145-year-old group that calls itself the second-oldest multilateral organization.
>
> UPU members exchanged hugs, handshakes and high-fives after voting by acclamation in favor of the compromise. The deal, which is to be phased-in over the coming years, will allow countries to choose,

or "self-declare," the rates their postal operators can recoup from foreign partners.

"It's a big deal for a couple of reasons: One is the U.S. got immediate self-declared rates that saves us a half-a-billion dollars. It eliminates market distortions. It creates tens of thousands of jobs for America. It also helps our friends and allies in other nations," said Navarro, insisting countries like Brazil, Norway and Finland were "getting hammered" under the current system.

The United States will fast-track to "immediate self-declared rates" as of the end of June next year, which is the fastest technically possible, Navarro said. The administration has sought to end a decades-old practice by which the United States in essence subsidizes postal operators from developing countries, insisting that rising rival China in particular has been benefiting unfairly.[24]

Yep. It doesn't get much better than that, and I did it all with a massive toothache that made me more gnarly than ever. Maybe that helped me put on my game face as nobody in Geneva—particularly the UPU's director Bishar Hussein—thought I was bluffing. And I wasn't. We were ready to bolt.

And did I mention: This would be the one and only time I was ever on the same side as the US Chamber of Commerce, which otherwise liked to keep itself busy trashing Trump trade policy and offshoring American jobs. Again, wrote the Associated Press:

In what had shaped up as a test of U.S. diplomatic clout against China's interest in the status quo, Navarro said: "China is certainly going to pay more for the privilege of shipping to our market."

"We'll buy less Chinese stuff and we'll buy more stuff from other countries, and we'll make more stuff in America—and the market will be free of distortions," he said. "We call it a hat trick in hockey."

The U.S. Chamber of Commerce, which supported the administration in its push, applauded the deal.

"The administration deserves a tremendous amount of credit for their leadership in tackling an antiquated, market distorting global pricing arrangement that for too long has seen the United States footing the bill to deliver the rest of world's mail," said Sean Heather, the chamber's senior vice president for International Regulatory Affairs, in a statement.[25]

I Get Cohned and Kushnered

On December 12, 2016, as I was neck deep drafting presidential actions, the news that the position that Jared Kushner had promised me—director of the National Economic Council—had instead been awarded to a globalist, Party of Davos, duplicitous Wall Street hack from Goldman Sachs would hit me like a ton of gold bricks. Here's how this news was reported in the *Wall Street Journal*:

> President-elect Donald Trump announced Monday that he was appointing Goldman Sachs...President and Chief Operating Officer Gary Cohn as director of the National Economic Council, a position that will make him one of the most influential voices on economic decisions in the White House.
>
> Mr. Trump...said Mr. Cohn would be his "top economic adviser." "He will help craft economic policies that will grow wages for our workers, stop the exodus of jobs overseas and create many great new opportunities for Americans who have been struggling.... He fully understands the economy and will use all of his vast knowledge and experience to make sure the American people start winning again."[26]

Just think about that for a minute—I sure the hell did. President-elect Trump had just hired a Goldman Sachs pirate who had spent his entire career screwing American workers by offshoring their factories and jobs. And here, a press release under the name of the president-elect was spinning the fantasy that this very same Wall Street globalist would "stop the exodus of jobs overseas."

Just how had this abomination happened? According to Bannon, as he told it to me years later, President Trump had been disrespected so many times by the haughty elites at Goldman Sachs that he simply couldn't resist bringing in one of their top executives, presumably to have under his thumb and service him. So when the opportunity came the Boss's way, he jumped at the chance—Kushner's handshake deal notwithstanding.

Of course, the underlying presumption was that a guy like Cohn would obey the commander in chief and be content to stay under the president's thumb. Instead, all Cohn did in the White House—besides smooch the Boss's derriere whenever he was in the Oval Office—was first expand and then consolidate his power in a way designed to constantly thwart the president's agenda, for example, the Andrew Bremberg gambit.

I can honestly tell you here, with more anger than pride, this:

Had I not been in the White House, Gary "Goldman Sachs" Cohn likely would have served the entire four years, the president would never have implemented policies like steel and aluminum tariffs much less tariffs on China, and the Trump White House and trade agenda would have looked far more dysfunctional than transformational.

To be clear here: Neither Wilbur Ross nor Bob Lighthizer were a match for the conniving Gary Cohn, particularly after Cohn formed an alliance with Mnuchin, and it would indeed have to be me who would have to get Cohn out the door. More about that later.

At any rate, after Cohn's appointment was announced in the morning, that afternoon I once again found myself in Jared Kushner's office asking him what exactly had just happened. Said I to him after hearing his lame excuse: "So is that all you have to say, Jared? Oops? If so, then see you later, bye."

Yes, I was hotter than a marshmallow in a bonfire and ready to make my great escape out of the East Coast and back to Laguna Beach.

Yet once again, Kushner would play to my loyalty to the president. He kept saying how much they needed me in Washington. And he kept asking what it would take to keep me around.

After thinking about it for a day—and in the clear light of day—I came up with the idea for a national trade council. This would be a council inside the White House that would be on equal footing with Cohn's National Economic Council and the National Security Council as well as the Domestic Policy Council when it came to initiating policy.

The focus of the NTC would be on the formation of trade and manufacturing actions which were embodied in the kind of executive orders and presidential memoranda I was writing for the president. And, as director of the National Trade Council, I would also have the rank of assistant to the president for trade and manufacturing policy. Without that highest rank in the White House, I would find myself subservient to the likes of Cohn and Bremberg when it came to the policy process.

When I pitched the idea to Jared, he once again quickly responded with: "Consider it done." And consider it done I did when the transition

TAKING BACK TRUMP'S AMERICA

team released this press release announcing my consolation prize on December 21, some nine days after the Gary Cohn screw job:

President-elect Donald J. Trump today announced the formation of the White House National Trade Council (NTC) and his selection of Dr. Peter Navarro to serve as Assistant to the President and Director of Trade and Industrial Policy.

The formation of the National Trade Council further demonstrates the President-elect's determination to make American manufacturing great again and to provide every American the opportunity to work in a decent job at a decent wage. Navarro is a visionary economist and will develop trade policies that shrink our trade deficit, expand our growth, and help stop the exodus of jobs from our shores.

The mission of the National Trade Council will be to advise the President on innovative strategies in trade negotiations, coordinate with other agencies to assess U.S. manufacturing capabilities and the defense industrial base, and help match unemployed American workers with new opportunities in the skilled manufacturing sector. The National Trade Council will also lead the Buy America, Hire America program to ensure the President-elect's promise is fulfilled in government procurement and projects ranging from infrastructure to national defense.

The National Trade Council will work collaboratively and synergistically with the National Security Council, the National Economic Council, and the Domestic Policy Council to fulfill the President's vision of peace and prosperity through military and economic strength. For the first time, there will be a council within the White House that puts American manufacturing and American workers first, and that thinks strategically about the health of America's defense industrial base and the role of trade and manufacturing in national security.

As a Harvard Ph.D. economist and UC-Irvine professor, Navarro has been instrumental in challenging the prevailing Washington orthodoxy on so-called free trade.[27]

If only this promise and commitment had been kept, I am completely and utterly convinced that Donald John Trump would still be in the White House today as I would have had the high ground from which to launch our policy initiatives in the trade arena. Yet even this commitment would not be kept, and it would be one of the worst days of my life—the president's Inauguration Day—that I would find out how I had been betrayed yet a second time.

An Ominous Prelude to the Priebus Daze

The first inkling of that betrayal would come a week before Inauguration Day and a few days before I was going to board the Acela train to Washington to start my new career as a senior White House official in the Trump administration.

At about eight o'clock that night, as I was cleaning up some tasks on my computer, none other than the chief of the November 9thers Reince Priebus—by then, the president-elect's new chief of staff—walked into the War Room and walked right over to me for what would turn out to be a very uncomfortable chat.

Now, the best thing I can say about Reince Priebus is that he is a very likable sort. A little gnome of a guy with an infectious smile, you just kind of feel happy around him. That is Reince's charm, and that is why you put a guy like him as chairman of the Republican National Committee, which is nothing more than a glorified fundraising operation specializing in glad-handing.

By the way, Reince's favorite form of *Game of Thrones* treachery was to make up something the Boss had allegedly said to throw you off the policy scent. For example, Reince might say to me as he did that night: "The President-elect says he doesn't want to do tariffs right away and that we will have to wait." Of course, that was complete and utter BS.

Now here is what made me so uncomfortable at that meeting: In his "aw shucks" kind of manner, Reince started raising the issue of me perhaps going over to the Department of Commerce to help Wilbur Ross out instead of coming to the White House as the director of the National Trade Council.

Of course, my antenna immediately went up, and I saw this—as it would turn out correctly—as what would be the opening salvo of a sustained campaign waged by Priebus, Steve Mnuchin, and Gary Cohn to ease—nay, shove—me out of the White House, out of their RINO globalist hair, and under the thumb of Ross.

I told Reince flat out that night "no way," that I had been announced as an assistant to the president, and I had a National Trade Council to run at the White House.

Thus rebuffed, Reince went on to make it clear that trade policy would indeed have to take a back seat early in the administration to what had been decided to be other top priorities.

"So what exactly are you talking about here Reince? The campaign I participated in had trade at the top of the list of action items to be done."

Reince responded by saying the first priorities of the administration would be to repeal Obamacare and pass a tax cut.

I said, "Oh really? How do you think that is going to play in Peoria with our blue-collar manufacturing swing voter base? Or, more precisely, how do you think that's going to play in Michigan, Pennsylvania, and in your home state of Wisconsin?"

After hemming and hawing, Reince didn't have much more to say, and we left it at that. But that conversation left me with a huge uneasy feeling about what awaited me in the DC Swamp. And as an empath who is rarely wrong about such bad feelings, I had indeed accurately sensed an ominous future before me. Little did I know just how bad it would immediately get shortly after the president was sworn in on January 20, 2017.

PART THREE

Let the West Wing
Games Begin &
Lessons Learned

NINE

American Carnage, Cheap Seats, and a Cabinet of Clowns

Americans want great schools for their children, safe neighbor-hoods for their families, and good jobs for themselves. These are the just and reasonable demands of a righteous public.

But for too many of our citizens, a different reality exists: Mothers and children trapped in poverty in our inner cities; rusted-out factories scattered like tombstones across the landscape of our nation; an education system, flush with cash, but which leaves our young and beautiful students deprived of knowledge; and the crime and gangs and drugs that have stolen too many lives and robbed our country of so much unrealized potential.

*This **American carnage** stops right here and stops right now.*

—President Donald John Trump, Inauguration Day, 2016[1]
[emphasis added]

This cold, damp, and dreary Inauguration Day would turn out to be, hands down, the worst day of my entire Trump tour—and I can assure you here that there were some very bad OTHER days.

Like the day after I lit up Canadian prime minister Justin Trudeau and got chewed up every which way but Sunday by the Boss. Like the day John Kelly told me I had to report to Gary Cohn and cc every one of my emails to one of the biggest rectal cavities I have ever met. Like the day I was told that the chief executive officer of Kodak had likely engaged in insider trading and thereby killed the best deal I have ever done in my life—one which would have established America's independence in essential medicines manufacturing. And yes, like the day Larry Kudlow got appointed to replace Gary Cohn as the director of the National Economic Council. I could go on and on.

Two days earlier, a new demon had entered my life via email with some beyond devilish news. That demon came by the name of Rob Porter in the corporal form of a man who President Trump himself might have said, as he often did, "was right out of central casting."

This man, really an angry and repressed little boy in a man's body, looked to be right off the cover of *Gentlemen's Quarterly*, if, that is, *GQ* had an edition for RINO Republicans only.

Tall, lean, chiseled, and charming, with a Reaganesque coif and a large rack of impeccably tailored pinstripe suits in a closet that hid so many of his secrets, Rob Porter had a resume to die for: president of the Harvard Republican Club, summer internship at the White House Domestic Policy Council, Rhodes scholar at Oxford, Harvard Law School. He could check every single box on his way up the ladder to the White House.

Oh, did I mention that Porter's father, Roger, was famous in and of himself, working in the Ford, Reagan, and H. W. Bush administrations. In fact, there's more than one photo of little Rob with Poppa Roger in the Oval Office with President Reagan.

Clearly, from his early years, Rob Porter's dream was to get back to the White House, and that dream would come true when he was appointed as the White House staff secretary—a position that would turn out to be one of the most important, mismanaged, and therefore consequential in the Trump White House.

Of course, the dirty little secret about Rob Porter which both White House Legal Counsel Don McGahn and two chiefs of staff in Reince Priebus and John Kelly would hide from President Trump and the world to their everlasting shame was that Rob Porter was a walking anger management issue. In fact, Porter had not one but two former wives alleging significant spousal abuse *and* a former girlfriend with similar complaints.[2]

By the way, Porter's anger was a peculiar kind of incendiary and white hot rage that could erupt in a matter of seconds. I know this because I would experience it on more than one occasion while Porter was in the White House.

On one such occasion, I was in Rob's office with several members of the White House press team, including the sweet, smart Natalie Strom and the soon to be Trump *Team of Vipers* author and Trump turncoat Cliff Sims. In a nanosecond, as he slammed a big stack of papers down on his desk, Porter morphed from Barney Fife of Mayberry into Jack Nicholson in *The Shining*.

Porter proceed to then falsely accuse me and several people in the room of being the source of a damaging leak. When Porter finished reading us the riot act, I calmly told him I didn't care if he vented his rage at me, but he had no right to cast his anger either at, or in front of, the good people in the room who had been working so hard on the project.

Later in the day, Rob would come meekly to my office and contritely apologize. It was a similar kind of behavior described by his ex-wives. So I was not surprised at all by the scandal.

But here is what remains the bigger point: The fact that Porter, the only person in the White House other than President Donald John Trump who would handle every single document that would pass over the President's Resolute Desk, would never get a top security clearance was one of the great failings of the Trump White House.

Of course, there are many reasons why people are denied security clearances in the White House, and a big one is they might be open to blackmail. Certainly, there were plenty of people who could have held those spousal abuse allegations over Porter's head for their own game.

That said, let me turn now back to the devilish news that this new demon in Rob Porter had brought into my life several nights before. This news came in the form of an email containing substantial edits to the executive order I had drafted to establish the National Trade Council I was supposed to be the director of.

A National Trade Council Stillbirth

Recall here that as consolation prize for being elbowed out of the way as the director of the National Economic Council, President Trump had announced I would have my own policy council dedicated towards the rebuilding of America's manufacturing base. However, when I opened the attachment to Rob Porter's email and saw the proposed edits, it was a gut punch.

In the new version of the executive order, my beloved National Trade Council had been downgraded from a true policy council to a unit *within* the National Economic Council. That meant in order to get anything done, I would have to report to none other than the man who had taken my original job, Gary Cohn.

The most frustrating part about the whole situation was that for the next several days leading into Inauguration Day—the day the order was supposed to be signed, formalizing my position—I couldn't get a hold of anybody. Not Rob Porter. Not Reince Priebus. And certainly not Gary Cohn.

I should say here that if I had known then what I know now, I might have been able to stop what was about to be heaped upon me along with the decimation of Donald Trump's trade agenda. To fight back, my first best option would have been to call the Boss directly and explain to him how dark forces within his White House were up to no good. But I didn't yet know how to do that. In fact, the only way I could reach the Boss in those days before I had his private cell phone number was to go through the very people who were trying to crush me.

That obvious constraint still left me a second option, the art of the strategic leak. The equally obvious gambit here would have been to call up Jonathan Swan at *Axios* or Daniel Lippman at *Politico* or Maggie Haberman at the *New York Times* or Damian Paletta at the *Washington Post* or Jennifer Jacobs at *Bloomberg* or any one of a number of reporters on the prowl for the latest scoop about the Trump administration and come out guns a blazing.

The headline here might have been something like "Policy Coup at White House as National Trade Council Arrives Stillborn." As part of my big reveal, I would have tried to spin the story in a way where Gary Cohn and Goldman Sachs were attempting a leveraged buyout of the White House behind the president's back by taking out one of the president's most loyal advisors—with the new RINO Chief of Staff in full collusion.

Of course, there were problems with this gambit as well. First, I did not yet know which reporters to call or trust—none of the ones I just named were as yet on my radar.

Second, most of the folks in the press were as eager to kill me as my enemies inside the perimeter were. I was, after all, the highest profile Populist Economic Nationalist among the president's advisors, and I had been often mocked and ridiculed during the campaign by a corporate media seeking to marginalize me.

The upshot of all of this was that resistance was futile at this point. This *was* my first rodeo, I was about one hundred miles up the DC Swamp without a paddle, and, much to my chagrin and dismay, I would soon be even without a lifeboat, much less a canoe.

A Sea of Pink Hats Amidst Trump Red

After cooking breakfast for my wife and stepson who had arrived from California for the occasion, we all bundled up and began what would be a two-mile slog in the cold wind and occasional rain to the inauguration ceremony on Capitol Hill. Yes, it was as cold as a CNN anchor interviewing Kellyanne Conway—I never get tired of that line.

After this long march, there would be more bad news as I wended my way with my family to what would turn out to be some of the cheapest seats at the event. Strictly nosebleed on the West Lawn of Capitol Hill amongst the masses we would sit.

Yes, this was yet another insult and message hurled my way by Reince Priebus and Katie Walsh letting me know that I was being walled off from the halls of power. As I looked around at others sitting in the section where I had been assigned, I saw plenty of familiar faces from the campaign and transition teams. But unlike me, every single one of them was a lower echelon staffer who would serve many rungs below where I had been slated to land—as an assistant to the president. Yet, there would be one more big insult to come—and very soon.

Oh, and by the way, please don't consider me a diva here. I didn't care one whit that I was sitting in a crappy aluminum chair in the mud. The point was simply that I was being sent the message and the message was loud and clear: I was not welcome in the White House.

These cheap seats notwithstanding, it still was quite a show.

The moment DJT put his expansive hand on not one but two Bibles—the 1861 Bible used to swear in Abraham Lincoln and the president's personal Bible given to him by his mother in 1955—it began to lightly rain. As a microcosm of the press and Twitter wars that would dog the administration, journalistic opinion was split as to whether this precipitation was a good or bad omen.

Time magazine would report:[3] "Supporters of the new commander-in-chief took Mother Nature's timing as a sign of cleansing, while his opponents perceived it as the sky joining them in mourning the transition of power." Liberal angst tweets ranged from "Mother Nature cries" to the "skies are weeping" while the religious right noted that in the Bible "Rain is a sign of God's blessing."[4]

The inauguration speech itself was vintage campaign DJT with a nice presidential burnish. My favorite passage perfectly captured the underlying rationale of the Trump trade agenda as well as the broader spirit of Make America Great Again. Said the newly minted President as the sun tried to peek through the gloom:[5]

> *We've defended other nation's borders while refusing to defend our own. And spent trillions of dollars overseas while America's infrastructure has fallen into disrepair and decay. We've made other countries rich while the wealth, strength, and confidence of our country has disappeared over the horizon.*
>
> *One by one, the factories shuttered and left our shores, with not even a thought about the millions upon millions of American workers left behind. The wealth of our middle class has been ripped from their homes and then redistributed across the entire world. But that is the past. And now we are looking only to the future.*
>
> *We assembled here today are issuing a new decree to be heard in every city, in every foreign capital, and in every hall of power. From this day forward, a new vision will govern our land.*
>
> *From this moment on, it's going to be America First. Every decision on trade, on taxes, on immigration, on foreign affairs, will be made to benefit American workers and American families.*

As I took all of this in, the contrast from where I sat in the cheap seats with what I watched upon the stage on the Capitol building could not have been more stark. Through the water-smeared lenses of my small set of binoculars, there was my brother-in-arms Wilbur Ross smiling and waving to his adoring fans.

Truth be told, the Trump cabinet beyond Wilbur would turn out to be one of the worst cabinets ever assembled by a president-elect.

Indeed, far too many would leave in some form of disgrace, disloyalty, or disarray. Talk about American carnage.

Some of the cabinet choices were simply monumental mismatches. For example, Ben Carson is a good, intelligent, loyal man with a broad skill set. But that skill set in no way translated well to the Department of Housing and Urban Development.

Carson, as you may recall, was really the only one of the gang of sixteen Republican candidates in the 2016 primary who would give Trump an initial run for his money. And perhaps for that reason, Carson was the only one of those sixteen who Trump didn't dare demean. Nope, there would be no "Little Marco," "Low Energy Jeb," or "Lyin' Ted" moniker for the good Dr. Ben.

With his extensive medical background, Carson *should* have been the secretary of Health and Human Services (HHS). And when the pandemic rolled around, Carson—not the hapless Pence—should have been the China virus czar.

Instead, HHS wound up with a Big Pharma fan in Alex Azar orchestrating a comedy of tragic errors that would needlessly kill hundreds of thousands of Americans.

As another monumental mismatch, there was Jeff Sessions. As I have noted, Sessions had been the first US senator to endorse Trump; he was (and is) a rabid China Hawk, and there is no man more loyal to President Trump to ever have walked God's good earth than Jeff.

Of course, Jeff's main flaw is that he is not exactly the sharpest tool in the shed. That's why throwing Jeff as attorney general to the lions and jackals at the Department of Justice was even more darkly funny than backwatering Ben Carson at HUD.

Sessions would quickly be screwed over by the very same bureaucrats at the Department of Justice who had schemed and dreamed of taking Trump down with their phony Russia Hoax. When these bureaucrats seduced Sessions into recusing himself from investigating that Russia Hoax, it was like a Democrat dream come true.

The rest is, of course, history. With that single ill-advised decision, Sessions plummeted from Trump grace like a comet crashing to earth. The Russia Hoax itself would never get properly investigated before the 2020 Election Day, and it was only a matter of time before Sessions would get tweeted out the Trump door.

The tragedy here is that if Jeff had simply been appointed to be the secretary of Homeland Security, he would likely have served with distinction for the entire four years of the administration, and we damn well would have had a far superior border security policy then we wound up with.

Of Dim Bulbs and #MeToo Victims

Besides these kind of mismatches, President Trump simply had some very bad luck. For example, Andy Puzder was the chief executive officer of CKE Restaurants, which includes fast food chains like Carl's Jr. and Hardee's.

I had met Andy on the campaign trail and loved the guy. He was one of those free market and free trade business types who, after you sat him down and explained the six ways from Sunday that Communist China was stealing American jobs, would quickly become a Trump trade policy convert.

During the campaign, Andy had indeed done yeoman's work writing pro-Trump op-eds—he had a direct pipeline to the influential editorial page of the *Wall Street Journal*. Both telegenic and articulate, Andy also performed as one of our best TV surrogates preaching the gospel of Trump on business-friendly cable networks like Fox Business and CNBC.

Well, as soon as Andy Puzder got nominated for secretary of labor, all hell broke loose. It was a hell ginned up particularly by the AFL-CIO, which took great umbrage with the fact that Puzder had had the gall to oppose the minimum wage.

The next thing we all knew, the piranha of the left-wing press were wrapping a decades-old set of false spousal abuse allegations against Puzder in the new fish wrap of the #MeToo movement. Never mind that Puzder's ex-wife had recanted all her false claims shortly after Trump won the election in November.

Never mind indeed. The knives were out, and faced with an onslaught of bad press, Andy, a brilliant, decent, and honorable man, would withdraw his nomination on February 15. He would become the first cabinet appointee of the Trump presidency to fall, and this would be another case of subtraction by addition.

This is because the man who would be added to the cabinet to take Andy's place would be a ticking time bomb that would blow up in another kind of scandal several years into the administration. The man in question was Alex Acosta.

Don't Cry for Me Lolita Island

Let me give you a funny story here before I dish on the Alex Acosta tragedy *cum* soap opera. While Wilbur Ross was waiting for his confirmation as secretary of commerce, I invited him to set up shop in my office at the White House. And Wilbur would quickly take me up on that offer and pretty much come and go as he pleased.

One day when I returned from lunch, I found Wilbur sitting there with a guy who he simply introduced as "Alex." Wilbur was interviewing this lean, broad-nosed, and vaguely Latino-looking gentlemen as his possible deputy secretary at Commerce, and when this guy left my office, Wilbur groused about how this "dud" lacked the kind of energy and financial acumen that were prized in the Ross calculus.

Of course, the very next day, this very same Alex Acosta—I now knew his last name—would be announced as President Trump's second nominee for secretary of labor. Boy, did I get a laugh out of that—and an equal laugh out of Wilbur's sheepish grin when he heard the news. Acosta, by the way, who had been recommended to the president by White House Legal Counsel Don McGahn, would cruise through a rather easy confirmation process and be approved on a 60 to 38 vote.[6]

Alex Acosta and I would go on to do some very good work together. Unlike Wilbur, I found him to be razor-sharp and eminently sensitive to getting stuff done in Trump time, which is to say as soon as possible, and truth be told, I was sorry to see Acosta go. This was particularly true because his replacement, Eugene Scalia, the son of Supreme Court Justice Antonin Scalia, was another poor Trump cabinet choice and yet another George W. Bushie RINO.

Not only did this anti-labor ideologue in Scalia make it more difficult for President Trump to woo the Teamsters and autoworkers and plumbers and pipefitters and carpenters and other labor unions we might well have gotten into the Trump fold in 2020. When it came time to crack down on American pension funds investing in highly risky and nontransparent Communist Chinese companies, Scalia, who as labor secretary had broad authority over such pension fund investments, simply would not cooperate with the White House.

As to why Acosta would prove to be such a ticking time bomb, the fuse was lit during his tenure as the US attorney for the Southern District of Florida. In that post, Acosta had approved a "get out of jail card free" deal for the sexual predator Jeffrey Epstein, who molested or sexually abused an estimated eighty women over a five-year period.[7]

The worst part of the Epstein deal was that it was conducted in secret, without *any* consultation from the victims. The *Miami Herald* would castigate it as the "deal of a lifetime,"[8] and Acosta would later be slapped on the wrist by a federal judge for violating the Crime Victims' Rights Act.

It is an open question as to why Alex cut the deal, but it was no secret that Jeffrey Epstein had friends in very high places and across the political aisle. These friends included everyone from Democrat Bill Clinton and Prince Andrew to Wilbur Ross himself, and Trump confidant Tom Barrack.

No doubt white hot pressure had been applied on Acosta from multiple vectors of attack, he had folded, and his cowardice under political fire would come to blindside him and the Boss years later.

By the way, one of the things I hate most is watching grown men cry. And that's exactly what I had to see on July 12, 2019.

Just by chance, I was traveling with POTUS and taking a rare trip with him on Marine One. While waiting under the portico of the East Wing as the Boss conducted one of his impromptu press conferences, he was joined by Acosta who gave a teary-eyed goodbye to America.

Truth be told, Acosta was doing nothing other than feeling sorry for *himself* when he should have been feeling sorry for the young women he had sold out. Sometimes, you just have to own it.

Corruptions R Us

As for some of the other cabinet secretary choices involving moral turpitude, there would be a surfeit. These included most notably Scott Pruitt at the Environmental Protection Agency, Tom Price at Health and Human Services, David Shulkin at the Veterans Administration, and Ryan Zinke at the Department of Interior. Each would resign in their own kind of disgrace because of an ethics scandal, and all would weaken the Trump administration in their own way by doing so.

While Price and Shulkin would turn out to be nothing more than grifters with a weakness for traveling first class on the taxpayer's dime, both Pruitt and Zinke would be far more dangerous.

Maybe it is because of my love of the ocean having grown up in Florida that I thought that the appointment of Pruitt, a rabid anti-environmentalist, was a particularly unnecessary punch in the nose to an American public that likes to be governed from the middle. I wasn't surprised in the slightest when he was embroiled in a sweetheart deal with a gas industry lobbying firm. Good riddance, I thought, as soon as he was gone.

As for Ryan Zinke, I have the greatest respect for anyone who serves as a Navy SEAL. Yet, I would lose that respect for Zinke within minutes of meeting him at a showdown at the White House over the Jones Act in the office of then OMB director Mick Mulvaney.

The Jones Act is America's oldest expression of Buy American legislation. It requires that all ships carrying cargo between two US ports be American-built, -owned, -crewed, and -flagged. It is the single most important piece of congressional legislation bolstering America's shipbuilding industry.

Given that the two most simple rules in the Trump White House were supposed to be Buy American and Hire American, stewardship over the Jones Act was clearly in my remit as the director of the Office of Trade and Manufacturing Policy.

As for my showdown with Ryan Zinke, Mick Mulvaney had called the meeting ostensibly to review a proposal by Customs and Border Protection Commissioner Kevin McAleenan. It was a proposal that had literally been years in the making, and it was designed to strengthen a critical part of the Jones Act related to oil and gas drilling offshore by closing a glaring loophole forged at one point by the Big Oil lobby.

At the Mulvaney meet, I quickly discovered that Mick's real agenda was to kill the Customs and Border Protection proposal. As to why Mick wanted to do so despite President Trump's professed support for Buy American, there was this:

Mick is an extreme version of a Libertarian opposed to any kind of intervention in the marketplace. Accordingly, any form of Buy

American policy was simply not his cup of Tea Party tea. Yep, that kind of anti-Buy American zealot was in the Trump administration—and I would clash repeatedly with him, first at OMB and then when Mick became the third chief of staff of the Trump White House.

In point of fact, Ryan Zinke really didn't belong at the meeting—he was the secretary of the interior, not the secretary of energy. Yet Zinke would perform admirably as both a useful idiot and puppet for the Big Oil lobbyists who had taken dead aim at McAleenan's Jones Act proposal.

You might imagine—and you would be spot on—that I would quickly get into a heated argument with both Zinke and Mulvaney. Meanwhile, Kevin McAleenan sat there like the milquetoast he was and wouldn't even fight for his own damn proposal. As this is going on, I am thinking to myself: "You have to be kidding me. Exactly what White House am I sitting in?"

Of course, the other guy I had to fight that day was none other than White House Legal Counsel Don McGahn. As I had quickly found out early in the administration, McGahn was another Never-Trumper, and sure enough, here he was, opposing a Buy American policy on libertarian grounds just like Mulvaney.

In his opposition, McGahn unnecessarily weighed in with a bogus legal view questioning the legality of the CBP proposal. It was flat out disingenuous as a critique. He knew it. I knew it. But Mulvaney would seize upon McGahn's opposition to kill that CBP proposal.

In this way, a golden opportunity to create more American manufacturing jobs was scattered to the ideological winds. At least Ryan Zinke did not last very long—and his replacement in David Bernhardt as interior secretary would turn out to be one of the best appointments Donald Trump would ever make.

The Real Clown at This Cabinet Clown Show

Now, this may sound unkind—heck, it is unkind, but what the heck—the Trump cabinet member who most looked like a clown with his red cheeks and bulbous red nose and perennial huge grin was Sonny Perdue, Trump's secretary of agriculture.

Perdue was not, however, to be underestimated, and I would battle him repeatedly because of his stiff opposition to the Trump tariffs.

It wasn't the tariffs *per se* that Sonny opposed. Rather, Perdue knew full well—like we all did—that any tariffs the president might impose, particularly on China, would inevitably lead to some form of Chinese retaliation.

Of course, it would be his farmer constituents who would bear the brunt of that retaliation. So Sonny did everything he could to subvert the Trump tariff paradigm.

The irony of the situation was that America's farmers were some of the staunchest Trump supporters, and most were more than ready to take the Chinese retaliation bullet for the greater good of cracking down on China's economic aggression. But not Sonny Perdue.

Call him a hero if you want—they loved the SOB on Wall Street. I just marked Sonny Perdue down as yet another sapper inside the perimeter trying to scuttle the most critical part of the president's trade and economic policy.

Interestingly enough, the worst thing Sonny did to the Boss's trade policy had nothing to do with the China tariffs. Instead, it had every-thing to do with the president's imperative to fast track the renegotiation of the toxic NAFTA trade deal with Mexico and Canada. Sonny didn't like that fast-tracking because he feared Mexican and Canadian retali-ation against his farmers if we pushed too hard for a quick NAFTA renegotiation.

I vividly remember the April 26 day I arrived at the Oval Office with an executive order that the Boss the previous day had asked me to draft. This little one-pager packed a neat little punch because it would have pulled us out of NAFTA within nine months if a successful negotiation wasn't consummated before that date.

This was a genius strategy if I do say so myself, and one that I had pushed hard for in the Oval Office. This was a genius strategy because the nine-month deadline would have put appropriate pressure on both the Mexicans and the Canadians to get off their rear ends and start negotiating in far better faith than they had up to that point—and nine months was a Goldilocks deadline, just long enough to give everybody time to get a detailed renegotiation done.

Unbeknownst to me, Sonny snuck into the Oval before I arrived for the signing with a map filled with red dots that purported to show how important the farm vote was across the country. It was pure deception on Sonny's part because if he had overlaid all of the *manufacturing* jobs at risk from bad trade deals like NAFTA, that would have dwarfed any possible job losses in the farm belt from the threatened NAFTA withdrawal—and anyway, the whole point of the threat was simply to get a quicker NAFTA renegotiation.

Remember here that direct on-farm employment only amounts to only 1.4 percent of US employment.[9] In contrast, manufacturing accounts for about 8.5 percent of the total nonfarm workforce.[10]

This disparity notwithstanding, Sonny would use that *faux* farm vote map to get the Boss to back off his NAFTA threat. By the time I got to the Oval with the requisite executive order ready to be signed, Sonny's dirty deed—with an assist from Gary Cohn and Rob Porter—was done.

Sonny Perdue saw it as a great victory. I saw it as yet more Bad Process pulled off by Bad Personnel and yet another missed opportunity.

Of course, we eventually got NAFTA renegotiated. But it took far, far longer than it should have. If we had simply put the right pressure on the Mexicans, and particularly the Canadians, as my executive order would have done, we would have had a much stronger agreement much quicker.

A KORUS of Fools

Besides Treasury Secretary Steve Mnuchin, two of the most damaging cabinet picks would be Jim "Mad Dog" Mattis at the Pentagon and Rex Tillerson at the State Department.

The first time I met Mattis was in the Oval Office on May Day, May 1, 2017. It was not pleasant for either him or me.

On this date, the Boss was chewing out both Mattis and Tillerson for opposing his efforts to renegotiate a grossly unfair trade deal with South Korea. It was the very deal that Hillary Clinton had originally been responsible for getting to the finish line during the Obama administration and the very same deal that the Boss had promised to renegotiate in his June 2016 Jobs Plan speech.

KORUS, as it was called, was just a horrible deal that was helping to destroy our auto industry and would eventually decimate our pickup truck industry. In the mercantilist process, KORUS would destroy tens of thousands of high-paying, blue-collar manufacturing jobs in key battleground states like Michigan, Ohio, and Wisconsin.

Memo to Mad Dog Mattis: in the Oval Office, the term "battleground" generally refers to the states in America where presidential elections are won or lost. Yet old Mad Dog just could never wrap his head around that kind of political reality so he inevitably had a knee-jerk negative reaction whenever we tried to stir up any kind of trade policy trouble with our putative military allies.

On this day in the Oval, both Mattis and Tillerson were opposing any renegotiation of the Korean deal because they didn't want to upset either the delicate military calculus (Mattis' view) or diplomatic alliance (Tillerson's) with the South Koreans.

The Boss had brought me over to the Oval to wax eloquent both on how the mercantilist South Koreans were screwing us and thereby destroying a key part of our defense industrial base as well as to explain a core principle of the administration to these Trump trade policy apostates, namely, that *economic security is indistinguishable from national security.*

As President Trump would say eloquently, when you sacrifice economic security on the altar of national security—for example, by allowing bad trade deals like the one with South Korea to fester—you wind up losing *both* economic and national security. "Hey Jim Mattis: how do you think we are going to build those tanks you need if we don't have the factories to do so?"

At any rate, I would pay a heavy price for my candor that day. Mattis would torment me every which way but loose whenever I needed anything from the Pentagon. Tillerson would just ignore me—just as, I might add, Tillerson did the president.

As for the rest of the assortment of gypsies, tramps, thieves, clowns, misfits, and occasionally competent bureaucrats that would make up the original Trump cabinet, Linda McMahon at the Small Business Administration was as tough and smart and good as Betsy DeVos was bad to the point of often embarrassing at the Department of Education.

In a similar vein, Trump loyalist Mike Pompeo at the Central Intelligence Agency was, dare I say, as intelligent a choice as the appointment of the far too ambitious Never-Trumper and Nikki Haley as ambassador to the United Nations was unfortunate.

Oh Nikki, Nikki, Nikki. The only politician more treacherous, deceitful, and dangerous from South Carolina than you is Senator Lindsey Graham. More about each of these two much later.

TEN

My Hard Pratfall
from Trumpian Grace

Katie Walsh, Deputy White House Chief of Staff, former RNC staffer and notorious Never Trumper, has been exposed as the White House leaker... With so many enemies in his own camp and his own party, our new president... must scrutinize closely the potential Judases working around him.[11]

—Thomas Madison, Powdered Wig Society, February 21, 2017

After the Boss's Inauguration Day speech, it was time to get to work. So I headed over to the rendezvous point for staffers at what had been the headquarters for the Presidential transition. This was a General Services Administration office building just west of the White House grounds at 1800 F Street.

I hadn't visited this paean-to-drab 1950s-style architecture for more than a month. My one enduring memory of that first visit was a rather eye-opening meeting with the then nominee for secretary of state, Rex Tillerson. He had set up shop at the HQ to practice for the tough grilling he could expect during his confirmation hearings in sessions that were accurately, but not so affectionately, called "murder boards."

During this visit, King Rex let me know in no uncertain terms that as secretary of state he would be balancing the promises of Donald Trump to crack down on the unfair trade practices of countries around the world with his own need for judicious diplomacy, and as Tillerson quite openly expressed his intentions to subvert the Trump trade policy paradigm, he made copious references to the need for well-functioning global supply chains.

Reading between Rex's lines, he, as the former chairman of Exxon— one of the biggest multinational corporations in the world—was telling me to forget about all that Populist Economic Nationalist stuff where we would bring our supply chains home. In Rex's world, that's not the way the world should work—at least when it came to allocating resources "efficiently," that is, in a way to maximize corporate profits. Let the devil and blue-collar workers take the hindmost.

At least Rex was honest about his intentions to sabotage our trade policy—despite the fact he had gotten *not* a single vote in the election, and I would remember that day well almost a year later at a big showdown in the Roosevelt room over the possible imposition of tariffs on China.

Virtually every top cabinet member with a stake in trade policy was there. Besides Tillerson, there was Treasury's Steve Mnuchin, Commerce's Wilbur Ross, the Pentagon's Jim Mattis, Agriculture's Sonny Perdue, and even Secretary of Labor Alex Acosta. Every single person in that room, including National Security Advisor H. R. McMaster, the Director of the National Economic Council Gary Cohn, and the always lurking Staff Secretary Rob Porter argued *against* the tough measures President Trump was proposing.

In fact, the only guy in the room supportive of the president was yours truly, and this unified opposition in the Roosevelt room to the centerpiece of his entire campaign and economic strategy seemed to be a wake-up call for the Boss.

As I had watched this showdown all unfold, I thought to myself: "Yes, the Boss is finally smelling the coffee that many of those on his putatively nationalist team might be playing for the other globalist side."

In fact, whenever I saw President Trump's eyebrows go up, it suggested an epiphany was at least percolating. When Rex Tillerson pointedly said to me that day in the Roosevelt room in his slow Texas drawl, "Peter, you simply don't understand the global supply chains," and I had quickly retorted, "Rex, you simply don't understand the president's trade policy," I at least might have climbed up a few notches in the

Boss's respect for me. Yet, in that first year, as with so many showdowns on trade policy, it would be all for naught.

At any rate, it had been on that brief trip to Washington, DC, where it had become crystal clear that the real locus of power and center of gravity of the transition was in New York at Trump Tower rather than in the DC Swamp. And I vowed never to return to DC until it was time for the president to be inaugurated. That time had now come, and this, my second visit to the DC presidential transition team headquarters, would make the first tawdry visit seem like an all-expense paid trip to Tahiti.

Stabbed in the Front

There would be nothing subtle about what Reince Priebus and Katie Walsh were about to do to me. As I moved slowly through security like a cow moving through a cattle pen to the slaughterhouse, I looked around and saw no familiar faces other than some low-level staffers.

Inside, I was given my welcome kit, and in the cover letter, there was this shattering news: I was addressed as a deputy assistant to the president rather than a full assistant. And here, I must confess that in my then naïveté, I had never imagined that they would stick *that* particular knife in my chest.

Sure, they looked like they were trying to take away my National Trade Council. And yes, there might be jockeying over whether I would have an office in the coveted West Wing or be exiled to the Eisenhower Executive Office Building. But I *never* thought they would strip me of the rank that President Trump himself had bestowed on me in a press release.

And to be clear here lest you again think I'm some kind of diva: I have never been particularly rank conscious. But I knew damn well right then that this deputy versus assistant rank mattered, and I would be horribly right.

As an assistant to the president, I would have been entitled to walk-in privileges to see the Boss anytime in the Oval Office or East Wing residence. That alone was literally worth the price of admission as it would be impossible to wall me off from President Trump.

As an assistant rather than deputy assistant, I would also have an open invitation to all senior staff meetings and walk-in privileges to virtually any senior staff member. At the convenience and perquisite level, I would likewise be able to reserve at a moment's notice a staff car to take me anywhere I wanted.

At a personal level, I would even have free Cadillac health care at Walter Reed Hospital. This was not an inconsequential benefit as it would play out in the first several years of my tenure at the White House, as I would be plagued by a series of nagging medical issues that were a direct result of the stress I was under—issues that I was unable to get proper medical care for because of the lack of ready access to Walter Reed.

To this point, I came down with a bad staphylococcus infection on my right ankle early in 2017. For a few days, it made my whole leg look like I had elephantiasis. I'm still grappling with a bit of residual damage from that.

At any rate, this demotion was, if not the biggest, then certainly the most consequential F-U that anybody had ever given me. And when I say "anybody" in this particular case, I mean Reince Priebus and Katie Walsh, in all likelihood acting as the water boy and water girl for the likes of a gleeful Gary Cohn and a Machiavellian Jared Kushner.

When I confronted Katie Walsh about what I hoped was simply an oversight, she simply told me that there weren't enough assistant positions to go around. As we talked, Walsh could barely suppress her smile and disdain. She was having a good screw with me, and she was clearly enjoying it. Message received.

An Office Lost and Found

Things didn't get any better once I got over to the White House to get my badge, cell phone, and laptop computer and find what I thought would be my new office. That "office" turned out not to be in the West Wing where all power does indeed reside in the White House. Instead, as I had feared, I had been exiled to the Eisenhower Executive Office Building across the street from the White House.

And here was the biggest joke of all that Priebus and Walsh would play on me: my "office," such as it was, consisted of a little windowless cubbyhole that had been assigned to about ten other people. In other words, I didn't have an office at all—I had another Dilbert-style big F-U.

In fact, for the next month, I would wander around the EEOB— and sometimes in the hall outside Stephen Miller's office in the West

Wing—like the Flying Dutchmen working on my laptop while trying to figure out a way both forward and out of the box—nay, coffin—Priebus and Walsh had put me in.

The story of how I made what would be a spectacularly successful escape out of that box would be one that likely saved my entire White House career. It goes something like this:

On yet another cold February day, I would trek into the White House along some very icy streets, and the first thing that would hit me was a frantic call from my one and only deputy Alex Gray. He had been prevented from coming into the West Wing complex because of an alleged badge malfunction.

Given all the crap I had been facing, I immediately jumped to the conclusion that Priebus and Walsh were screwing around not just with me but now with my deputy as well. To this day, I don't know if it was an innocent mistake. I do know that I stomped over to Kushner's office, told him in no uncertain terms that it was one thing to F with me, but he and the clowns over the West Wing needed to draw the line at screwing around with a young man who was simply trying to serve his country.

My rant finally got Jared's attention. Fearing that I might take this all way up to the top of the chain—that possibility did come up in the conversation—he made one call and told whoever it was at the other end of the line to make sure I had an office by the end of the day.

For whatever reason—that was my first inkling that Jared might be the *real* chief of staff—that office turned out to be a four-hundred-square-foot suite on the first floor of the northeast corner of the EEOB with a kick ass outer office that could accommodate up to eight staff—an accommodation I would eventually make as my star rose over the four years of the administration and I steadily added staff.

At any rate, with a twenty-foot-high ceiling and a beautiful view of the north lawn media complex and the White House itself in the background, heaven—at least political heaven—could not have been any prettier. In other words, I had just landed one of the best offices inside the entire White House perimeter.

I can safely say here that if Walsh and Priebus had simply put me in a little office with no view at the outset, it is unlikely that I would have lasted more than a few months. But that big, beautiful office suite—not just one of the very best in the EEOB but three to four times the size of anything most staffers had in the West Wing—would be where my comeback and numerous counterattacks would officially begin.

Indeed, it would be from that office where I would create dozens of executive orders, write dozens of memos (including many that would save hundreds of thousands of American lives during the pandemic), author nearly one hundred articles and reports, solve countless problems, and especially on the weekends, kick back and relax during my breaks, often with a little sports on the two big screen televisions inside the suite.

So at least now this truth can be told: Reince and Katie, you had me on the ropes. But you blew it by overplaying your hand. And you both would be gone long before I would leave—Walsh in just sixty-nine days for leaking.

Memo to the Boss: You might want to make sure that Katie Walsh has nothing ever to do either with your 2024 campaign or in your POTUS 47 White House. She sandbagged you when she was in the West Wing, and, as we will discuss later, Walsh milked you for all your campaign was worth during the 2020 tilt.

Deputy Down, Down a Deputy

Now the other thing I need to tell you about my worst day in the Trump White House is this: Not only was I *unceremoniously* demoted. I also lost one of the two deputy slots I had been promised.

In losing that deputy slot—and this is the buried lede—I was also stripped of my responsibilities for moving a Trump infrastructure bill forward. Both the deputy slot and the infrastructure portfolio were absorbed—no surprise here—into Gary Cohn's National Economic Council. And yes, as with so many things that Priebus, Cohn, and Walsh did at the outset of the administration, this particular move would come back to haunt President Trump and his 2020 reelection chances.

Why? Because for all four years of the Trump administration, Gary Cohn, and then his successor Larry Kudlow, would fail miserably in moving an infrastructure bill on Capitol Hill. This failure—likely the result of these Wall Street hacks not caring a whit about all the jobs an infrastructure bill might create for blue-collar Americans—bordered on the criminal. For no piece of legislation was more important to the

MAGA blue-collar and manufacturing agenda of President Trump than a robust infrastructure bill. None.

In the process of rebuilding our roads and bridges and airports—not to mention our digital infrastructure like fiber and 5G—a robust infrastructure bill would have created millions of manufacturing jobs. Such an infrastructure bill would also have dramatically increased both productivity and wages. Here, a central tenet of economics is that investment in the *public good* of infrastructure inevitably boosts productivity in the *private sector* and therefore increases real wages.

For example, when you build better roads and bridges, you will have more efficient domestic supply chains and shorter transit times to get goods to market. Upgrade your airports and similar good things happen.

It broke my heart to lose this infrastructure portfolio. It broke my heart again when first Cohn and then Kudlow failed miserably in delivering a infrastructure bill. It broke my heart for a third time when Joe Biden, with the help of a lot of the same Democrats and RINO Republicans who had been so unhelpful to President Trump in his bid to pass his own infrastructure bill, gave full throated support to a *faux* Biden "infrastructure" bill.

I say "*faux*" because Biden's abomination dedicated only a relatively small fraction of expenditures to actual infrastructure like roads and bridges. Instead, the rest of Biden's bucks will be squandered on a gaggle of Green New Deal and Robin Hood schemes that will benefit workers in Shanghai and Mumbai a lot more than those in Akron and Scranton.

Here's the broader point:

So many of the mistakes made early in the administration would come back to haunt us in the 2020 election—including this massive Trump legislative miss with infrastructure.

It wouldn't just be the infrastructure bill the 2017 West Wing cast of characters would screw up. It would be virtually the entire Trump legislative agenda for the year.

In considering the politically preferred order of that legislative agenda, it is important to remember this: On the strength of Donald Trump's coattails, the Republican party had seized control of *both* the Senate and House of Representatives on Capitol Hill. By all accounts and measures, we had the Democrats by the proverbial shorthairs, and we should have been locked and loaded to push forward the Trump agenda as expressed in the campaign of Donald Trump.

Instead, however, because of all of the Bad Personnel in the West Wing, the Trump presidency almost immediately went off the legislative rails. The precipitating event was the really inexplicable decision to make repeal and replacement of Obamacare the very first priority of the White House.

When I heard about that decision, I thought this was sheer political lunacy. If Hillary Clinton's experience during the early years of the Bill Clinton presidency had taught us anything, it is that healthcare is an issue where presidencies come to die.

Of course, my second thought was that there was no way in Hades this particular repeal-and-replace-Obamacare initiative would pass. It was just too politically divisive.

Instead, all this tilting at Barack's windmill would do would be to burn precious presidential capital in the first critical hundred days of the administration. But what did I know? I was just that pesky trade advisor in exile across the street in the EEOB.

The Short and Long of It

So just how did this lunacy happen? Here, the blame can squarely be laid on Chief of Staff Reince Priebus and his Legislative Affairs Director Marc Short along with Reince's fellow Badger State compadre, newly minted Republican House Speaker Paul Ryan.

As a reminder from my book *In Trump Time*, Marc Short wormed his way into the White House as an advisor to Vice President Mike Pence during the 2016 campaign. He would turn out to be a very destructive worm as a *de facto* emissary for a Koch network of dark conservative and globalist money dedicated to the defeat of Donald Trump. And Marc Short would play a key role as Iago in the Shakespearean tragedy otherwise known as the *et tu Brute* betrayal of the American Caesar Trump by his own vice president on January 6, 2021.

At any rate, Speaker Ryan would convince Reince that he had the votes to repeal and replace Obamacare,[12] Marc Short was too stupid or arrogant to push back, and pretty soon Ryan, Reince, and Short convinced President Trump to get a quick win on Obamacare before moving on to the next favorite piece of legislation on Reince's RINO list. Nope, not infrastructure but rather the Trump tax cuts.

Now, as I just noted, but it is worth repeating: any damn fool with any sense of history knows that healthcare policy is the mother of all tar babies when it comes to dragging down political careers and presidencies. The fact that this issue almost killed the Clinton presidency in its crib should have been warning enough not to go there. But Reince, Ryan, and Marc Short said that this time would be different.

It was like thinking you could go into Iraq in March of 2003, simply topple Saddam Hussein, and have the troops home by Christmas. Mission accomplished. Right? Wrong!

Of course, we would get bogged down in the battle over Obamacare for six long months, and, as I feared, in the process, the Boss would indeed burn incredible amounts of political capital.

On top of all this, John McCain's famous two thumbs down July 28, 2017, killing of even a weak compromise bill vehemently and venomously turned what had been a simmering squabble between McCain and Trump into a full-blown Hatfields versus McCoys blood feud.

This blood feud would, in turn, help contribute to President Trump's contested loss of Arizona in the 2020 race. Not only did the McCain wing of the Republican Party in Arizona actively campaign against Trump.[13] Key Republican officials in that McCain wing like Governor Doug Ducey, former Senator Jeff Flake, and Cindy McCain herself helped thwart efforts to investigate widespread fraud and election irregularities in Arizona in the 2020 race—Ducey, Flake, and McCain would all be censored by the Arizona Republican Party for their turncoat behavior while Biden would reward McCain with an ambassadorship.[14]

A Flawed Tax Bill Loses the House

President Trump's deeply flawed tax bill that ultimately passed in Congress on December 20, 2017, would have even more far ranging Bad Personnel equals Bad Politics consequences as it would directly contribute to the loss of the House of Representatives to the Democrats in the midterm elections of 2018.

Follow me here: If, for example, Steve Bannon had been chief of staff instead of Reince Priebus and I had been director of the National Economic Council instead of Gary Cohn, we would have pushed for a tax bill just like Priebus and Cohn, albeit only after we had passed an infrastructure bill. However, the Bannon-Navarro version of that tax bill would have *truly* targeted the middle class and done so with far greater political sensitivity.

In particular, both Bannon and I would have pressed *hard* on President Trump to include a tax on the *uber*-wealthy—the top 1 percent of earners. By simply including such a provision, we would have immediately blunted the criticism that this was a tax cut for the wealthy.

Note to the Steve Moores of this world: Any negative *economic* consequences from such a "tax the *uber*-rich" provision would have been negligible. In contrast, the *political* benefits would have been huge. As Steve Bannon might have said with successful passage of such a provision and thereby having secured the president's left flank: "Suck on that Bernie Sanders and Elizabeth Warren."

Even more important politically, neither Bannon nor I would have crafted a piece of tax legislation explicitly designed to screw the Democrats' Blue States in a way designed to redistribute income and tax dollars to the Republicans' Red States. Priebus and Cohn, on the other hand, working in league with Treasury Secretary Steve Mnuchin, Office of Management and Budget Director Mick Mulvaney, and both Paul Ryan and his partner in tax crime on Capitol Hill Kevin Brady, came up with this anything but brilliant idea: the Trump tax bill would significantly reduce the tax deduction on state and local taxes—the so-called SALT provision.

When the Trump tax bill capped the SALT deduction at $10,000, it was a giant SCREW-YOU to middle class homeowners in general. However, that cap disproportionately hit property owners in Blue States like California and New York where home prices and associated property taxes were far higher.

For libertarian purists like Mulvaney, this was a dream come true. His textbook thinking—I sure heard Mick voice it enough—was that by sharply curtailing the SALT deduction, that would lead to a more efficient allocation of investment resources and therefore stronger economic growth. Never mind that nuking the SALT deduction would be a wallet and hammer blow to many middle-class families living in homes in Blue State country, homes that would have cost half as much for the same amenities in flyover Red State land.

As for Priebus and Ryan, they could barely hide their glee at the prospect of kicking the dung out of the Deep Blue States. And the more politicians like Nancy Pelosi and Chuck Schumer and Dianne Feinstein squealed and whined as the debate unfolded, the more pleasure Priebus and Ryan—and a whole gaggle of myopic Republicans on the Hill— took from it.

Yet, here is what these Republicans, along with Mulvaney and Priebus and Ryan and Marc Short—and of course Mnuchin and Cohn— all missed:

Even though there wasn't a snowball's chance in hell that the Republican Party would ever grab a Senate seat in any of the Deep Blue States where the elimination of the SALT deduction would most wound, and even though there was not an ice cube's chance in boiling water of a Republican presidential candidate ever getting any Electoral College votes in these Deep Blue States, *there were still a hell of a lot of Republican-leaning congressional seats in those states.* And ALL of these Republican-leaning seats would suddenly be put up for grabs by the anger engendered by this big SALT SCREW-YOU and assault on middle-class homeowners.

For my part, I had a particularly keen sense of the political dangers and tried my best to warn everybody I could, including the president, that nuking the SALT provision could be politically catastrophic. I understood that because I had lived for more than twenty-five years in the very Reddest part of one of America's Bluest states—Orange County, California.

For any of you who have ever flown into Orange County, you might have noticed the statue of that most famous Republican cowboy John Wayne at the airport. Orange County was also the home of a "Western White House" during the halcyon days of the Nixon administration, and it is the home of Ronald Reagan's Presidential Library.

Knowing all this, you may not be surprised to learn that when Donald Trump took office in January of 2017, Republicans held fully six congressional seats that included some or all of Orange County. We would lose fully four of those seats in 2018 at a time when the Democrats seized the House of Representatives by a count of just thirty-six seats.

As an example of how the Trump tax bill and loss of the SALT deduction hit middle-class Blue Stators so very hard, just consider how hard this alleged "tax cut" hit yours truly. To be clear here, I am a man of modest means—not by choice but rather by bad choices.

In 1992, I squandered a relatively small fortune doing what you should never do in politics, spending your own money on your campaign, in that case, my 1992 San Diego mayor's race. Over time, I fought my way back, and by the early 2000s, I was able to buy a small starter home.

I then parlayed that Laguna Canyon pillbox into a down payment on a $1 million fixer-upper in Laguna Beach. After a half a million dollars in upgrades, and steady property tax escalations over time, I had, along with the interest payments on my jumbo mortgage, more than a nice little SALT deduction every year.

Enter stage right the Trump tax cut. My tax bill the following year would pop up by over $25,000. Moreover, the market value of my beloved ocean view house would fall, along with my net worth, by at least $1 million.

In short, I was living proof right inside the White House that the Trump tax bill was indeed designed not for middle class professors like me—at least not middle classers from a Blue State—but rather more for the *uber* rich. And this was entirely the product of the screw job Paul Ryan, Reince Priebus, Steve Mnuchin, Gary Cohn, and Mick Mulvaney all ginned up to gleefully screw the Deep Blue States.

Of course, all this SALT into the wounds of the Deep Blue States would indeed come back to bite us big time in the 2018 congressional midterms. In Orange County alone, as I have noted, we lost four seats, and this was in no small part because the real estate industry spent a ton of money on the Democrat challengers.

Harley Rouda, a Republican turned Democrat from my own hometown of Laguna Beach, would lead the way, vanquishing ten-term Republican and fellow China Hawk Dana Rohrabacher. Wrote a gleeful *Politico*:

> *Rouda and three other Democrats swept the congressional races, eradicating the GOP from the electoral map in a place that Ronald Reagan once described as the place "where good Republicans go to die." Democrats' blue wave in 2018 was more like a blue tsunami in this affluent and scenic sanctuary nestled between the urban sprawls of Los Angeles and San Diego.*[15]

If only we had instead swapped out a Bannon-Navarro income tax on the *uber*-wealthy for the SALT gambit to get us to the required revenue stream necessary to pass the tax bill, we would have been living high on the political hog—and maybe even held on to a House of Representatives.

It's the House, Stupid, Not the Senate!

Now, I would be remiss here in not pointing out one other big bad decision within the West Wing that would help grease the skids for the Democrats to seize control of the House in 2018. The feckless fools responsible for this particular fiasco would go by the names of Bill Stepien and Johnny DeStefano.

Bill Stepien had come to the White House from Governor Chris Christie's House of Corruption Horrors, yet somehow, by the grace of either God or the Devil, Stepien had avoided a jail cell for his alleged role in Chris Christie's infamous Bridgegate scandal.[16]

Johnny DeStefano was—and remains—a quintessential Deep Swamp RINO political operative right out of the John Boehner School of Glad-Handing—Johnny jumpstarted his career with Boehner. At the White House, Johnny's best qualities included his height, winning smile, and wavy hair. After that, he was a pure zero. If you don't believe me, all you need know is that after he departed the West Wing, John Boy cashed in as a lowly lobbyist for a low-life e-cigarette company.

At any rate, in 2018, Bill Stepien was working at the White House in the Office of Political Affairs while DeStefano was in the Office of Intergovernmental Affairs. It would be their bright idea to focus primarily on Senate, rather than House, races as a way of economizing President Trump's travel time and campaign costs.

By focusing on Senate races, these geniuses would be able to send the Boss on Air Force One to as many states as possible, but as a trade-off, the Boss wouldn't be able to take the time to actually visit many of the key congressional districts that were at risk.

This was because many of the key congressional districts up for grabs did not have an airport that was long enough for Air Force One to land and therefore close enough for the Boss to take a simple limo ride in the Beast directly to the event. Instead, the Boss would have to deplane from Air Force One at a more distant airport and then travel on a fleet of Nighthawk Helicopters to some landing zone nearby the event—often a high school parking lot or football field. From there, the Boss could motor in quickly to the event in the Beast.

By the way, "the Beast" is the nickname for POTUS's heavily armor-plated limousine. It comes with a refrigerator full of the president's own blood type, is sealed for any bioweapons or chemical weapons attack, and tips the scales at an astonishing 10 tons.[17] That's about five times heavier than the average pickup truck.[18]

Sadly, although I did get to ride the Marine One helicopter several times, a trip in the Beast remains on my bucket list.

The more pertinent punchline here, however, is that adding the Nighthawks to the journey substantially increased not just the travel time but also the cost of campaigning. And Stepien and DeStefano along with Kushner simply didn't want to bear that freight.

It was an incredibly stupid "penny-wise, pound-foolish" strategy to focus on Senate races rather than the House of Representatives in this manner. It was stupid because, all things being equal, a president like Trump—arguably the greatest presidential campaigner of all time—would much rather have control of the House of Representatives than the Senate leading into a presidential reelection campaign.

The reason, as I have alluded to, is that members of the House tend to behave like feral cats when it comes to abusing their investigatory powers, and of course the Boss had all manner of investigatory targets on his back. These ranged from possible impeachment proceedings and guilt by association with the Russia Hoax to alleged shady real estate dealings and the release of his tax returns.

Sure enough, once Nancy Pelosi and henchmen like Adam Schiff and Jerry Nadler got control of the House, they would quickly weaponize the House's investigatory powers in a way designed to inflict maximum political damage on the Boss every hour of every day leading up to November 3, 2020. As Yahoo would note:

President Trump has had a rough go of it since the midterms in November.... [T]he elections on November 6th handed Democrats control of the House of Representatives. In addition to being able to thwart Republican legislative efforts, House Democrats will now helm several congressional committees that have the power to investigate— and, if necessary, subpoena—the Trump administration.... [N]ow that Democrats are in charge, the White House should be prepared to field a flood of inquiries into how it's chosen to run the country since Trump took office.[19]

Truth be told here, this was not just a Stepien-DeStefano screw up. It was also a Mitch McConnell screw job.

As Senate Majority Leader, McConnell quietly lobbied the White House to focus on the Senate, constantly raising the specter of not being able to fill seats on the Supreme Court if we lost the Senate. And he would play both Bill Stepien and Johnny DeStefano like fiddling fools to achieve his goal.

Truth be told here once again: Mitch McConnell absolutely hated the Trump trade and border security agendas, and on behalf of his corporate donor base, McConnell did everything possible during our four years to block any progress on moving these agendas—and thereby preserve Corporate America's access to the sweatshops of Latin America and Asia.

And now hear this: Even as Mitch was doing everything he could to smooth the way for appointing conservative judges, he would drag his heels on all of the Trump political appointees we needed to get confirmed by the Senate so that they could begin serving the president and his agenda.

Yes, I hated Mitch McConnell from the moment I was onto his game; and that was just days after I arrived in Washington watching him work—and work against us. Unfortunately, it would take four more years before the Boss would finally go off on McConnell.

Better late than never, I guess, but Mitch sure did a lot of damage to the Trump administration for a guy who was supposed be playing on our team, not the least of which was to help us lose the House. For once the House of Representatives fell to the Pelosites, the stage was set for what would be not one but two supremely politically corrosive impeachments of the president.

For added measure, we would indeed have to endure a wide array of other politically motivated House investigations into everything from the Russia Hoax to alleged malfeasance and mismanagement by the White House during the pandemic—with me caught in the middle of that last cluster puck.

* * *

These were all self-inflicted wounds directly traceable back to Bad Personnel in the White House *who never should have been there to begin with*. And if there ever were a canary in that particular coal mine gasping for a breath of fresh MAGA air, it was me as I entered the White House on Inauguration Day.

At least I had one small piece of good news come my way on my purple haze of a hazing day at the White House. Priebus and Walsh gave me as a consolation prize a blue, rather than a green, badge. With that blue badge, I could at least walk without the humiliation of an escort from the EEOB into the West Wing.

ELEVEN

Process Delayed, Diluted, or Derailed Is Trump Policy Denied

Chaos isn't a pit. Chaos is a ladder.

—Littlefinger, *Game of Thrones*[20]

Day four—the first Monday and business day of the administration—would turn out to be almost as bad for me as day one's Inauguration Day. For it was on this day four that President Donald Trump decidedly did *not* sign all of the executive orders and presidential memoranda I had been working on during the transition. These actions included:

- Branding China a currency manipulator;
- Canceling the proposed US-China Bilateral Investment treaty;
- Renegotiating NAFTA;
- Retooling Secretary of State Hillary Clinton's equally toxic South Korea deal;
- Immediately cracking down on the unfair trade practices of our major trading partners;
- Levying tariffs—including those on China—to dramatically reduce the trade deficit;
- Strengthening and expanding Buy American, Hire American in government procurement;

- Stopping the offshoring of American jobs;
- Imposing steel and aluminum tariffs in the interests of national security; and
- Formally establishing the National Trade Council I was slated to direct.

As an oeuvre, these executive orders and presidential memoranda were pure expressions of both Steve Bannon's philosophy and strategy of Action, Action, Action and Donald J. Trump's Populist Economic Nationalism.

By signing these orders, President Trump could have, in one historical swoop, fulfilled almost every single trade policy promise Candidate Trump had made.

Instead of this red letter day, I felt like the primary target in a *Game of Thrones*-style Red Wedding massacre. That is because when I finally tracked down Rob Porter in his staff secretary office early that day, he told me that all of the actions I had prepared were not ready for the president's Resolute desk.

"Not ready?" I asked him, "How can that be?"

In fact, each of these actions had gone through a careful legal vetting during the transition. This vetting included the very last step in the legal blessing of any presidential executive order. This is to get the approval stamp of "form and legality" from the Office of Legal Counsel within the Department of Justice. And this Stephen Vaughn, Gil Kaplan, and I had certainly done working with a special transition team unit within the Office of Legal Counsel in the weeks leading up to this day.

"Be that as it may," said Porter, "Chief of Staff Priebus has directed me to submit all of these actions to the White House Staff Secretary process."

"What the hell is the Staff Secretary process?" thought I to myself. Oh, would my eyes soon be opened to one of the worst horror shows I have ever had to watch this side of *The Exorcist*.

The Most Powerful Bureaucrat in the West Wing

Before I explain the staff secretary process and why it would prove to be such a poisonous and pivotal element in the Trump White House, it may be useful to describe the role of the staff secretary—and thereby come to understand why the staff secretary can become one of the most powerful people within the West Wing.

It is the staff secretary who is responsible for managing all of the paper flow that comes across a president's desk. If left unchecked or unsupervised, however, as Rob Porter, and later his successor Derek Lyons would be, this staff secretary paper-pusher can quickly become one of the most powerful people in the White House. This is for two reasons.

First, as a censor, the staff secretary can control the flow of news and information that winds up in the president's reading packets and briefing books. This power allows the staff secretary to *exclude* certain information that might otherwise influence the president to take action.

For example, a globalist staff secretary like Porter or Lyons might decide to conveniently omit any articles critical of the president's failure to impose steel tariffs or any letters from steel executives imploring POTUS to do so. So the Boss would be less likely to push for their tariffs.

This power over information flows also allows the staff secretary to *place greater emphasis* on news that might push the president in a particular direction. For example, pile up the Boss's evening reading packet with articles from globalist writers about the possible dangers of tariffs to consumers or the stock market, and the Boss might be more cautious about moving forward with his trade agenda.

This kind of selective censorship hit me personally as one of the things the Boss loved to do to get feedback from his advisors was to scrawl big notes and questions on newspaper articles and then send them by courier over to us for comment. "What do you think of this Peter?" in big red letters. Stuff like that.

When I would answer his question either with a brief memo or a red ink scrawl of my own on the same article I had received, Porter, and later Derek Lyons, would invariably refuse to put it on POTUS's desk or in his overnight reading packet. They claimed it had to go through "process." This was despite the fact that the president had asked me a direct question.

I am sorry, but that is just plain wrong. And in the Trump White House, where the president loved the free flow of information, it was also destructive to his agenda. But that was Rob Porter's and Derek

Lyons's mission all along: destroy at least those parts of the Trump agenda that ran against their globalist grain.

An Intercepted Memo Changes History

By the way, the very worst and perhaps most consequential case of Rob Porter cutting off the free flow of information to the president involved a memo I tried to send POTUS very early in the administration. Here's an excerpt from that memo that illustrates how Porter would put his thumb on the information scale (emphasis added):

March 27, 2017

MEMORANDUM FOR THE PRESIDENT

FROM: PETER NAVARRO, NATIONAL TRADE COUNCIL

SUBJECT: FUTURE DIRECTION OF TRADE POLICY

Thank you for forwarding an article that appeared in the Wall Street Journal entitled "Trump's Trade Vows at Risk." The Trump trade agenda does indeed remain severely hobbled by political forces within the West Wing. At present:

- *It's impossible to get a trade action to your desk for consideration in a timely manner.*
- *Any proposed executive action on trade that moves through the Staff Secretary process is highly vulnerable to dilution, delay, or derailment....*

As accurately reported in the media, G. Cohn has amassed a large power base in the West Wing and [he and his] skilled political operatives [are] fundamentally opposed to the Trump trade agenda. Not reported in the press is that Treasury Secretary Mnuchin is part of Cohn's "Wall Street Wing," which has effectively blocked or delayed every proposed action on trade since [you] the President signed the order withdrawing the US from the [Trans-Pacific Partnership].

If this situation is allowed to persist, **this Administration is likely to fail on trade and suffer catastrophic political consequences.**

Peter Navarro, Memorandum to the President, March 27, 2017

Now you might expect that if a senior White House official writes a memo to the president of the United States that such a memo should and would find its way to the president's desk. And I do believe that if the Boss had actually read this memo, it would have transformed history.

At this early critical juncture, a mere two months in, the Boss would have known exactly what he was up against, and with such knowledge, he would likely have done something about it, at least something much faster than he would finally do.

But here's the thing: POTUS *never even got that memorandum.* He did not get that memo precisely because of Bad Process—but I wouldn't find that out until *several years later.* That's right, several years later.

The reason is that, in my naïveté, I believed that when Rob Porter looked me squarely in the eyes and told me with all due solemnity he had delivered my memo directly to the president, that he had actually done so. Au contraire, mon bozo.

I'm sure Rob had a pretty good laugh about the whole thing. But it was yet one more supreme act of disloyalty both to the president this man served and to the process he was supposed to protect and respect.

Game of Thrones Redux

As important as controlling the flow of information is as a lever of power for the staff secretary, it is the second sphere of staff secretary influence that is ultimately more important. By nature of the job, the staff secretary has more access to the president than any other official in the White House, including the chief of staff. This is because every single document handled by the president must come and go through the staff secretary.

This virtually unlimited access provides the staff secretary with the opportunity to develop a relationship of trust with the single most powerful person in the world. Given that one of the most prominent qualities of President Trump was his constant querying of people for their opinion on something, his staff secretary would get numerous opportunities to whisper all manner of sweet globalist nothings into the president's ear, and nobody would ever be the wiser.

"Rob, what do you think about this? And what about this, Rob? Boy this seems odd, can you explain this to me, Rob?" I think you get the unlimited access picture.

In fact, if Rob Porter were a character out of *Game of Thrones*, he would certainly be closest to the cunning and conniving Littlefinger.

Like Littlefinger, Porter moved with a seductive combination of obsequiousness and deferential grace. Like Littlefinger, he was always weighing the odds and only making his moves at the right time.

Because of the way he operated, Rob Porter would quickly become, for me, the poster child of the Trump senior staffer who believed that *the only way he could be loyal to the president was by being disloyal to the president's trade agenda.* While Cohn and Mnuchin flat-out rejected that agenda, Porter did his damage the old-fashioned way using the very ample levers of bureaucracy he had quite literally at his fingertips.

In this sense, Rob Porter reminded me of the Chinese concept of influencing history, as China scholar Mike Pillsbury once explained to me. Porter *cum* Littlefinger did so not by forging boldly and bluntly ahead as was President Trump's style but rather by attempting to nudge things towards the preferred outcome.

At one critical meeting in the East Wing on August 14, 2017 about whether and when to impose steel tariffs, Porter watched for over thirty minutes a ping-pong match between me on the side of *immediately* imposing the steel tariffs and Mnuchin and Cohn on the other side of *waiting* to impose the tariffs until after the tax bill passed.

At a key moment, Porter put his finger on the scale and moved the president to the "wait" side of the aisle. It was a clear process foul—the staff secretary is not supposed to be part of the policy process. But given the president's familiarity with Porter—the Boss was as yet unaware that Porter was a dyed-in-the-wool globalist—Porter took his Littlefinger shot and won that terrible day.

Over time, as Porter would work his Littlefinger magic time and time again, Bob Lighthizer, Wilbur Ross, and I would walk into trade meetings with the president and wonder what fresh globalist hell Porter would next serve up.

At one point, in the Oval Office, the Boss would finally look at Porter and say: "You are globalist. I didn't know that." All Rob could do at that point is look sheepishly back at the president, finally having been outed.

I could not resist chiding the Boss: "What took you so long Mr. President? I been fighting this guy for a year."

At the end of the day, I can say unequivocally that in his own subtle and conniving ways, Rob Porter was every bit as destructive to the president's trade agenda as Cohn's frontal assault, Mnuchin's back channeling, Ross's bumbling and Lone Rangering, and Priebus's stacking of the White House personnel deck. But on this first business day of the administration, as I was trying to salvage all the work I had done during the transition on behalf of both President Trump and American workers, I did not yet know any of this.

All I knew when I walked for the first time into Rob Porter's relatively spacious basement office in the West Wing on day four was this: The "staff secretary" process Porter was demanding that I follow with my executive orders and presidential memoranda would spell nothing but trouble ahead.

The Ghost of George Bush

When I probed Porter further that day about just what this staff secretary process was, he explained that the Trump White House, per the direction of Chief of Staff Reince Priebus, was going to rely on a policy process that had been the backbone of decision-making within the Bush administration.

As Porter explained it, the staff secretary process is a "bottom-up" approach that starts with a Policy Coordinating Committee. This PCC is made up of lower echelon bureaucrats across the so-called—and we shall soon see, dreaded—Deep State interagency, and any policy bound for the president's Resolute Desk would have to start at this sub-deputy level in a PCC framework and work its way laboriously up the chain through numerous layers of numerous cabinet departments and agencies. In the case of trade policy, the list of participants in this interagency process could include staff from departments ranging from Agriculture, Commerce, and Labor to Treasury, the Pentagon, and Homeland Security.

From this description, it should be obvious why the staff secretary *cum* Bush PCC policy process would prove to be so toxic in Trump Land. If every proposed presidential action had to start at the sub-deputy level with *career bureaucrats* with no clear allegiance—or outright antipathy—to the president's agenda, you would not have an honest broker review process but simply a Deep Administrative State gauntlet which would open every proposed Trump action to endless mischief.

That said, the problem with the staff secretary process did not stop there. Once a proposed action cleared the PCC sub-deputy layer, it then had to go through two additional layers of approval before reaching the president's desk for a decision and possible signature.

The first is a deputy-level review whereby the undersecretaries to the various cabinet secretaries take a cut at the proposed action—and it often would quite literally be a cut.

Second, the proposed action then had to go to the cabinet secretaries themselves for further approval. Of course, along this long and winding road, there would be endless opportunities to amend, alter, or even veto a proposed Trump action.

As Porter described this process to me that day in his office, I thought it was absolutely crazy. Intuitively, I had assumed that the only way the policy process would and should work in the Trump White House—never mind what came before it, especially if it was from a Bushie—was that if POTUS wanted something done, we damn well ought to do it.

Moreover, we ought to do it in what I had already begun to call "Trump Time," which is to say as quickly as possible. And nowhere was this truer than with the dozen or so executive orders and presidential memoranda I had locked and loaded and ready for the president's signing that very day—but were now dead on arrival.

A Bad Process Stranglehold

As bad as the bottom-up structure of the staff secretary process was, it would not be the only thing that would get in the way of the timely signing of the numerous executive orders and presidential memoranda I would pen for the Boss over the course of my four years in the White House.

As I noted earlier, before any president can issue an executive order, it must be reviewed for "form and legality" by the Office of Legal Counsel within the Department of Justice.[21] At least in principle, this requirement is a very good thing as any executive order worth its policy salt is likely to be challenged in the courts.

In practice, however, the Department of Justice's OLC under first Jeff Sessions and then Bill Barr would turn out to be the ultimate bottleneck and stranglehold in the process of churning out executive orders from the Trump White House in a timely manner. There were two reasons why this was so.

First, there was OLC's risk aversion on steroids and concomitant legal review equivalent of a zero-based budgeting process. To wit: Every proposed presidential action not only had to go through three or more layers of review. Every time an action would clear one layer of review, it had to be rereviewed at the next level as if no lawyers at OLC had ever looked at it.

This was obviously a tremendously lawyer-intensive process—and that observation leads us to the second reason why OLC was such a bottleneck. This DOJ backwater where Trump MAGA dreams would come to die was dramatically and grossly understaffed.

That's right. In an office where there were nowhere near enough lawyers, OLC relied on a highly risk-averse process that used as many lawyers as possible for every single action.

Over the course of the administration, I warned both Jeff Sessions and Bill Barr *repeatedly* that the best way they could help the president—besides indicting the likes of Comey, Clapper, Brennan, Page, and Strzok—would be to triple or quadruple the staffing of OLC. However, my pleas and plaints always fell on deaf ears.

A Zero-Sum OLC Game

OLC's dilatory process would have been comical if it were not so tragic. Over the course of the four years of the Trump administration, executive orders and presidential memoranda that urgently needed signing would stack up like jets trying to land at Kennedy Airport. And yet there was even more Bad Process associated with the OLC.

In the spirit of "excrement rolls downhill," bottlenecks at the OLC also sparked tremendous infighting within the White House policy units over whose actions would get to clear OLC first. Invariably, those with the most juice in the White House were able to jump the long queue, and one of the worst offenders was none other than the president's daughter Ivanka Trump. Indeed, every time Ivanka jammed the OLC channel with another one of her liberal Democrat ideas—or worse, jumped the queue—she pushed other policy actions out of the way that were much more likely to help boost her father's chances for reelection.

This was a matter of sheer triage math: in OLC's zero-sum game, if its lawyers were reviewing some things, they were *not* reviewing others.

A similar "jam the OLC channel, jump the queue" problem arose with Brooke Rollins after she was installed as the director of the Domestic Policy Council in the home stretch just five months before the 2020 Election Day. Brooke is one of the sweetest and most genuine people I've ever met, but once she got ensconced at the DPC, she was like a bulldog pushing her own particular brand of conservative Texas policies.

It was real raw red meat stuff for the Trump conservative and Evangelical base. But it was also nothing that would really help us in the Blue Wall and battleground states to swing persuadable voters.

The Man Without Qualities

I don't blame either Ivanka or Brooke at all for pushing their own agendas. That's just power politics in any White House. I do, however, squarely blame Chris Liddell.

Particularly in the home stretch as we barreled forward towards the 2020 Election Day, Liddell, as the White House deputy chief of staff for policy coordination, should have prioritized all proposed presidential actions moving through his and OLC's pipelines based on their *political* impact. Instead, Liddell viewed his job as to simply play traffic cop and deft juggler for the competing power centers, and one of his top priorities was always to keep those happy who had helped him into his job, particularly Jared and Ivanka.

Chris's approach to managing the policy process and priorities at the White House was consistent with his journey to that position of power. A former Microsoft executive worth millions of dollars, Chris was perhaps second among equals behind only Reince Priebus as a November 9ther guy.

Remember: these were the people who came into Trump Land the day *after* the November 8, 2016 election without ever having paid any real campaign dues.

This November 9 crowd simply elbowed the Make America Great Again (MAGA) folks aside as they assumed positions of power. And Chris—a key player in the 2012 Romney for president campaign—was particularly adept at moving MAGA people out of his way.

I knew Chris would be trouble the moment I saw him at Trump Tower shortly after Election Day cozying up to Gary Cohn. That was

Chris's MO—obsequiously attach himself to people of power. First it was Cohn. Then Kudlow. And always Jared and Ivanka. Liddell would then use those relationships to work his way up the ladder.

In my interactions with Chris, he reminded me of the title of one of the philosophy books I had read in college that had a tremendous impact on me—*The Man Without Qualities*. That seemed to be Chris. Even though he professed to fully support the president, he had no strong attachment to the President's vision or agenda. He was effectively a man without any strong ideology or world view, that is, a man without political qualities.

Even more curious to me, he frequently admitted that he wasn't interested in policy—this, the guy who had "deputy chief of staff for policy coordination" after his name. Rather, Chris viewed his job as simply to make the policy trains run on time—and he couldn't even do that.

Together, Rob Porter, before he resigned in disgrace, along with Chris Liddell collectively added months of delay to the actions my office alone would eventually get through the staff secretary and OLC processes.

Process delayed is indeed policy denied, and the biggest loser was not me. It was POTUS, who missed opportunity after opportunity to briskly move his trade agenda forward. Over time, he would have far less political and policy ammunition to fire during his reelection campaign.

In fact, the only one of my actions POTUS would sign that first business day in office was a presidential memorandum directing withdrawal from negotiations related to the Trans-Pacific Partnership.[22] And the only reason why we were able to nuke the dreaded TPP was because the president literally screamed at Porter and Priebus to get the damn thing on his desk. NOW!

Economically, the TPP followed in the globalist tradition of opening up our markets to countries like Vietnam and Malaysia with their vast reserves of cheap labor, state-owned enterprises, and illegal government subsidies without appropriately reciprocal access. If the TPP had been signed, they would have absolutely slaughtered our manufacturers.

The deal also would have given Japan's humming factories in cities like Hamamatsu, Nagoya, and Yokohama even further access to

America's auto and auto parts industries—Japan already exports 100 cars to the US for every one car the US exports to Japan. The net result would have been the further erosion of the US manufacturing base, and the likely death knell of the US as an automobile manufacturer.

So make no mistake here: The signing of the presidential memorandum to withdraw from the TPP was indeed a grand historic gesture as it signaled a sea change in American trade policy. It was, however, only a gesture as the withdrawal would create no new American manufacturing jobs. Withdrawing from the TPP negotiations merely prevented even more of American manufacturing jobs from being taken by the forces of globalization.

And that was why all the other executive orders and presidential memoranda I had teed up for President Trump to sign that first business day of the Trump administration *would have been far more important over the arc of American economic and manufacturing history.*

To make one last thing clear on this subject—and to give credit where credit is due—I was only standing there in the Oval Office that day by President Trump's side as POTUS signed the TPP to the scrap heap of history because of Steve Bannon. He had shoehorned me into the Oval as a prop to signal that the Trump trade agenda was alive and well. Never mind at the time, my fledgling career at the White House was already on life support.

It would be fully forty-six "Where's my Peter?" days before I would see the Oval Office and POTUS again. That was how effective the White House's Bad Personnel were at keeping me, the tip of the president's trade and manufacturing policies spear, out of what they presumed was harm to their globalist ways. But once that day came, it was one hell of a good day.

TWELVE

A "Where's My Peter" Battle Cry and Oval Office Resurrection

Clear eyes, full hearts, can't lose.

—Coach Eric Taylor, *Friday Night Lights*

I've seen you guys can shoot but there's more to the game than shooting. There's fundamentals and defense.

—Coach Norman Dale, *Hoosiers*

Observe calmly; secure our position...hide our capacities and bide our time;...and never claim leadership.

—Deng Xiaoping, *The 24-Character Strategy*

On day five of the Trump administration, I woke up to the reality that I was a beaten man. I had no rank of assistant to the president and therefore no walk-in privileges to see the Boss. Katie Walsh had literally physically barred me from senior staff meetings. I had no office, and I was down to only one staff member while my primary antagonist Gary Cohn had over forty troops to pummel, pound, and outflank me.

In addition, my opportunity to run a beautiful table of MAGA executive orders and presidential memoranda had slipped through my fingers even as my knuckles had been repeatedly mashed and process smashed by the likes of Reince Priebus, Rob Porter, and White House Legal Counsel Don McGahn.

This was as big a beat down as one could possibly imagine, and at least at that moment in time, the well-worn cliché about "if you don't know who the mark is in the poker game, you are probably the mark" seemed to fit me like a glove.

Or I was at least a marked man because Cohn, along with his new best buddy Treasury Secretary Steve Mnuchin, would spend idle time trying to either get me fired or get me moved over to the Department of Commerce to work for my old "good buddy" Wilbur Ross who already was beginning to stick stilettos in my back.

About that "good buddy" thing, I might remind you here that Wilbur and I had worked beautifully together and as equals on the campaign trail. Our report on how President Trump would spur economic growth after eight years of Obama-Biden stagnation had been a *tour de force* and media home run, and our op-ed articles had integrated our skill sets beautifully.

On that note, Wilbur, the finance guy and consummate accountant's pencil pusher, would grind out all manner of numbers for whatever problem we were writing about, He'd do it all with a stubby pencil on the back of a proverbial envelope. I would then take Wilbur's scribblings, press them through the mill of my economics training, and then turn Wilbur's drier than dust discourse into something at least a little more prosaic. It was all good between us—at least until the day *after* the election when Wilbur went full DC Swamp native on me.

My canary-in-the-coal-mine signal that all might not be well in Wilbur World was when the newly minted secretary of commerce refused to say anything particularly nice about me to a *Bloomberg* reporter who was doing a "trade warrior" profile on me. The *Bloomberg* reporter himself described Ross's comments as "restrained" and pointedly noted in the profile how Ross had "added a sentence about the administration's intention to fix bad trade deals that made no mention of Navarro."[23]

It became abundantly clear to me the day I read that profile that Brother Wilbur had indeed gone full DC Swamp on me, and he was no longer content to share a limelight that we had shared quite cordially during the campaign. Going forward, *he* was going to be *the* trade guy, and it wasn't just me who was in the way. It was also the guy who was *actually supposed to do that job*, United States Trade Representative Bob Lighthizer.

I vividly remember attending a dinner with Bob along with Gary Cohn over at Wilbur's mansion in the posh Massachusetts Heights section of Washington, DC. In typical Wilbur fashion, he had paid cash for the mansion a mere days after the election outcome and dispatched his sweet wife Hilary down to decorate said new digs in the style to which both had become accustomed.

Yes, Hilary was indeed a sweet person, and she had done me a few nice favors during my time in New York on the campaign. And that was all the more reason why it bugged me when Wilbur mistreated her.

In fact, when I was with the two of them, I sometimes felt like I was in Saudi Arabia. This is because Hilary would always walk a few steps behind Wilbur rather than by his side—no burka yes, but head held down.

The only thing that bugged me more was how Wilbur treated his maids and hired help. I should have known when I first saw such barking abuse at his New York apartment that all might not end well—and I will be candid with you here. One BIG reason why I steadfastly refused to go over to the Department of Commerce to serve Wilbur was because of what I had observed.

At any rate, on that winter's night nightmare in Wilbur's new digs, as a new set of servants scurried back and forth from the kitchen to lavish us with *haute cuisine*, Gary Cohn, Bob Lighthizer, and I sat with Wilbur at the dinner table, and each of us was quickly astonished by the lecture that Wilbur began to give us about how he was going to commandeer trade policy.

In this particular delusion of grandeur, I was going to be Wilbur's little bitch, Bob Lighthizer was going to be Wilbur's big bitch, and presumably, Gary Cohn was going to stay out of Wilbur's way. That night was the only night that Gary Cohn and I would ever share any common cause as we kept glancing over at each other with a bemusement in our eyes as steam began to pour out of Bob Lighthizer's ears. Yes, Bob was hotter than a junk bond during the housing bubble.

Of Hives and Green Bananas

Lest I digress, this day five in the Trump administration had me as low as I ever get. Day five was also the day I started to get hives, and this stress-related ailment would stay with me for the better part of a year.

Towards the end of the administration, I read with interest that George Stephanopoulos had been afflicted with the same problem when he served in the Clinton White House. Unlike me, however, George probably never had to worry about *his* job security.

True this: from the day I walked into the White House on January 20, 2017, to the day I left, I always thought each new day would be my last day. Particularly in those early months, while Wilbur Ross and Jared Kushner and Steve Mnuchin were all buying mansions and Gary Cohn was settling into a luxury suite at the Ritz-Carlton and snoring in silk sheets, I was like a modern day Claude Pepper, daring neither to buy green bananas or sign anything that looked like even a month-to-month lease on an apartment.

At such points in my life, I have learned that you must never let the weight of the world crush you. Instead, you must say screw it and fight back. And you fight back by trying to beat whoever is beating you up at their own game.

It is not for nothing that *Friday Night Lights* is my favorite TV series. By day five, I did indeed have clear eyes, I would find that full heart because I owed it both to the Boss and this country, and I damn well would and could not lose.

It is not for nothing that *Hoosiers* is also my favorite movie. Sure, even by day one, I could shoot off executive orders like three-pointers from Steph Curry. But with the likes of Priebus and Porter and Cohn and Mnuchin and Ross as my adversaries, I had to learn a lot more about the fundamentals of how the White House and this new curve-ball otherwise known as the staff secretary process worked, and I sure as hell needed to build up a much better set of defenses.

So that's what I decided to do. By mastering the ways of the White House and the staff secretary process—and by hiding my capabilities and biding my time as Deng Xiaoping did indeed once advise—I would be ready if and when the Boss ever called me.

True this too: over the course of my four years in the White House, I would shepherd more presidential actions through the staff secretary process than any other single senior White House staff member, and do so by a large margin. That winning streak would begin on March 27 and day sixty-six of the administration when I would hear for the very first time a battle cry from the Oval Office that would, like a modern-day Lazarus, raise me from the dead.

Whenever I softly say that battle cry to myself, it still puts a grin on my face, warms my heart, and lifts my spirits: That POTUS battle cry was: "Where's my Peter?"

Gary Cohn Mano a Mano

On that March 27 day, I was at my stand-up desk working up an idea to help resurrect what had already become my beloved but flagging Philadelphia shipyard when Madeleine Westerhout, the Boss's executive assistant, called me from her perch in the Outer Oval and asked me to come over immediately to see the president. The funny thing about getting the call was that I was in gym shorts, socks, and a T-shirt—not exactly West Wing attire, particularly with a boss who is always meticulously dressed.

I was in this locker room attire because I had jogged into work and had as yet not changed into my suit, and that was basically my routine. Jog or ride my bike into work and change in my office where I kept all three suits that I owned in a small wardrobe armoire I had commandeered from a store room in the basement of the EEOB.

This was not exactly the best day to be caught half naked because it added five minutes to the journey over to the West Wing. But all's well that ends well, and this meeting would end even better than it began.

Despite the fact that almost every single person in the Oval that day except the president had had a boot to my neck for the better part of two months—Steve Mnuchin, Gary Cohn, Reince Priebus, Wilbur Ross, Don McGahn, and Jared Kushner—I walked into that Oval like I owned the damn place. I do not remember exactly what I said to President Trump, but it went something along the lines of, "Well, are we ready now to actually get some stuff done on trade?"

Within nanoseconds, Gary Cohn and I began going at it like Ali and Frazier in the "Thrilla in Manila." How about I let the *Financial Times* provide you first with a sanitized version of the confrontation as it was leaked to the press:

> *A civil war has broken out within the White House over trade, leading to what one official called "a fiery meeting" in the Oval Office pitting economic nationalists close to Donald Trump against pro-trade moderates from Wall Street. According to more than half a dozen people inside the White House or dealing with it, the bitter fight has set a hardline group including senior adviser Steve Bannon and Trump trade adviser Peter Navarro against a faction led by Gary Cohn, the former Goldman Sachs executive who leads Mr. Trump's National Economic Council. At the centre of the debate is Mr. Navarro, a firebrand economist who has angered Berlin and other European allies by accusing Germany of exploiting a "grossly undervalued" euro and calling for bilateral discussions with Angela Merkel's government over ways to reduce the US trade deficit with Europe's most powerful economy. The officials and people dealing with the White House said Mr. Navarro appeared to be losing influence in recent weeks. But during the recent Oval Office fight, Mr. Trump appeared to side with the economic nationalists, one official said. The battle over trade is emblematic of a broader fight on economic policy within the Trump administration.*[24]

Not surprisingly, the staid *FT* left out all the good and funny parts. To wit: every time Gary Cohn tried to pull his usual globalist gibberish crap, I quickly corrected him on his flawed economic analysis. After just a few minutes of this Harvard-style skewering, the former Goldman Sachs Kingpin, who was not exactly used to being challenged in this manner, lost his cool.

Now, the thing you have to know about Gary Cohn is that when he was at Goldman Sachs his most disgusting *modus operandi* when he wanted to intimidate subordinates was to get up close and personal into their space and lift his leg up onto their desks. In this case, Cohn did not dare get into my personal space. But what tone-deaf Gary did do—and I still cannot believe he was dumb enough to do this—was put his leg up on one of the couches in the Oval Office as he tried to harangue me. Of course, POTUS—along with everyone else in the room—was aghast. And that was not even the best part.

The best part was when the leader of the free world tried to interrupt Cohn to disagree with him, Gary dismissed him with a wave of his hand, and, spittle flying, Cohn continued his harangue.

I knew right then—and I was right—that that day would be the high water mark of Gary Cohn's reign in the West Wing, and it would be all downhill from there.

It was at this point in the confrontation that I noticed Brother Bannon leaning slyly against one of the back walls. As usual, he looked uncomfortable in his suit and shorn locks—Steve was born to form governments, not run them. But on this day, he did have a twinkle in his eye as he watched me go head to head with Cohn, and there was no way I was going to lose that debate that day because I not only had economics on my side. I had the Boss.

Yes, as the *Financial Times* noted: "Mr. Trump appeared to side with the economic nationalists."[25]

At any rate, with both Gary Cohn's guts and brains now on the floor—truly, a self-inflicted wound—I assured POTUS that I was indeed locked and loaded with close to a dozen executive orders that had been held up since day one of his administration.

"So how about we get moving, Boss?" said I. And his reply was the first time I would hear POTUS say that signature phrase of his: "Let's go!"

And go we did, with pedal to the metal for what would be one of my most beautiful thirty days in the Trump White House. During that time, I would finally get steel and aluminum tariffs rolling on what would be an albeit long and winding road to implementation.

POTUS would also sign actions on both reducing the trade deficit and eliminating unfair trade practices around the world. He would provide for the significantly enhanced collection and enforcement of antidumping and countervailing duties from trade cheats and sign what would be the first of my many drafted orders to strengthen and expand Buy American and Hire American provisions in government procurement.

The Boss would even put his John Hancock on the order formally establishing my Office of Trade and Manufacturing Policy—regrettably, a pale shadow of what should have been my National Trade Council.[26]

And throughout this beautiful month, there was no way on God's good earth that either Reince Priebus or Rob Porter—much less Gary Cohn—was going to get in the way after that showdown throwdown in the Oval Office. In fact, on the way out of the Oval in the wake of that confrontation, Reince had been positively gushing. All he could say was "Navarro! Navarro!"

A Priebus Deathbed Populist Conversion

By this point, less than seventy days into the administration, Reince had realized that he was as much a marked man as I was. Cohn was openly lobbying for his job, Chris Liddell was quietly lobbying for it, and Jared Kushner and Ivanka Trump were taking turns simply doing it. Beyond desperate, Reince Priebus was looking for allies like a drowning man prays for a lifeguard.

You may be surprised here to learn that Reince would find those allies in both Steve Bannon and myself. Reince's epiphany was this: The only way he was going to stay in the Trump White House was by moving forward the Trump trade agenda and thereby pleasing the president. And the only two people in the White House likely to help him to do that were me and Steve.

Regrettably—and it was regrettable because of what I am about to tell you—Reince came to that realization far too late to save his sad, sorry ass. Still, over the course of the next several months, as Reince helped both me and Steve move action and action through the staff secretary pipeline, we would devise what we would dub (in one of my more vanilla marketing moments) our "Trade Agenda Timeline."

This master strategy laid out a six-month plan beginning on August 1 to effectively run the trade policy table. We would begin renegotiating NAFTA on August 16 and Hillary's toxic South Korea deal on August 22. On September 1, POTUS would then direct the United States trade representative to start the ball rolling on possible tariffs on automobile imports.

Much to my own great delight, the day after Labor Day we would impose the by-now-long-overdue tariffs on steel imports and be poised by November 1 to impose a similar tariff on aluminum imports.

It was all good, and it was all so good that I had produced one of my oversized and colorful poster board charts to illustrate and memorialize this "Trade Agenda Timeline." This kind of chart had become a signature analytical tool of my office after I had, several months earlier, quite accidentally stumbled across the White House print shop in the basement of the Eisenhower Executive Office Building while scrounging around for some furniture for my office.

That printshop could pop out these charts in record time, particularly if I told the always friendly operators I needed the chart for a POTUS meet. Since that time, I rarely had appeared at a briefing without one or more of these colorful charts, which got me the nickname of "poster boy" around the West Wing—and it was never said with affection.

At any rate, Reince loved my chart and agreed to get us in to see the Boss and get his blessing for our sustained trade policy blitzkrieg. As I left Reince that day, he even asked me to autograph the chart for him, which I thought was pretty funny given our earlier sordid history.

What was not funny at all was that Reince would be fired a few days later, Bannon would be exiled shortly thereafter to the Eisenhower Executive Office Building on his way out the White House door, and our great Trade Agenda Timeline, which in one fell swoop, may well have done everything we needed to win the 2020 election, would be put into the deepest of freezes.

Never Claim Leadership

Truth be told, I had had a premonition that my future ally and brother-in-arms Steve Bannon would not stay the White House course when I saw him in an absolutely gorgeous photo in the *Washington Post* coming off the stage at the annual CPAC event arm in arm with none other than Reince.[27]

CPAC—the Conservative Political Action Conference—was, at least at that time, the undisputed leader of the PACs in conservative politics, and Reince and Steve just looked too damn good and powerful in the photo.

I am sure that when the Boss saw that photo in celebration of Reince and Steve as White House kingpins he was not pleased. Note: One of the reasons why I lasted five long years at the side of the president is that I always followed Deng Xiaoping's dictum: "Never claim leadership."

The Trump-Bannon split would be a breakup for the ages—although, as I will relate later on in this book, this Simon and Garfunkel of politics *almost* got back together in 2020.

Kelly Comes, Trump's Trade Agenda Goes

The loss of Reince Priebus and Steve Bannon in the summer of 2017 would be devastating both for me personally and for the Trump trade agenda. This is because the man who would replace Priebus, US Marine Corps Four Star General John Francis Kelly, would be even more ill-equipped for the Chief's job than Priebus.

As to why Kelly was so opposed to the Trump trade agenda from the git-go, it boiled down to three things: Kelly had nary a clue about economics, he knew less about politics, and he had no idea about how to manage either the time or space of Donald Trump.

Because Kelly had no training in economics, he easily fell prey to the facile globalism of virtually everyone in the West Wing—including Cohn, McMaster, Kushner, Porter, and Mnuchin. In that scenario, I immediately became the odd man out—and once again I had a big target placed on my back by a chief of staff.

Because Kelly had no training in politics, he failed to understand the importance of trade policy in holding the high political ground of Blue Wall manufacturing states like Pennsylvania, Wisconsin, and Michigan that Trump had won the election with in 2016.

Because Kelly did not know how to "let Trump be Trump"—as the great Corey Lewandowski once advised—there was no way in Hades that John Boy was going to let me or anyone else with deviant trade policy thoughts anywhere near the Oval Office.

To say that I would be in for a very rough time with the coming of John Kelly would be one of the great understatements of this book. Kelly tried to fire me so many times that I lost track.

What I do remember indelibly is sitting with General Kelly at my right shoulder on December 2, 2018 at the end of a long table in Buenos Aires, Argentina. We were there with President Trump who sat at the center of the table flanked on either side by the rest of his trade team.

Of course, sitting across from us on the other side of the table were our counterparts from the Chinese Communist trade side, with the Chinese dictator Xi Jinping at center stage right across from the president.

Before the meeting began, a by-then broken and broken down Kelly, no doubt aware of his soon-to-be exit, apologized for treating me so poorly. In doing so, he further acknowledged that he had failed to see what George Bush might have called the real evildoers in the West Wing—both Gary Cohn and Jared Kushner in particular came from his muted lips.

I thought at the time that while Kelly had done a very bad job, he was at his core a very good man who had simply borne too much stress in his life—right to the breaking point. A son lost in war. Too many wars lost. And now Kelly was, as he once confessed in a jarring manner in a senior staff meeting, "in a very dark place."

At the time, I really had nothing to say. I just gently put my hand on his forearm, looked him in the eyes briefly, and then turned my own eyes back to the Chinese Communists as the meeting began. Kelly would be fired six days later.

THIRTEEN

Bad Personnel PLUS Bad Process Is Bad Policy Is Bad Politics

The returns from [President] Nixon's failure to staff his government with loyalists who would follow his lead and carry out his policies were now in…The chance to seize control of and redirect the government of the United States passed us by. It would not come again.

—Patrick J. Buchanan, *Nixon's White House Wars*[28]

At the end of this chapter, we are going to strap ourselves into a time machine and jump forward to the last few months of the 2020 presidential election. There, we will see how Five Strategic Failures committed in part by key White House personnel and in part by the Trump Campaign would inexorably lead to the loss of the 2020 race and the fall of the White House of Trump.

The reason why we have thus far spent so much time on the 2016 campaign, the presidential transition, and the early 2017 days of the Trump administration has been to illustrate how, in many ways, the foundation for that 2020 defeat was already being laid by a toxic combination of the Bad Personnel, Bad Process, Bad Policy, and ultimately, Bad Politics that define those early years.

Accordingly, as a capstone to this early journey, I want to do what we often do in my native academia. This is "formalize" the underlying principle that most succinctly explains the broad thesis of this book. That thesis is an offshoot and refinement of the famous Ronald Reagan-era dictum that "Personnel is Policy."[29]

By this dictum, the people that you put in positions of power in any White House will tend to advance their own policy agendas. It follows that if a president fails to appoint personnel who share his or her own agenda, things can go very wrong and very quickly.

If you don't think that is true, just reread the Pat Buchanan quote leading off this chapter to see how long lasting such a "Personnel is Policy" problem can be. Richard Milhous Nixon forever lost a golden opportunity to redefine the federal bureaucracy in his practical conservative image because of Bad Personnel choices.

By parallel construction in *this* book, Donald J. Trump lost a *platinum* opportunity to institutionalize a Populist Economic Nationalism across the economic and national security policy spectrums of the US government. These reasons for this crushing loss are best captured in this refinement and extension of the Reagan-era dictum:

Bad Personnel PLUS Bad Process is Bad Policy is Bad Politics

Bad Personnel are those who do not share, and are unwilling to advance, the vision and policy agenda of the president they serve. When you have such Bad Personnel—particularly if they are able to access Bad Process such as the Staff Secretary process we have discussed, you will have Bad Policy. This I further define as any policy that substantially deviates from the president's vision and agenda.

Of course, when these Bad Personnel use Bad Process to advance Bad Policies, the inevitable result must be Bad Politics in the following sense:

When policies are put in place that fail to implement a president's campaign vision, or that deviate substantially from policies necessary to implement and advance that vision, or, in the most extreme case, outright contradict that vision, these Bad Policies will inevitably disappoint those who voted for that president.

If the deviation is substantial, that disappointment may even rise to a deep feeling of betrayal, and the likelihood in either case—from mild disappointment to deep betrayal—will be the failure of that president to retain enough of his or her original supporters come Election Day for a second term.

To put this in *realpolitik* terms, Candidate Trump promised in 2016 to be tough on Communist China, secure the southern border, bring our globalized supply chains back on shore, and bring our troops home from endless wars. Yet, some of President Trump's very top officials within both the White House and across the cabinet agencies and departments charged with fulfilling those promises would pursue just the opposite policies.

Again, at least from a *quasi*-academic point of view, let us think about these critical Bad Personnel within the context of at least *six* distinct, at times overlapping, mischievous Madisonian factions that often ruled the White House roost.

The Wall Street Transactionalists

At the top of the disloyalist pyramid, at least in terms of the sheer ability to lean directly on the president and twist the arc of history, there were the Wall Street transactionalists.

The essence of Wall Street transactionalism is that all that matters is The Deal. There are no moral, ethical, or national security issues that must ever be allowed to get in the way of The Deal, not even when, to these high-net-worth, low-brow rug merchants, it comes to a godless, authoritarian, concentration-camp-strewn, military-expansionist, intellectual-property-stealing Communist China.

Through the dollar-green colored lenses of these Wall Street transactionalists, every policy action is always about somewhere and somehow finding an accommodation that enriches both parties. And the best deals during the Trump administration were those where the United States would tactically gain more than the other country—never mind any broader economic, human rights, or strategic national security concerns.

The most prominent Wall Street transactionalists in the White House of Trump included Treasury Secretary Steve Mnuchin, son-in-law Jared Kushner, Secretary of Commerce Wilbur Ross, and the two who would serve as the director of the National Economic Council in first Gary Cohn and then Larry Kudlow.

Here, it is well worth noting for the history books that arguably the worst act of disloyalty ever perpetrated in the Trump White House by a Wall Street transactionalist was the theft of documents from the president's Resolute Desk by National Economic Council Director Gary Cohn. It didn't just happen once. It was a pattern.

If Cohn objected to the president signing an executive order or presidential memorandum that was in conflict with Cohn's free trade view of the world, Cohn would literally try to make the document disappear, even if the president wanted it to be implemented. Cohn, himself, would even brag about doing this to reporters, as if it were some heroic act.

A poster child was Cohn's theft of a document I myself had drafted at the president's request which would have pulled us out of a toxic trade treaty with South Korea within a specified timeframe. What this felony-dumb Cohn never understood was that these kind of presidential actions were designed not necessarily to exit such agreements but rather to put pressure on other countries like South Korea so that we could quickly negotiate better deals for American workers and companies.

If I had had my way when I found about Cohn's thievery, I would have had him charged with both a felony and treason. I just hope that anybody who ever thinks about employing Cohn factors in his lack of moral fiber in their hiring decision.

The Traditional Globalist Republicans

As a second important Trump disloyalist faction, there were the hordes of traditional globalist Republicans spread out across the Trump bureaucratic diaspora. These often balding and gray-bearded punks in pinstripes were as enthusiastic about the Trump policies of deregulation and tax cuts as they were horrified by the idea of using tariffs to bring about fair trade or sealing off our southern border from a flood of cheap, illegal immigrant labor.

While there was no shortage of traditional globalist Republicans resistant to the more disruptive and transformational aspects of the Trump agenda in the White House itself—Joe Hagin, Chris Liddell, Rob Porter, Marc Short, and Derek Lyons come immediately to mind—some of the most significant damage would be done by "quasi-Bad Personnel" in the Republican-controlled Senate.

Key among these "quasi-personnel" Senators were then Senate Majority Leader Mitch McConnell, Iowa's Chuck Grassley, Nebraska's Ben Sasse, Pennsylvania's Pat Toomey, South Dakota's John Thune, Utah's Mike Lee, and the now retired Orrin Hatch (it would be from Hatch's office that Rob Porter would come, having served as Hatch's chief of staff).

Quick aside on the Utah front: Senator Mitt Romney also fits like a glove into this traditional globalist Republican category. However, Romney has been such a pompous, self-righteous ass from the moment he got elected to the Senate—after President Trump graciously endorsed him—that Mitt deserves his own category. We'll call this category: Bitter loser and forever jealous of a president who did what Mitt never could.

None of these traditional globalist Republican Senators—many from farm states—gave a lick about the plight of American manufacturing workers. These "quasi-Bad Personnel" were continually firing warning shots at, and lobbing grenades into, the White House, and one or more of them was always seeking to pass new legislation to constrain the power of the president, particularly on tariffs and trade.

Of course, none of these politicians worked directly for the president—ergo the term "quasi-personnel." However, many had former staff members working in high positions directly inside the White House perimeter. And here's the quasi-personnel punchline: These termites in the Trump house tended to be far more loyal to their old Capitol Hill bosses than the new POTUS in the Oval Office—making them a particularly virulent strain of disloyalist.

Take, for example, Emma Doyle. You probably never heard of her, and you probably never will hear of her again after reading this book. Yet, because of the White House positions she would hold, she was a consummate bureaucratic saboteur when it came to derailing the Trump agenda.

Doyle started as Mick Mulvaney's chief of staff at the Office of Management and Budget and then became his deputy chief when Mulvaney became acting White House chief of staff. As to where Mick found a saboteur like Doyle, he plucked her straight from the Senator Pat Toomey globalist tree.

Here, all you need to know is that Toomey rose to prominence as the chairman of the globalist-on-steroids Club for Growth and represents the most extreme version of a traditional Republican free trader as chairman of the globalist-on-steroids Club for Growth.

Toomey, hands down, was perhaps the oddest choice that Pennsylvania, with its working-class and manufacturing base electorate, has ever made for a Senator. In fact, the only reason Toomey got elected was because Donald J. Trump endorsed him at the last minute in 2016.

Talk about biting the hand that feeds you: Toomey would prove to be a perennial thorn in the side of the Trump administration. And the president would lament on more than one occasion in the Oval Office that his single worst endorsement was that of Toomey. Yet Emma Doyle would wind up doing far more direct damage.

Down the pecking order, there were big problems from seemingly smaller appointments as well.

For example, Gary Cohn's principal deputy on trade was Everett Eissenstat. He held the coveted "sherpa" role whose job it is to orchestrate key international meetings like the G20 and the G7.

Like Rob Porter, Eissenstat was a pure Orrin Hatch guy, and Orrin is as pure a traditional globalist open border endless war free trader Republican as the Good Lord ever conceived. Eissenstat's specialty was watering down the joint communiqués that country leaders would issue with President Trump at the G20 and the G7 in a way that would weaken the Trump trade and America First agendas. Lighthizer had to watch that guy like a hawk.

When Eissenstat left to become a high-priced lobbyist for General Motors, he was succeeded by two more lobbyists in training, first Clete Willems and then Kelly Ann Shaw. Willems, for example, fought me tooth and nail on a pure Trumpian Open Skies initiative designed to put an end to the United Arab Emirates predatory trade assaults on American airlines like Delta and United.

Of course, Clete wound up working for the mega-lobbying firm Akin Gump,[30] which has the United Arab Emirates as a client.[31] Cursed be the lobbying ties that blind.

As for Kelly Ann Shaw, she joined Hogan Lovells. [32] That's one of the largest lobbying firms in the United States[33] with a client list that reads like a who's who of multinational corporation offshoring companies opposed to Trump trade policies.

Shaw's bio on the Hogan Lovells website claims "she was directly involved in almost every major economic decision made Trump White House."[34] In truth, she was constantly throwing sand in the gears of every Trump trade and economic policy that did not conform to her globalist ideology—or future lobbying prospects.

My broader point is that the Trump White House was riddled top to bottom with these kinds of globalist termites eating away at the very foundations of the Trump presidency—and those little termites like Doyle and Shaw can sometimes do as much damage as sharks like Cohn and Kudlow.

The Freedom Caucus Nut Jobs

As a third category of disloyalists—and a particularly toxic strain of traditional Republicanism—there were the Freedom Caucus Nut Jobs. These nut jobs represent the "just say no" to any form of government or government expenditure wing of the Republican Party.

This anti-Trump agenda faction gets its name from the House Congressional Caucus that would be established in January 2015 by two particular nut jobs who would serve as the president's chief of staff—Mick Mulvaney and Mark Meadows. And throw in for bad measure here, Meadows's deputy chief of staff John Fleming.

Yet a third Freedom Caucus founder and libertarian acolyte, Fleming would almost single-handedly kill any last chance American lives could be saved from the China-Fauci virus by lifesaving therapeutic otherwise known as hydroxychloroquine.

Said former House Speaker John Boehner of the Freedom Caucus: "They can't tell you what they're for.… They're anarchists. They want total chaos. Tear it all down and start over. That's where their mindset is."[35] Here I must use the three most favorite words I learned in Washington: "I don't disagree."

A big source of friction I had with these Freedom Caucus Nut Jobs was their opposition to President Trump's two simple rules: Buy

American, Hire American. Neither Meadows or Mulvaney—or, for that matter Kudlow—ever met a Buy American, Hire American executive order they liked or didn't want to (and often did) shoot down. Dealing with their continual sniping and sabotage was as exhausting as it should have been unnecessary.

On October 17, 2019, the hapless Mulvaney would almost get the president impeached with a flippant "get over it" remark in arguably the worst press briefing ever given by a chief of staff. In his remarks, Mulvaney falsely implicated the Boss in a "quid pro quo" impeachable offense with the Ukrainians, and in this case, a punk's smartass character almost determined the president's fate.

As for Meadows, as we shall soon see, he would spectacularly crash and burn any hopes for a Phase 4 stimulus and relief package. But, that would be just a small sliver of damage that Meadows would do to the Trump agenda and the president's reelection bid.

The Broken Chain of Command Commandos

As still a fourth category of disloyalists, there was the "Broken Chain of Command Commandos." These were the generals—Gulf War hero and tank commander H. R. McMaster, Jim "Mad Dog" Mattis, and John "Just Always Mad" Kelly. These top brass, along with other high-ranking military officers serving in the administration like Four-Star General Mark Milley, would repeatedly ignore *direct* orders from their commander in chief. Yes, that would be the guy at the very top of *their* chain of command.

Their treasonous conduct—a court-martial offense in the military—always reminded me of the quip Bob Lighthizer, the United States trade representative, would often make about some gaggle of globalists seeking to subvert the President's agenda. To Lighthizer, there were only two types of people in the Trump administration: Those people who thought they had to save the world from President Trump, and those who thought President Trump would save the world.

You could put every single Break the Chain of Command Commando, including McMaster, Mattis, and Kelly, into the former "save the world from Trump" box, and wrap that box up with a neat and treasonous little John Bolton bowtie.

The Deep Administrative State Bureaucrats

The fifth disloyalist faction included a broad array of Deep Administrative State Bureaucrats who were constantly throwing sand into the gears of the Trump Populist Economic Nationalist machine.

Here, I have already told you about how the firing of Michael Flynn aborted the normal housecleaning of detailees at the National Security Council. As a result, for all four years of the Trump administration, the NSC was riddled with Obama appointees to the NSC who often worked at cross purposes to the Trump agenda.

The White House NSC wasn't, however, the only Deep Administrative State problem. Besides sappers like Gina Haspel at the CIA, Dan Coats as the director of national intelligence, and just about everybody at the top of the FBI—Comey, Wray, Rosenstein, Page, Strzok, and so on—the president and his agenda also had to contend with the slings and arrows of the administration's sprawling healthcare bureaucracy.

The most dangerous of these healthcare bureaucrats was the media savvy, passive-aggressive Tony Fauci, director of the National Institute of Allergy and Infectious Diseases (NIAID). But there were others of this ilk with names like Francis Collins at the National Institutes of Health, Robert Redfield at the Centers for Disease Control, and Steve Hahn at the Food and Drug Administration.

Each of these Never-Trumpers would contribute in their own way to the fall of the White House of Trump—Fauci with the stilettos he would stick in the president's chest and back every time he got on TV, Collins with subtle subversion, Redfield with incompetence, and Hahn with weakness.

The inevitable Bad Politics and fall in President Trump's approval rating that would follow would be no accident but rather a clear expression of the partisanship and personal animus of Fauci and his disciples.

The Political Climbers

As a final disloyalist faction, there was the Political Climbers. These were typically registered Republicans and often young kids—20- and 30-somethings with no well-formed ideology or strong commitment to the transformative and disruptive Trump agenda. These Political Climbers were simply upwardly mobile opportunists who saw the

White House on their resumes as a cool steppingstone to fame or fortune (likely as a lobbyist), or to some higher political position.

It always amazed me that on weekends at my office in the Eisenhower Executive Office Building I was virtually alone. The long, almost 100-yard hallways of the EEOB were devoid of human life—except for the occasional tour that came through—and much of the marbled building resembled a mausoleum come Saturday and Sunday.

This amazed me because I always saw my work at the White House not as a job but rather as a mission to serve both the president and the country. It was a mission that necessarily required long hours at short pay and weekend duty.

The fact that the EEOB was mostly deserted on weekends—even during the critical crucial weeks before Election Day—was a function of the fact that the offices in this building were largely populated by either the National Security Council's 9-to-5 Deep Administrative State Bureaucrats or the Political Climbers for whom work at the White House was merely a Monday through Friday grind and stepping stone job.

The poster child for the Political Climbers was, hands down, Madeleine Westerhout. She literally wept the night Hillary Clinton was vanquished by Donald J. Trump. Yes, *Madeleine literally wept for Crooked Hillary*.[36] Against all odds and logic, she wound up in the Outer Oval as the gatekeeper to the Oval Office sanctum.

As for what might go wrong with such an odd Hillary-lover choice, with Westerhout, it would turn out to be quite a bit. For starters, she was allegedly one of the biggest leakers in the West Wing. To that point, it was always a puzzle to me how we could hold our trade team meetings in the Oval Office with the president and there would only be a few of us in the room—typically Mnuchin, Kudlow, Ross, Lighthizer, and myself.

Yet, within hours of virtually every meet, hostile publications like *Axios* or *Politico* would publish stories with verbatim quotes and often very damaging details—damaging at least to the president's ability to prosecute his trade policy without massive blowback as a result of the leaked material.

Here, it must be said that while Mnuchin, Cohn, and Kudlow were no strangers to strategic leaking, even they would not leak at least some of the poison arrows and quotes that came out of the Oval Office. That left as the only other possible explanation the fact that the door to the Oval Office was typically open during the trade team meetings and Westerhout was a mere thirty feet away. And our conversations were often as loud as they were contentious. And yes, as another piece of circumstantial evidence, after Westerhout left and was replaced by Molly Michael, the amount of leaking fell dramatically.

Original Sin Redux

Of course, at this point you might be thinking: "How in the world did all these people with personal and policy agendas so opposed to that of POTUS 45 wind up serving in his administration?" Indeed, all that has transpired thus far in this chapter begs the very big question as to why a president who is supposed to be one of the greatest assessors of talent—wasn't that the whole talent-picking premise of *The Apprentice*—would make such Bad Personnel choices across so many White House and cabinet-level positions.

I think the answer to this question boils down to five main reasons.

First, at the beginning of the administration, many within the Trump inner circle believed that the only way the administration could effectively govern was to be accepted by the power elites and establishment figures of Washington, at least on the Republican side. That meant making an accommodation, first and foremost, with a Republican National Committee that had often worked against the president during the campaign, particularly prior to his locking up the Republican presidential nomination.

This "after you licked them, join them" mentality also meant making an accommodation with traditional globalist Republicans on Capitol Hill like the aforementioned McConnell, Grassley, Lee, Thune, and Toomey.

With McConnell in particular, he was always playing a double game. The Boss would say to Mitch, "You give me passage of my repeal-Obamacare bill and I'll give you a bunch of judges to appoint." Double Game Mitch would say "sure."

Yet all we ever got from McConnell was the appointment of judges. Judges by the boatload. Judges by the ton. More judges appointed up to that point than any in presidential history. Conservative judges coming out of your eyes, ears, nose, and throat. Just not a lot of Trump agenda policies passed.

And here's what was even worse about McConnell. Yes, the "Turtle," as Mitch was derisively called, would move his conservative judges faster than Usain Bolt. But when it came time to moving President Trump's key personnel appointments, these would move at, dare I say, a turtle's pace. And because President Trump couldn't quickly fill his top deputy and undersecretary political slots across many of the departments and agencies, his policies would fall prey to the Deep Administrative State career bureaucrats—just as Turtle Mitch no doubt intended.

As we have discussed, it was this traditional Republican accommodation by President Trump that the 2016 campaign strategist Steve Bannon would refer to as the "Original Sin" of the administration. This Original Sin, which I have likewise already waxed at least semi-eloquent on, would lead, for example, to the disastrous decision by President Trump to give RNC Chairman Reince Priebus the keys to the White House by making him chief of staff.

Note: That would be the same Reince Priebus who implored, indeed demanded, that Candidate Trump quit the race after the infamous 2016 October Surprise Billy Bush tapes broke.[37] At that time, Bannon and Trump told Priebus to pound sand, and Reince, cute little puppy dog though he is, never should have been let back into the fold.

Once, however, Priebus got his snoop dog nose through the door of the White House, he would bring a whole parade of Never-Trump traditional Republicans with him. The seed of Priebus would begat Cruella Katie Walsh, the hyperbolic Sean Spicer, the Bushie Joe Hagin, the Never-Trumper Don McGahn, the Littlefingering Rob Porter, and so on down the West Wing Original Sin chorus line—just a host of bad seeds that would sprout all manner of poisonous trees across the West Wing and beyond.

Straight Out Of Central Casting

As a second reason for the president's Bad Personnel choices, there is the president's well-known weakness for glamour, good looks, and characters that he refers to as coming "straight out of central casting." Exhibit A was Rex Tillerson, the president's first secretary of state.

How can you resist a guy like King Rex, Lord of the Exxon Manor, with his beautiful mane of hair, deep tan, and deep, soothing baritone? Of course, this Oil Barren turned out to be, as they say in his native Texas: "All hat and no cattle." And Rex would leave the State Department with the president's Twitter door hitting him right in his silk underwear on his way out.

And by the way, it is absolutely true—not West Wing legend—that John Bolton did NOT get the National Security Advisor job the first time around because the president hates mustaches. Trump Rule #247:

Mustaches are *not* in the Good Guys wardrobe when it comes to central casting—they are only for villains. And yes, Bolton would turn out to be a real lying-about-the-rooms-where-it-happened villain.

Rich Guys Rule

By this rule, President Trump would often judge an individual by the size of his bank account. The thinking was: "If this guy is rich, he must be smart and therefore a good appointment."

Never mind that being a profit-hungry Wall Street sociopath doesn't always—indeed rarely—translate into a propensity for honorable public service. But it was this kind of "billionaires have bigger brains" thinking that would saddle the president with Wall Street transactionalists like Steve Neville Chamberlain Mnuchin, the kleptomaniac Gary Cohn, and the octogenarian Wilbur "Lost a Step" Ross.

By the way, I heard from more than one Yalie that Mnuchin was one of the dumbest guys in his class at Yale and only made it into the Goldman Sachs sanctum on the coattails of his daddy, a high-ranking Goldman executive. That story certainly resonated with me: Mnuchin is the dumbest smart guy I have ever met this side of Larry Summers.

As for Cohn, he at least had street smarts. He would make a bundle by agreeing to serve in the Trump administration because, by a loophole in the tax code, Cohn was able to defer hundreds of millions of dollars in capital gains taxes that he otherwise would have had to pay when he divested his Goldman Sachs stock so he could enter the White House.[38]

Of course, by the time Cohn left, he had been part of the effort to significantly reduce the capital gains tax rate. Ergo, by being in the

Trump administration, Cohn was able to increase his net worth in two ways—once through the deferral of the tax on his capital gains and twice by paying a lower rate when he finally had to pay the tax.

Dazzled by the Brass

As a fourth reason for the president's Bad Personnel choices, there was also and always the president's fascination with military brass—the more stars on the shoulder the better. Perhaps it was because the president had never served in the military. Perhaps it was his love of war movies—according to Steve Bannon, the president's favorite movie of all time is the documentary series *Victory at Sea* about World War II.

His fascination with military men would, however, saddle the president with a renegade secretary of defense in General Jim "Mad Dog" Mattis; a globalist, endless war National Security Advisor in General H. R. McMaster; and the dark, brooding, and bullying chief of staff John Kelly.

In a story relayed to me by Matt Pottinger that reveals a lot, Kelly continually treated McMaster with condescension because he had "only" three stars. Never mind that McMaster was a four-star war hero in anybody's book and had twenty IQ points on Kelly—to Kelly, it was only the stars and bars that mattered.

As for my relationship with the bullying Kelly, I would physically have to steel myself every time I got a call from his office as it would inevitably mean some type of abuse or threat. Some men lead by inspiration. Some *try* to lead by intimidation. Kelly was clearly the latter, and I can't imagine serving under his command in a combat situation.

Here's the broader military brass lesson that the president never learned in his own worship of stars and bars. It was a stark lesson that became painfully obvious to me after interacting repeatedly with Mattis and Kelly:

Four-star generals like Mattis and Kelly typically reach the pinnacle of their profession because they are generally the sharpest tools in their military shed. Yet put Mattis or Kelly in a room in the West Wing with uber-elite civilians drawn from academia, the corporate world, and Wall Street, and these guys were often the dumbest guys in the room. Just checker players thrust into a chess world.

Yet, that wasn't what bothered me the most about Trump's generals. Rather, it was their utter failure to obey their commander in chief—and therefore the chain of command.

Just think about that: These generals knew, above all else, that without an ironclad respect for, and adherence to, the chain of command, *the military would fall apart in a heartbeat.* Yet once Trump's generals got to the pinnacle of civilian power, they figured no one was above them, apparently not even their president.

And please take note of this: what Mattis and Kelly and McMaster all did in ignoring the chain of presidential command would be a court martial offense in the military punishable with a dishonorable discharge, forfeiture of all pay and allowances, and confinement for two years. From my perch in the White House, I'd say that punishment would have more than fit their crime. I would have put them in the same cell as Gary Cohn.

Both Nepotism and Excrement Roll Downhill

As a fifth and final reason for the president's Bad Personnel decisions, there was this nepotistic abomination: the president would often delegate tasks to his son-in-law Jared Kushner. Yet Kushner was nothing more than a young and rich, run-of-the-mill liberal New York Democrat *cum* slumlord with a worldview totally orthogonal to the father-in-law and president he would putatively serve.

Kushner, himself, considered himself to be the ultimate "DJT whisperer," first on the 2016 campaign, and then within the White House itself. In private, Jared would often boast about how he had brought the president back from whatever the brink of the day was—shut the border down, get out of NAFTA, slap tariffs on China, get tough on the Koreans, whatever.

This "neuter the Boss" role Jared had chosen to take on in the White House quickly became a source of friction between us. This is because Kushner believed that yours truly, more than just about anyone else inside the perimeter, would, and could, "rile up" the president, as Jared put it, to take actions that in fact were totally consistent with Donald Trump's campaign promises. But as this particular Wall Street transactionalist liked to say—and it always made me cringe: "That was the campaign. This is reality."

In the cold light of a January West Wing day, there was simply no other scenario than a nepotistic one where this decidedly unqualified Clown Prince would wind up sitting as a modern-day Rasputin at the right hand of a Washington God.

When Margaret Mead Met Richard Nixon

To end this chapter, I would like to clear up at least one misconception that may already be forming in your mind. That misconception may be that I had little regard for *anybody* at the White House that I worked with and, more broadly, even less regard for those I interacted within the broader Washington Swamp.

You would not necessarily be wrong to think that thought at this juncture in this book. After all, all I have mostly done so far is dump on a lot of people, many of whom have had, by traditional DC metrics, distinguished careers—people, for example, like Mattis and Fauci that the anti-Trump media have lionized. But the truth is far more textured.

The truth of the matter is that, in the White House and DC Swamp, I worked with some of the most amazing and intelligent people I have ever encountered in my life—and you will meet many of them at the end of this book when I offer up my "MAGA Dream Team" for a 2024 Trump administration.

For now, the simple point I have been trying to make is embodied in that most famous quote of the cultural anthropologist Margaret Mead:

Never doubt that a small group of thoughtful, committed citizens can change the world; indeed, it's the only thing that ever has.

The point of this chapter—and a key theme of this book—is that Mead's wisdom can very much cut the *wrong* way.

Under the weight of the Bad Personnel facilitated by Bad Process in the Trump administration, many of the Mead-like Bad Policy changes that came to the Trump World were certainly not for the better, at least when it came to Bad Politics and the reelection prospects of the Boss.

If, on the other hand, we had simply followed a more top-down policy process in the image of President Trump himself, and if we had avoided the trap of Bad Personnel, it is likely we would have avoided most or all of the Five Strategic Failures that we will now begin to work our way through.

PART FOUR

From China Hawks to China Appeasers

FOURTEEN

The Road to Reelection Runs Through Beijing

In numerous meetings, the President has...expressed his affection and admiration for China's president Xi Jinping. The clear danger here is that our president may be "charmed into submission," and this possibility likewise represents a signal failure of President Trump's intelligence briefings.

—Memorandum to the President from Peter Navarro,
October 25, 2017

I meet Jason Miller at the campaign headquarters and we go over some [internal] polling data. The data shows very clearly that about two-thirds of the respondents blame China for the pandemic [and] want reparations.... They like the idea of a Presidential Commission...and it appears to move voters off the fence [towards Trump]. This is a hot buttered croissant ready to eat....

I tried fruitlessly to call Mark Meadows. What the heck is going on? The campaign headquarters is a ghost town. The White House is a ghost town. And I can't reach anybody on the phone, including the Chief of Staff.

This is why we are going to lose. I can almost guarantee it right now, and I can taste the bitter fruit that is going to be served on November 3rd because we are not getting done what we should be getting done, and people are not working.

—Navarro Journal Entry, September 6, 2020, Labor Day Weekend

Of the Five Strategic Failures that would lead to the fall of the White House of Trump, the failure to make Communist China *the* most important issue of the 2020 campaign must rank head and shoulders above all others. Contributing mightily to this failure was the collateral and companion inability to *credibly* run on a Tough on China platform. It was all because of just too many Bad Personnel screwups and just piss-poor political judgment.

In fact, dating back to the nanosecond after President Trump was inaugurated in January of 2017, I believed that a Tough on China message—matched with Bannonite Action, Action, Action—should be the foundation of our 2020 campaign platform. After all, we had run hard on Communist China's theft of American manufacturing jobs in 2016. Not coincidentally, the Democrat's Blue Wall had crumbled under the weight of blue-collar factory workers rising up to dance with Donald J. Trump on Beijing's mercantilist grave. Yet, in 2020, it was not to be.

A Beijing State of Mind

As I watched this strategic failure and train wreck of a China appeasement policy unfold, my state of mind was one of outrage. This was a controlled outrage yes, but an incandescent rage as well.

It was a rage directed not just at Communist China for its blatant and obvious bioweapons attack on America—obvious at least to me. My outrage was also directed at both the corporate media and the Democrat Party.

These two institutions, which are so critical to American democracy and the security of our nation, simply hated Donald Trump so much that they were willing to sweep under the rug any blame for a pandemic that should otherwise have been prudently and rationally assigned to Communist China.

Most of all, my rage was directed at my putative colleagues within the West Wing—Kudlow, Kushner, Meadows, Chris Liddell, Marc Short, Derek Lyons, always Mnuchin (who spent more time over in the West Wing than at his own Treasury Department), and even the vice president himself. It would be all of these politically tone-deaf mandarins who would fight me tooth and nail on my efforts to convince POTUS of the strategic imperative to run on a Tough on China platform.

This was a platform that necessarily had to be constructed with a set of policy planks as solid as Tennessee oak. These planks could, and should, have included everything from:

- A presidential commission to hold China accountable for the virus,

- A ban on Communist Chinese investment in American pension funds,

- Unyielding sanctions aimed at ending human rights abuses— including concentration camps in Xinjiang Province,

- A no-holds-barred response to China's crushing of Hong Kong's democracy, and

- The banning of all manner of Chinese social media companies like TikTok and WeChat.

Yes, I had a long list of Bannonite actions that would be as politically potent as morally and strategically necessary. And make no mistake about this: the American people and 2020 electorate were more than primed for such Action, Action, Action.

We're All China Hawks Now

During the first three years of the Trump administration, as POTUS 45 became America's first president to crack down on China's unfair trade practices, the American people's distrust of Beijing had only grown stronger. Consider that in a Pew poll during the last year of the Obama administration, 55 percent of the American people viewed China in an unfavorable light.[1] Yet by the end of the Trump administration, that number had risen to 73 percent.[2]

Moreover, under President Trump's leadership, nine of ten Americans would come to view Communist China as a threat while[3] at least two-thirds of Americans also would see a wide range of issues with China as "serious concerns." These issues included everything from Chinese cyberattacks and our massive trade deficit to environmental degradation, American job losses, and Communist China's growing military might.[4]

History will no doubt judge this sea change in American attitudes towards Communist China during the Trump administration to be *one of the president's greatest achievements.* As I was fond of saying during the last year of the administration when accused by the media and other critics of being a "hardliner" on China, my response was an homage to Richard Nixon and his famous quote: "We are all Keynesians now."

My new Trump line in this old Nixon bottle was simply: "We are all China Hawks now."

What Donald Trump had done to affect this China Hawk sea change was to rip the Band-Aid off a shop-worn bipartisan gospel of American economic engagement with a Communist enterprise that had wounded millions of American workers and all but killed America's manufacturing and defense industrial base. According to this now thoroughly debunked globalist gospel, if America simply engaged economically with the big bad Communist Dragon, Xi Jinping's brutal, authoritarian beast would somehow morph peacefully into a free and democratic system and society.

It was President Bill Clinton who would most famously preach this gospel of economic engagement to sell America and the American Congress on the single worst trade deal in US history. This was the shoehorning of Communist China into the World Trade Organization. Said Clinton in naively pimping for this trade policy disaster: "Economically, this agreement is the equivalent of a one-way street."[5]

Bill Clinton was certainly right about that. He just got the direction wrong, as more than five million American manufacturing jobs would head offshore to the factories of Beijing, Shanghai, and Guangzhou—even as over fifty thousand American factories would close.[6]

President Trump saw right through this gospel of economic engagement as nothing but free trade insanity.[7] In the clear light of a Populist Economic Nationalist day, a strong majority of the American people now see Communist China for exactly what it is: a dangerous, predatory, mercantilist, and militarizing strategic rival intent on rising up across the globe by tearing America down.

And it is well worth noting here that it wasn't just POTUS who brought about this sea change in American attitudes. It was fearless China Hawk warriors like Secretary of State Mike Pompeo, White House Senior Counselor Steve Bannon, National Security Advisor Robert O'Brien, the Director of National Intelligence John Ratcliffe,

Customs and Border Protection Commissioner Mark Morgan, and dare I say, yours truly.

It's not for nothing that literally four minutes into the Biden administration, Communist China imposed sanctions[8] on Pompeo, O'Brien, Bannon, and myself. Here is what the ministry of foreign affairs of the People's Republic of China had to say about us:

> Over the past few years, some anti-China politicians in the United States, out of their selfish political interests and prejudice and hatred against China and showing no regard for the interests of the Chinese and American people, have planned, promoted and executed a series of crazy moves which have gravely interfered in China's internal affairs, undermined China's interests, offended the Chinese people, and seriously disrupted China-U.S. relations.... China has decided to sanction...Michael R. Pompeo, Peter K. Navarro, Robert C. O'Brien...and Stephen K. Bannon. These individuals...are prohibited from entering the mainland, Hong Kong and Macao of China.[9]

Of course, the Skinny Ass Trade Deal China Appeaser trio of Mnuchin, Kudlow, and Kushner, along with Bob Lighthizer were noticeably absent from that list.

A Dead OMG Biden-Trump China Heat

Given President Trump's leadership on the China issue, and given the dramatic shift in American attitudes, it was a no-brainer to make Communist China the number one issue of the 2020 campaign and to firmly position POTUS as the Tough on China candidate. This would, however, prove to be far more difficult than I would ever have imagined given the *bona fides* President Trump had established in the first three years of the administration with his bold tariffs and tough sanctions.

Our political problem was quite visible in the polling data after Joe Biden locked down his nomination as the Democrat Candidate to take on Trump. Throughout the spring and summer of 2020, polls began popping up showing that the American people saw little difference between Joe Biden and Donald Trump in their ability to handle the Communist China issue.[10]

Mind you, this was the same Sleepy Joe career politician who had not only sat on his hands for more than forty years on the China issue and voted to shoehorn Communist China into the World Trade Organization. This was also a candidate saddled with a coked-out unregistered foreign agent of a laptop-from-hell son in Hunter Biden who had gone into business with Communist China for the express purpose of selling American manufacturing companies to Beijing.[11]

OMG! WTF! Just pick your own internet acronym, clean or filthy, and you get the drift of what was going on in my mind as I grappled with what seemed to me cognitive dissonance in the American electorate. If after Donald Trump's tough actions on Communist China, the Boss was only marginally ahead or in a statistical dead heat with Joe Biden on this pivotal and salient issue, then I did not know what the Hades was going on. At least, I didn't know what was going on until I thought about it just a little bit.

After just a bit of reflection, it all boiled down to two specific problems. First, there was President Trump's very public "bromance" with his counterpart in Beijing, Xi Jinping. Every time POTUS referred to this authoritarian murderer as "my good friend,"[12] this didn't just turn my own stomach. It turned off a good portion of the America's swing voters—and likely all of the Trump base—who, in their own guts, knew quite better.

Second, there was also the quite legitimate perception that the president was pulling his punches on a wide range of China issues. Mnuchin's weak-kneed, run up the white flag, Skinny Ass China Trade Deal was just the tip of this "pull our China punches" iceberg. There was also the very public embarrassment of a Wilbur Ross bellyflop on ZTE[13], a Mnuchin- and Kudlow-driven waffling on the 5G network bandit Huawei,[14] a Kushner Devil's bargain on TikTok,[15] and a truly unforgiveable Mark Meadows-driven "see no evil" accommodation to the most brutal of human abuses in Xinjiang Province.

Cumulatively, these pulled punches would make us punch drunk in the polls, and this would turn out to be yet another case of Bad Personnel leveraging Bad Process to turn Bad Policy into profoundly Bad Politics.

About That Toxic Trump Bromance

In the weeks leading up to the first major summit with China in April of 2017 at the Boss's Mar-a-Lago resort in Florida, I had frankly been bummed out that I was being left behind in Washington, DC. That's right, me, the guy who was supposed to be the administration's leading China Hawk was not on the Air Force One passenger manifest. Cherry blossoms yes. Orange blossoms no.

Of course, at some level, you could argue that that my exclusion might make sense if you were trying to make peace and a deal with the Chinese. Why bring the flamethrower?

On the other hand, through the Reagan lens of pursuing peace through strength, excluding me from the trip as a peace offering to the Chinese was fuzzy thinking at best. If you want to drive a good and hard bargain, particularly with the Butchers of Beijing, the likely best strategy is to show these beasts you mean business. What better way to signal this than to make me a key part of the negotiating team.

Fortunately, Steve Bannon, then still White House senior counselor and in his West Wing prime, would see it exactly that way. When Bannon noticed that my name was not on the travel manifest, he marched the thirty feet over from his cubby hole to Priebus's spacious suite and told Reince that I had to be on the trip.

At first, as Steve would later tell it, Priebus was his usual high-pitched whiny self. Said Reince, "I don't know, Steve. Navarro comes in kinda hot and he might get the Boss worked up. That's what I'm hearing from [H. R.] McMaster and Kushner and [Gary] Cohn. They're lobbying me hard to keep Navarro in Washington. So I just don't know, Steve."

Ever the strategist, Steve's answer was to make it in Reince's self-interest to have me on the trip. So he says to Priebus, "Reince, you know that the president, at some point during the trip, is going to ask 'Where's my Peter?' And when he's not there, it's going to be your ass on the line—not McMaster and Cohn and certainly not Kushner."

At that, Reince folded like a cheap suit, and that's how I got a last-minute phone call from the chief's office to get my own ass on the bus, and that's how I wound up in Palm Beach, Florida with nothing but the suit on my back—and a tooth brush that I had grabbed from one of the bathrooms in Air Force One.

And sure enough, on the very next day, at a critical pre-planning meeting with our team and the Boss—which Cohn and McMaster initially kept me out of—POTUS looked around the room and then looked at Priebus and bellowed: "Where's my Peter?"

So Reince came and got me from the adjacent room where Bannon had told me to hang out and be patient. And the rest is history—literally.

An Original Mar-a-Lago Sin

The Mar-a-Lago summit would turn out to be pure Trumpian pomp and circumstance—a truly grandiose summit where POTUS would wine and dine China's president in the hopes of out-foxing and out-negotiating the most powerful dictator in the un-free world.

In truth, this event was also a pure Wall Street transactionalist power play, a profiteer's pageant conjured up by Jared Kushner working—but really getting worked by—his Beijing back street channels. That's just one of many things the young but not-so-precocious Kushner never really understood.

> *Every time Jared thought he was working Beijing, Beijing and its Wall Street agents like Steve Schwarzman, John Thornton, Hank Paulson, and Henry Kissinger were really working Jared.*

Here, let me state what was obvious to everybody but Jared: What better way to slow down President Trump from imposing tariffs on China than for Xi Jinping to come and do a *faux* Florida kowtow leavened with extreme flattery?

Now let me state something perhaps more subtle: If the Original Sin of the administration was to bring far too many traditionalist globalist Republicans into key positions of power, the Original Sin of that first Mar-a-Lago Summit was to leave America's president completely alone with the president of China for a private meeting and let them, shall we say, "bond."

The story behind this bonding and the blossoming of what, at least from the outside, looked to be a very real Trump-Xi bromance brings to mind one of my favorite movie lines from the Paul Newman classic *Cool Hand Luke*: "What we've got here is a failure to communicate."

In the case of the star-crossed Mar-a-Lago Summit, what we got was a "failure to brief." What I am talking about here is not a failure to brief the president properly, but rather a failure to adequately brief the Boss *at all*.

During that Mar-a-Lago summit, POTUS and Xi would spend several hours alone together, with only their interpreters. During that intimate time, a literally teary-eyed Xi would spin his version of the well-known historical tale of woe known as China's "century of humiliation."

From 1839 to 1949, eight foreign nations, most prominently Great Britain, Germany, and France—the US was but a young pup at the time—would impose "unequal trade treaties" on China. These sometimes quite literally rapacious imperialists would also seize Hong Kong and Macau while turning rivers like the Yangtze and port towns like Canton effectively into international waters and trade zones.

In telling his teary-eyed tale of China's loss of sovereignty, Xi Jinping weaved in the hardships that had been imposed upon his family ancestors. "Oh the pain and suffering," weeped a wet-eyed Xi. Quick *House of Cards* aside: there is nothing scarier than a brutal dictator who can tear up on command.

Of course, what the weepy Xi left out of this tale of woe was that during the five thousand years prior to China's one hundred years of humiliation, *an imperial China had intermittently and brutally humiliated just about every other foreign country in Asia.* Vietnam alone would be invaded repeatedly and occupied by China for more than a thousand years while these Chinese mandarins treated the Koreans worse than slaves.

It should have been a simple matter for the National Security Advisor H. R. McMaster to actually do his frigging job and brief the president of the United States before he sat down with Xi Jinping. Any damn fool—even the dullard McMaster—could have anticipated that Xi Jinping would play the century of humiliation card. But neither McMaster or anyone from the intelligence community bothered to conduct such a brief.

Because of that failure, the Boss came out of that summit with what at least appeared to be an admiration and adoration for a teary-eyed sociopath who was running concentration camps in Xinjiang and Tibet,[16] pillaging the American economy, holding his own people hostage in digital and often actual Orwellian prisons, militarizing the South China Sea,[17] and continuing preparations to crush democracies in both Hong Kong and Taiwan—yes, history will note that Xi Jinping took Hong Kong on our watch and *shame on us.*

Of course, it may also be true that much of the apparent love that the president would demonstrate for Xi was simply strategic—in the very same ways, his bromances with North Korea's Kim Jong-un and Russia's Vladimir Putin were strategic. The president's philosophy here—often waxed eloquent in the Oval—was that, as the saying goes, you can get more with honey than with vinegar, especially with a despot.

Here, however, I must also be candid. If the Boss had to spend a few hours with a world leader, he much preferred tough and masculine brutes like Xi, Putin, or Turkey's Erdogan to effete, leftist, metrosexuals like Justin Trudeau of Canada or Emmanuel Macron of France. And with those two androgynous *GQ* gentleman in particular, I can particularly see the Boss's point of view as Trudeau and Macron were nothing but leftist and globalist trouble at every summit we ever attended—to the point where POTUS had made me light up Trudeau on TV in a "special place in hell" way that almost lit my own self up. But the story behind that story is one for another time.

Winnie the Pooh Kowtows

Whether the Boss's admiration for China's dictator was real or simply a strategic ruse, it would not be until more than two years later at the June 2019 G20 summit in Osaka, Japan, that POTUS would *finally*, albeit quite accidentally, unmask the real Xi Jinping.

During the meeting of the two trade teams—with Communist China on one side of the flag-festooned table and the good old USA on the other—the Boss and the Butcher started out in the usual way. POTUS bittersweetly talked broadly about the need for more reciprocity in the trade relationship and about how he did not *really* want to impose tariffs but might have to—his classic Dragon in the Pot strategy that I discussed at length in my *In Trump Time* memoir.

For his part, China's dictator in chief fawned and feigned to kiss the Boss's ring by telling him what a great leader he was and how important it was for him to get reelected. Right. The very last thing on China's Godless polluted earth Xi Jinping wanted was another four years of the Donald and his punishing tariffs.

Of course, by then, all of us on the trade team, as well as the president, were hip to Xi Jinping's game. We knew that the Butcher of Beijing would come to the summit with lips prepuckered and with the goal of using his obsequiousness to further delay any new tariff actions.

We'd seen that game before, particularly at the critical 2018 G20 Buenos Aires summit. In the room where *that* happened, as I sat next to the lame-duck chief of staff, John Kelly, Xi Jinping performed his own unique version of a kowtow on steroids to stop POTUS from imposing additional tariffs.

It was, hands down, one of the great masterful political seductions of all time. All I could think of as this quintessentially Chinese Communist flattery unfolded was that my president, who had had every intention of slapping on tough new tariffs as he had entered that summit room, was in no way going to follow through on that intention. Winnie the Pooh had gone down so hard on the president, the only climax I was going to witness at the end of that meeting was going to be a no-additional-tariffs *anti*-climax—which was exactly what happened.

And by the way, lest I get accused of using obscure lowbrow literary references in this opus, "Winnie the Pooh" is the derogatory nickname many cynics and dissidents in China use for Xi Jinping. Of course, anyone who gets caught using that term in China is in for a long one-way train ride to parts and gulags unknown.

Xi Jinping Unmasked

Now, unlike the 2018 G20 Kumbaya Buenos Aires summit, Xi's encounter with Trump at the Osaka 2019 G20 would not have the same happy ending. The Boss, in a quite accidental and offhand remark, claimed—with absolute historical accuracy—that if the United States had not come to China's aid during World War II, China would have been lost to Japan.

With that remark, Xi's flash of anger was so bright I thought I needed shades. Gone in a Beijing second was the façade of any obsequiousness. Vaporized was any hint of a kowtow. In this magic moment of the great reveal, Xi Jinping seemed to at least figuratively rise up on his Devil's haunches and went off on a long rant about how the noble Communist Chinese troops sacrificed blood and treasure to drive out the evil Nipponese.

Of course, Xi Jinping left out the fact that it was the nationalist Kuomintang troops of Generalissimo Chiang Kai-shek who mostly got slaughtered trying to drive out the Sons of Nippon while Xi Jinping's progenitors—Mao Zedong and his Long March band of Communists—hid out like cowards in the mountains.

Truth be told here—but never in any of Communist China's history books—it would be the bleeding out of Chiang Kai-shek's forces by the Japanese during World War II that would enable Mao and his Communist troops to quickly overcome Chang's severely depleted nationalist forces after the war. By 1949, the insurgent and decidedly cave-rested Mao Zedong would drive Chang and his loyalists offshore to Taiwan.[18]

Of course, we heard none of that during Winnie the Pooh's angry rant. Instead, we saw the total unmasking of Xi through his own harsh propagandist rhetoric.

As I watched this unfold, I had to restrain myself from laughing out loud—that certainly would have been an international incident. But at least I had a big "I told you so" grin on my face for all in the room to see.

Immediately after the meeting, there was an absolutely priceless moment as we on the American side went to a holding room before moving on to the next event on the calendar. With a wry or sheepish smile—I couldn't quite tell which—the president acknowledged that he had finally seen the real Communist Butcher of Beijing. Said the Boss as his eyebrows rose, "Wow, did you see that? Finally, the true Xi Jinping." True that.

My hope at the time was that with Xi Jinping's unmasking, the president would forever more abandon the "my good friend" rhetoric and get down to the real business at hand. Alas, this was not to be.

A Dark John McEnroe Moment

Right at the dawn of the pandemic, President Trump would twaddle up a poisonous pair of buddy tweets that would reinforce the growing public perception that the president had needlessly softened not just on Xi Jinping and trade policy but also on the looming pandemic. Tweeted the Boss on January 24, 2020:

> *China has been working very hard to contain the Coronavirus. The United States greatly appreciates their efforts and transparency. It will all work out well. In particular, on behalf of the American People, I want to thank President Xi!*[19]

At the time that I read that tweet, I was at my stand-up desk in my office at the Eisenhower Executive Office Building. As my normally very low blood pressure sharply spiked, I literally let out a loud expletive. It was so loud that Garrett Ziegler, one of my staffers, came running in to see if something was wrong.

"You bet something is wrong," said I to Garrett, pointing at the tweet on my screen, as I thought to myself: "This is full John McEnroe territory here. Boss, you cannot be serious!"

Yet serious it was, and the Boss's tweet would turn out to be a missive so far from the facts of the pandemic case that it would have made even Alice in Wonderland's head spin.

The killer here was not just praise for China "working very hard" at containing a virus that China was in fact responsible for genetically engineering and unleashing upon the world. It was also the absurd notion that Communist China—the most opaque large country in the world—somehow was exhibiting "transparency" when in fact it was hiding the genome of the virus even as it hid the potential of human transmission and a pandemic from the world.

And guess what: to this day, Communist China still has not divulged the original, genetically engineered genome of the virus. Such information would still be valuable today. But it would have been absolutely invaluable at that early stage of the pandemic.

Why? Because promptly having the exact genome would have allowed us to design a far more robust and complex suite of vaccines to fight China's virus. Instead, we wound up with a far inferior set of experimental gene therapy quasi-vaccines that have proven to be far less effective—and far more dangerous—then a gaggle of liars from both the FDA and companies like Pfizer once promised us.

Regrettably, that first buddy tweet would not be the last. Just two weeks later, on February 7, the president would double down on his "trust in Xi Jinping" rhetoric with yet one more twaddling tweet:

> Just had a long and very good conversation by phone with President Xi of China. He is strong, sharp and powerfully focused on leading the counterattack on the Coronavirus. Great discipline is taking place in China, as President Xi strongly leads what will be a very successful operation. We are working closely with China to help![20]

Talk about letting the Bully of Beijing off the hook. At this early stage in the pandemic, we damn well should have impaled Xi Jinping on the "demon" virus his minions had unleashed and kept our Trumpian boot to his damn neck throughout 2020. Instead, this pair of buddy tweets would set the stage for what would be the steady unraveling of the Boss's Tough on China image throughout 2020

These tweets would only be eclipsed by one that I shall share with you shortly regarding the tawdry "ZTE Affair."

FIFTEEN

A Wilbur Ross ZTE Belly Flop

Wilbur Ross has largely been sidelined in high-stakes trade negotiations with China in the latest signal that President Donald Trump is losing confidence in his commerce secretary.... Ross—whom Trump once affectionately called a "killer," a high compliment in the president's lexicon—has steadily become a bit player, with the president regularly leaning on Treasury Secretary Steven Mnuchin, U.S. Trade Representative Robert Lighthizer and White House trade adviser Peter Navarro.

The commerce secretary's standing took another hit this week when the president tweeted criticism of the department's recent decision to block the Chinese phone-maker ZTE from accessing U.S. technology.... "He's not a prime-time player here," said one trade strategist closely tracking the administration's trade discussions.

—*Politico*, May 14, 2018[21]

ZTE—formally the Zhongxing Telecommunications Equipment Corporation—is a poster child of a state-directed Chinese company that, as a matter of Chinese Communist Party strategy, uses stolen intellectual property from America and other Western countries to gain a competitive advantage. On behalf of the Chinese state, ZTE then uses that purloined advantage to kill American companies and steal American jobs.

ZTE is also a company that has made sure—while making billions of dollars along the way—that rogue regimes like Iran and North Korea have all of the technological baddies they need to build up their nuclear weapons arsenals—and thereby keep a poisonous potpourri of profane mullahs and blood-sucking dictators comfortably in power.

The ZTE tale itself starts very early in the administration. Under the gun of the Department of Commerce, ZTE was forced, in March of 2017, to pay a combined civil and criminal penalty and forfeiture of just over $1 billion. Not exactly small change.

ZTE had been found guilty of illegally shipping its telecom equipment to both Iran and North Korea. As the *Financial Times* succinctly put it:

> *The Chinese state-owned group was found to have conspired to evade the embargoes by buying US components, incorporating them into ZTE equipment and shipping them to Iran and North Korea. As part of its original settlement with the US, ZTE agreed to a 7-year suspended denial of export privileges, which could be triggered if the company failed to comply with the terms of the deal.*[22]

Throw in further the facts that ZTE executives had also made false statements and obstructed justice so as to "affirmatively" mislead the American government, and it had been time back in 2017 for the Department of Commerce to throw at least half a book at them.[23] Ergo, the more than $1 billion fine. So far, so good.

Fast-forward now to 2018 and, lo and behold, Commerce Secretary Wilbur Ross discovers that ZTE had violated its 2017 agreement with yet more false statements *and* by disregarding much of what it had agreed to in the original settlement. So Wilbur decides to go yard on ZTE—and here's an important detail: Wilbur throws what he thinks is a touchdown pass *without* informing the Boss.

The next thing we know at the White House on April 16, 2018 is that Wilbur has slapped a so-called "denial of export privileges" penalty on ZTE. This was effectively a death sentence for the company because the denial would prohibit ZTE from sourcing US components that it needed to build its phones and other products.[24] With such a death sentence, at least from afar, Wilbur's opening move on ZTE looked far more like a beautiful Greg Louganis dive than the bellyflop it would soon turn out to be.

All ZTE Hell Breaks Loose

Upon hearing of Wilbur's ZTE lightning bolt, I first thought: "Why do I, one of the top members of the president's trade team, have to find out about this in the *Wall Street Journal*? Isn't that what trade team meetings are for?"

Of course, my next thought was: "If Wilbur had actually brought the issue to the trade team, Mnuchin would've done everything possible to block Wilbur's action. So good for Wilbur's Bad Process end run around Bad Personnel."

Unfortunately, that simple and single congratulatory thought would be short-lived—and Bad Process and Bad Personnel would soon take its pound of flesh. To wit:

In the wake of Wilbur's announcement and the ensuing firestorm, the president got hit by the usual Silicon Valley lobbying shills. Implored these shills:

Pretty please, Mr. President, let us sell our computer chips to ZTE so they can continue assisting Iran and North Korea with their nuclear proliferation even as they continue to steal American jobs.

Well, Silicon Valley's lobbyists didn't put it *exactly* that way. But you get my drift.

Far more consequentially, POTUS also got an urgent personal call from Xi Jinping. With all the false humility Xi Jinping could muster, his message to the boss was clear (at least to me): "If you stupidly show mercy on ZTE, I will pretend to owe you."

In his own *Art of the Deal* mind, the Boss no doubt figured he could bank that Xi Jinping favor, and this would help get us to the bigger prize of a big deal with China on its Seven Deadly Sins of economic aggression. Truth be told here, there was also this:

The Boss loved the idea of getting another billion dollars more in fines from ZTE—$1.4 billion to be exact[25]—rather than just shutting ZTE down. And he figured that a *huge* fine would surely be enough to show he was Tough on China.

This, however, was a very significant political miscalculation, but I don't blame the Boss for stumbling into it so much as I blame two of the West Wing's in-resident Wall Street transactionalists, Ross and Mnuchin. Indeed, when POTUS told Wilbur to simply slap an additional Trump-sized fine on ZTE *rather* than put the company out of business, Wilbur should have told the Boss that was the absolutely wrong decision for two reasons.

First, there were the obvious national security issues associated with allowing ZTE to continue with its rogue nation business model. If you see a poisonous snake in the grass, don't wound it, kill it.

Second, and this is where Bad Politics came into the equation, Wilbur should have warned the Boss that all hell would break loose on Capitol Hill and in the anti-Trump media if we backed down even a whit from our *initial* tough position.

Specifically, Ross *should* have warned POTUS he would likely be excoriated by the likes of wannabe 2024 presidential candidates like Marco Rubio and Tom Cotton. They, of course, were quite strategically trying to demonstrate they were tougher than the president on the evil Commies.

> If Wilbur had been playing Four Star General rather the Lone Ranger, he would have told Donald Trump: "Never let a political rival outflank you."

And Wilbur should have also warned that POTUS would surely be taken to task not just by the left-wing *New York Times* and *Washington Post* but also by the *Wall Street Journal*—ZTE was just a very bad actor despised across party lines.

Unfortunately, Wilbur failed to warn the president about *any* of these political complications. Even more unfortunately, and as a further complication, the administration's Secretary of Appeasement Steve Mnuchin was up to his usual tricks back-channeling the Boss to ease up on ZTE, just exactly like his Wall Street and Silicon Valley Masters would have Neville Mnuchin do.

Again and again, that was Mnuchin's *modus operandi*—slide into the Oval Office and backchannel the Boss with his bitching and moaning. So when Xi Jinping called the Boss for his ZTE favor, POTUS immediately granted it, and we would begin at that point in early 2018 to exhibit a fairly consistent pattern over the next several years of looking more like rug merchants rather than sound policy implementers—effectively playing the modern version of the classic fools from the Vladimir Lenin definition of a capitalist as the Mnuchin willing to sell the rope to hang our country.

And yes, we indeed got lit up in the public arena. Rubio came out hot in a tweet warning, quite correctly, that "Trump's reversal on ZTE is [a] national security risk."[26] The anti-Trump CNBC noted, equally correctly, that "the Florida Republican's criticism marks the first backlash to the president's effort from a notable lawmaker with his own party."[27]

To make matters worse—incredibly worse—the president had himself teed up Rubio's tweet with a tweet of his own, which even today ranks as the single most tone deaf of his entire presidency.

This particularly ill-considered tweet starts off by reinforcing the Xi-Trump bromance which the public already hated with a vengeance. The tweet then, incredibly, expresses concern for the poor workers in China who lost their jobs rather than for all the Americans that the truly evil and mercantilist ZTE had screwed along the way. Tweeted and touted the president:

> *President Xi of China, and I, are working together to give massive Chinese phone company, ZTE, a way to get back into business, fast. Too many jobs in China lost. Commerce Department has been instructed to get it done!*[28]

When I saw that tweet, it was a WTF on steroids. "Too many jobs *in China* lost?" Surely you jest. What globalist body snatcher has taken my president?

SIXTEEN

Whiffing and Waffling on Huawei

Treasury Secretary Steven Mnuchin in recent days urged U.S. suppliers of Huawei Technologies Co. to seek licenses to resume sales to the blacklisted Chinese firm…The development reflects a recent reversal of the Trump administration's get-tough stance on Huawei….

—*The Wall Street Journal*, July 10, 2019[29]

As you read this, Huawei *remains* on the existential threat cusp of consolidating global control of 5G, one of the most powerful civilian and military technologies in world history.

The previous "Gs" represent the technologies that have powered your own cell phone and wireless communications. If you can hear me now, and you're in the middle of just about nowhere, you're probably connected to at least a 4G network.

5G is 4G on rocket fuel. It stands for "fifth-generation cellular communications technology," and 5G's dramatic increase in both speed and capacity suggests more of a *revolution* than an evolution.

This is very dangerous revolution because 5G is not just a way to make lightning-fast, no-drop phone calls to your friends or in a business environment. 5G also has the power to seamlessly interconnect both people *and machines* in ways that will lead to a dramatic increase not just in productivity but also in dangerous cyber vulnerabilities and military lethality.

To be macabrely specific here, just imagine Communist China using Huawei's 5G networks to turn off America's electricity grids and transportation systems—or to make US Air Force planes drop from the skies over the Taiwan Strait—and you get the existential threat picture.

My point is simply that you don't need a classified briefing—although I had plenty of those on 5G—to understand the potential pitfalls of allowing a Communist Chinese state-directed company like Huawei to seize the commanding heights of 5G. And when I say "commanding heights," I'm referring to Huawei's global strategy to be the technology and network of choice for the communication networks of *every* country around the world—from the salons of Europe and flyover country of America to the teeming cities of Africa and Asia.

In light of all we knew, we on the Trump trade team had a solemn duty to stop this particularly pernicious form of Chinese economic expansionism from occurring on POTUS 45's watch. So what exactly did we do—and not do—about the Huawei 5G threat?

Wilbur Strikes, Mnuchin Strikes Back

On the "do" side, I worked with warriors like Josh Steinman at the National Security Council and Nazak Nikakhtar at the Department of Commerce on Executive Order 13873, which the Boss signed on May 15, 2019. If properly implemented, this EO would have effectively been a *death sentence* for Huawei.

Not only would US telecommunications companies have been prevented from buying any Huawei equipment. Huawei would also have been denied market access to the computer chips it needs to manufacture the cell phones that consumers need to access Huawei's 5G network. This would have indeed hurt mightily as Huawei holds a significant share of the world cell phone market and relies on that market for an equally significant share of its revenues.

When POTUS signed the executive order, I thought: "This is as tough an approach as it gets. Good for us."

Soon, however, and once again, the Bad Personnel computer chips started hitting the "pull our punches" fan. Not surprisingly, the pressure started with Neville Mnuchin whining both privately in the Oval and publicly in the media that this latest crackdown on China would make it more difficult for him and Lighthizer to negotiate the Skinny Ass Phase One trade deal.

There was also relentless pressure from Deep Swamp lobbyists representing the semiconductor and telecommunications industries. Each of these sectors had their profit and loss statement panties in a twist but for a different reason.

America's semiconductor companies wanted to *sell* chips *to* Huawei to *boost revenues.*

In contrast, the wireless conglomerates wanted to *buy* cheap chips *from* Huawei to *decrease costs.*

Of course, nowhere in this profit maximizing calculus was any reference to either economic or national security. And that's what pisses me off so much about the Deep Swamp in Washington—all responsibility stops at the shareholder shore.[30]

We Fold Like a Cheap Pinstripe Suit

For (all too short) a time, POTUS held firm. However, a chink in the Oval Office armor began to develop when Mnuchin, Kudlow, and Ross argued that there was no point in *not* selling at least some chips to Huawei—specifically, the lower end *commoditized* chips.

As their Wall Street transactionalist argument went, Huawei would simply be able to buy these low-end chips from foreign competitors like Samsung and that would only hurt American companies like Intel and AMD. So why not give Huawei a short-term waiver for certain kinds of commoditized chips?

Why not indeed? This typical short term rug merchant thinking blissfully ignored any possible political blowback—as well as the core mission, which was to bring Huawei to its knees. And the reason for this rug merchant thinking is because of something that these Wall Street transactionalists could simply never understand during my four long years of trading sharp elbows with them:

To really stand up to Communist China, we as a country were going to have to endure some temporary pain—whether it be pain to our farmers or our chipmakers who would sell less to China or pain to American consumers who might have to pay a bit more for their goods.

However, in their purely *tactical* pragmatism, Wall Street transactionalists like Ross and Kudlow never wanted to endure such pain for the sake of the broader mission while Mnuchin himself never even embraced the mission.

If Steve, Larry, and Wilbur had been generals commanding our troops during the Korean War, they never would have tried to take Pork Chop Hill—or in this case Huawei Hill—for fear of taking casualties.[31]

Here, however, were the two *big* problems with giving Huawei waivers to keep buying at least the low-end commoditized American chips:

First, even as we were mitigating some of our own pain with these sales, we were doing the exact same thing for Huawei—making it less painful for them to make what they already saw was a necessary transition away from the American supply chain. And the more time that we gave Huawei to make that transition to independence from American semiconductor manufacturers, the less likely our attempt to take Huawei off the global chessboard would be.

To succeed, we had to hit them now with the weapon we had that would work now. That's because over time, that weapon would become increasingly ineffective.

Second, there was the hypocrisy of it all. Consider, here, that a major part of our Huawei foreign policy was to discourage our allies around the world from committing to the Huawei 5G system. If we could stop countries like Canada, Germany, and Japan from committing to Huawei networks, this would be an equally effective way of killing the Huawei teenager who had long since left the crib. But how could the US credibly demand that other countries wean themselves from the teat of Huawei's cheap, state-subsidized 5G milk if we were granting waivers to Huawei so America itself could keep sucking on that teat?

The answer, of course, is that you simply can't credibly implement a foreign policy on the foundation of such hypocrisy, and the granting of waivers to Huawei would significantly undercut the efforts of our State Department to go forth and preach the gospel of a free world free from the dangers and tyranny of Huawei.

So once again, with a series of Bad Personnel waivers to Huawei, the Wall Street transactionalists made us look like rug merchants in the eyes not just of our own people—and the 2020 electorate!—but also in the increasingly jaundiced eyes of the world.

Bad Personnel is Bad Policy is Bad Politics indeed. But we weren't done yet pulling our punches and eroding the image of Donald J. Trump as a Tough on China president.

SEVENTEEN

My TikTok Aaron Sorkin West Wing Moment

President Donald Trump was furious with Treasury Secretary Steven Mnuchin over the way the TikTok Global agreement was sold to him, two current Trump administration officials...confirmed to the Daily Caller.... Mnuchin has been the administration's lead official in searching for a U.S. company to purchase TikTok from parent company ByteDance, despite some administration officials—including White House Trade and Manufacturing Policy Director Peter Navarro—pushing Trump instead to ban the social media app entirely....

Mnuchin knew the TikTok Global deal undercut national security by failing to force ByteDance to turn over critical pieces of technology, including TikTok's central content algorithm, and not including an enforcement mechanism to ensure user data security.

—The Daily Caller, September 23, 2020[32]

The Trump administration's attempted ban on the Chinese social media app TikTok started with a Communist Chinese invasion of India. What's that you say?

Yes, the Trump TikTok gambit all started with this geopolitical reality: the Chinese Communist Empire has a long and particularly nasty habit of using periods of uncertainty and chaos in the world as opportunities to advance their imperialistic agenda. A case in point is the ChiCom's sneak invasion of India during the chaos and confusion of the 1962 Cuban Missile Crisis.

At that time of nuclear brinksmanship between two superpowers, India was a client state of the Soviet Union. With Nikita Khrushchev and the Soviets otherwise preoccupied with an eyeball-to-eyeball showdown with John F. Kennedy and the Americans, Chinese military troops poured into India.

With nary a peep or missile from Khrushchev, Communist China then bit off a nice little chunk of Indian territory known as Aksai Chin, which is located in the eastern portion of the larger Kashmir region. Small though it is, Aksai Chin is no small piece of territory strategically. The distance between Aksai Chin and New Delhi is only about the same distance as between Boston and Washington, DC—think lightning Chinese blitzkrieg in a war with India rather than a slow, Long March slog.[33]

Fast-forward now to May 2020, and, in a new fog of pandemic war, the ChiComs were back to pouring across the Indian border. At least this time, the Indians were able to fend off the Chinese invasion— but not before Chinese death squads slaughtered over twenty Indian soldiers in what newspapers described as "gruesome" and "bloody hand-to-hand combat."[34]

In retaliation for China's aggression, the Prime Minister of India Narendra Modi, on June 29, 2020, banned more than fifty Chinese social media apps, most notably WeChat, Weibo, and TikTok itself. When the Boss saw the decisive courage of Modi, a Tough on China light bulb immediately went off in the East Wing. With a late-night order from on high—or at least from the second floor of the East Wing—the National Security Council quickly went to work on an executive order that would impose a similar type of ban on select Chinese apps—including both TikTok and WeChat.

Banning Chinese social media apps like TikTok and WeChat was not just good Tough on China politics. It was very good policy. From both an economic and national security perspective, these Chinese social media apps pose an intricate and interrelated set of threats.

Most obviously, these social media apps collect a tremendous amount of personal and financial information from American citizens and businesses and routinely transfer that data over servers on the Chinese Communist mainland. By law, this data is accessible to the Chinese government and, by extension, China's large cadres of Chinese government hackers.[35]

Now most internet users tend to log on to multiple applications using the same username and password. So let's say you do that, and you log into TikTok. China's hackers can then access *any other applications* for which you may use that same username and password combination, including your bank accounts and credit cards.

Note: These hacker scum don't even have to know *if* you use these applications; they can simply go through a universe of such applications—or just have a bot do it—to see if they can hit a jackpot that will hit you like a jackhammer.

Beyond these dangers, social media apps can also archive all manner of photos and videos that can be used for nefarious state activities like facial recognition tracking. Travel to China, for example, and the government may already have a whole dossier ready to review on you as you step off the plane on your way to passport control.

For all these reasons, it was very good policy for the White House to swiftly move on an executive order that would, as Modi's India had boldly and swiftly done, ban a large number of social media apps within the Communist China cyber universe.

NSC Has the Pen, Treasury Has the Eraser

While the task of drawing up the TikTok ban fell to the National Security Council per the Boss's orders, I would have at least a hand in the matter. The problem the NSC lawyers and I quickly ran into, however, was that while NSC had the pen, Mnuchin's Treasury Department had the eraser.

Just why was this so? Simply because the real hammer in the executive order was the imposition of economic sanctions on any company that engaged in financial transactions with TikTok, and Treasury was in charge of imposing any such sanctions.

Mnuchin's Treasury minions didn't just drag their heels. They dug in, and as they dug in, Mnuchin began hatching a plot to blunt the order by engineering the sale of TikTok rather than going for an outright ban.

Now, once Mnuchin's "buy" versus "ban" option was in play, Microsoft was initially floated as a possible buyer. This was, of course, beyond laughable as the Microsoft House of Crappy Software that Bill Gates built has been one of China's biggest kowtowing lackeys for more than two decades and clearly not trustable.

Here, you should know that Microsoft has not just made billions peddling its software while bending to the Chinese government's censorship demands. Microsoft's engineers have also customized its software for both the Chinese military and cyber cops that use China's Great Firewall to monitor, and thereby digitally imprison, the Chinese people.

Today, as you read this, Vichy Microsoft is even partnering with the Chinese military on the development of artificial intelligence.[36] AI is a technology destined to be one of the most powerful weapons on the twenty-first-century battlefield.

So the idea of a Microsoft Corporation in bed with the Chinese Communist Party first buying the American slice of TikTok and then keeping American data safe was indeed more than laughable.

The Oracle Resistance

Of course, as was his backstabbing way, Steve Mnuchin did all of his backchanneling dirty work without *any* consultation of either President Trump or the White House Trade Team—much less the NSC and its top cop Robert O'Brien, and I myself would only find out about Mnuchin's backchanneling buggery by accident.

That big reveal happened when I got a call from one of the true patriots of the Trump movement, Safra Catz, the chief executive officer of Oracle. Safra let me know that Oracle had joined the hunt for TikTok and wanted to take my temperature on whether I would oppose the "buy" versus "ban" option.

When I got that call, I was simultaneously breathless and speechless. That's because I realized in an instant that if Oracle was a possible buyer, that meant a deal was very likely as Oracle had significant stroke inside the White House. Not a good thing in my mind by *any* stretch of the imagination as I clearly preferred the ban. Yet Oracle clearly was far more preferable as a suitor than Microsoft.

With albeit cold comfort, I also believed it was true—and Safra was trying to convince me of that truth—that if any company could provide assurances that an American standalone TikTok would *not* be exporting any data or information to the Communist Chinese, it would be Oracle.

Here, it must be said—to the credit of Safra Catz and Oracle's chairman of the board Larry Ellison—Oracle is one of the very few American corporations that has refused to kowtow while operating on the Chinese mainland. For that reason, Oracle is also one of the few American companies that has been successful in protecting its intellectual property and technologies from expropriation by the Chinese Communists.

So yes, Oracle clearly was *far* more preferable as a suitor than Microsoft.

Still, I hated the idea of a standalone American TikTok deal rather than an outright ban for a number of reasons. First, we would be handing over billions of dollars to Communist China for the purchase of TikTok—up goes the trade deficit.

Second, and far more importantly, as good as Oracle might be in searching the software code of TikTok for hidden bugs or blocking any escape routes with data, I was unconvinced that the company could maintain an adequate American Firewall between US consumers using TikTok and China's vaunted hacker cadres—along with the Russians, they are the best in the world.

Here was the problem: It wasn't like Oracle or Microsoft could just buy TikTok and run it as a completely safe and sanitized program in America. Rather, the real value of TikTok is in its computer code and the engineers and computer programmers who would be constantly updating and improving that code.

Of course, most of those Star Trekkies would be Chinese Nationals operating outside the Oracle firewall. So whenever the American version of TikTok had to be updated, there would always be the possibility of some Chinese Trojan virus being imported into American cell phones and computers through the update—*no matter how careful Oracle might be.*

Third, it was a terrible precedent to "buy rather than ban" as a strategy. We simply would not have enough American companies with the technical expertise and financial capital to purchase ALL of the Chinese social media apps that needed to be shut down. So the TikTok deal was at best a one-off deal.

As the last consideration in making the choice between an outright ban versus a purchase of TikTok—and foremost in my mind given the nearness of the impending election—there was the Bad Politics of the matter. We had made a strong case that this Chinese social media app had to be shut down immediately because of pressing national security reasons. After all, we were invoking the ultimate statutory authority hammer of the International Economic Emergency Powers Act to justify the actions we were taking.

Yet, by backing down now from an outright ban, we were shifting to an option that would still leave the door wide open to significant national security risks. That was a pulling of our punch that not only undermined the perception of the White House and President Trump as Tough on China. It also undercut our legal argument that there actually *was* a national security emergency we had to worry about—and yes, TikTok immediately took us into court upon imposition of the ban.

Urban Decay on K Street

Predictably, the Washington Swamp with a "K Street" lobbying crowd that salutes no American flag was working overtime to grease the skids for TikTok. To that end, TikTok's parent company ByteDance strategically showered one of the president's closest confidantes—and swampiest of Swamp Creatures—with obscene sums and a top executive position to sway the president. Here is how the website opensecrets. org reported this particular Washington ooze:

> *The most crucial lobbyist for TikTok's future might be David Urban, a key player in Trump's 2016 win in Pennsylvania and an adviser to Trump's reelection campaign. Hired by TikTok in January, Urban's firm American Continental Group has seen its revenue explode to new highs in the Trump era as companies attempt to leverage Urban's connection to the president.*[37]

For the record, I like David Urban. At least I used to like Urban until our TikTok blow up—he is no longer "David" to me. Whenever I needed help in Pennsylvania, I would give him a call. And over the past several years, Urban had been helpful to my efforts to both boost the fortunes of the Philly shipyard and get increased defense appropriations for a politically-sensitive combat vehicle plant in York, PA.

On the fun front, Urban had also been instrumental in organizing my trip to Pennsylvania in October of 2019 with the Secretary of the Navy Richard Spencer. Richard and I had hatched a plot to name a new San Antonio-class warship after the city of Harrisburg,[38] and sure, it was a gambit blatantly aimed at boosting the president's reelection chances in the Keystone—and key battleground—state. But that's just politics. If the Democrats were in power, they would do the same damn thing—if they ever bothered to build new naval ships.

At any rate, when Urban called to lobby me on behalf of TikTok, I was surprised for two reasons. First, while I knew he was a lobbyist, I didn't think he would be so venal as to represent the interests of Communist China. David knew better, and, more to the point, David knew that I knew that he knew better.

Second, and this is where it got really interesting, when Urban called me, I was surprised at his threatening tone. He had seen my negative public comments about Microsoft and TikTok, and thirty seconds into the call, he went off on a long rant about why I was wrong and why I needed to get in line—or else.

"Or else what," thought I. Now I have to add David Urban to my long list of enemies in Washington, DC? And what does this big lobbying dog think he can possibly do to me that my *very, very, very* long list of enemies in the DC Swamp and West Wing haven't already done or tried? Put a bad word in with the Boss? Oh please. Get in frigging line, Davey.

By the way, our phone call ended with me telling Urban he was one TikTok toke over the lobbying line. David Urban would never call or speak to me again. It just broke my heart.

Just kidding.

These Swamp Creatures *really* disgust me. Have I mentioned that before?

Life Imitates Sorkin

As all of this Swamp Creature maneuvering and Treasury Department treachery was unfolding, I once again feared—and I repeatedly warned the president about this—that this was yet again another stupid move by Wall Street transactionalists within our midst who were tone deaf to the political environment and unwilling to see the real dangers. And yes, feeling the urgency of the matter, I was holding nothing back in meetings with the Boss. Nothing!

In fact, during this whole TikTok debate—and eventual debacle—I had my single best, bluntest, and funniest fifteen minutes in the Oval Office of my entire career at the White House. It was a perfect Aaron Sorkin scene right out of the old TV drama with Martin Sheen, *The West Wing*—absolutely pitch perfect with respect to both the setup of the scene and the albeit purely *accidental* precision timing of my grand entrance into the Oval.

It all started out July 20, 2020, with an innocent mid-afternoon stroll from my office in the EEOB to the West Wing to see White House Legal Counsel Pat Cipollone. My sole mission was a quick brief on where we stood with the more than twenty executive orders that were backed up at various nodes of the bad staff secretary process.

Pat, like myself, had grown increasingly frustrated with the slow pace of both the internal wheels within the White House and the interminable delays of the Office of Legal Counsel over at the Department of Justice. So Pat and I, often joined by others like NSC attorney Sue Bai, had gotten into the habit of meeting once a day to see where any bottlenecks might be and how we might blow by them.

When I arrived at Pat's office promptly at 1 p.m., his receptionist told me he was down in the Oval but would be up shortly. So as I was cooling my heels, I started going through the newspapers on the coffee table in the waiting room. Almost twenty minutes later, after I had scanned the *Wall Street Journal*, the *New York Post*, and the *Washington Times*, I was getting antsy. So I innocently asked the receptionist what Pat was up to in the Oval. When she told me he was at a meeting about TikTok, I literally jumped up from the couch, raced down the stairs two at a time, and sprinted down the hallway towards the Oval.

Make no mistake about it. I was *pissed*. There were not supposed to be *any* decision meetings with POTUS about TikTok without me present—and that was a direction from POTUS himself. So this was a clear process foul.

Enter Navarro, Chased by a Lobbyist

Now here's the funny part, and why sometimes, timing is indeed everything. As I entered the Outer Oval reception area, I didn't even bother to ask the gatekeepers Molly Michael or Nick Luna for permission to enter the Oval. I didn't even look at them. Instead, I just walked up to the closed Oval Office door, gave the handle a good yank, and literally burst into the room. Navarro. Enter stage right, chased by the ghost of David Urban.

It was if I had arrived *exactly* on my Aaron Sorkin cue. Without missing a beat, I strode smartly towards the Resolute Desk as the Boss was asking the assembled throng whether he should just ban TikTok outright. Said I in midstride:

> Yes sir, just ban that puppy. If we do anything else, we will just look weak. It will [pointing at Mnuchin] be just more weak-ass, broke-dick, piece of Steve Mnuchin manure. We just have to stop doing this "pull our punches" rug merchant crap.

Not surprisingly, at this point, the unhappiest person in the room was Steve Mnuchin. It was not just because I had crashed his little Bad Process party. It was also because my pointed comments led the Boss to go off on a riff and rant about how Mnuchin was always weak on China, weak on trade, weak on currency manipulation, and weak on sanctions, how Mnuchin had screwed up the Jay Powell appointment at the Fed, had screwed up the stimulus and relief bill, and was pretty much Nancy Pelosi's little whiny bitch.

It was all just deliciously entertaining, and if looks could kill, the one Mnuchin gave me in that Aaron Sorkin moment would have been my very bitter end.

The chief of staff Mark Meadows, for his part, wasn't wild about the fact either that I had simply barged into the Oval uninvited. When he tried to give me a raft of dung about it afterwards, I told him in no uncertain terms that I wasn't wild about the fact that he had strategically excluded me from the meeting.

In fact, I was especially ripped at Meadows because literally everybody *else* who should have been at that meeting *was* at that meeting—Lighthizer, Kushner, Lyons, Cipollone, Kudlow, O'Brien, Ross, Liddell. Yep, everybody but me—once again the odd China Hawk out.

And to that not-so-odd point, everybody in that Oval Office knew damn well that when I walked in I would be the *only* guy who would give POTUS a strong, honest, and textured assessment as to why a TikTok ban was far more preferable to an Oracle, or especially a Microsoft, buyout. Which is exactly why Meadows—probably goaded by Mnuchin or Kushner—had at least tried to hold the meeting without me.

The *Washington Post* would correctly describe the meeting as a "'knock-down, drag-out' brawl" between me and Mnuchin.[39] I say it was just another West Wing day of Bad Personnel using Bad Process to make Bad Policy that would result in Bad Politics for the Boss.

Either way, I was at least heartened that day by the fact that the president seemed to side with my suite of arguments. In fact, by the time the meeting ended, I was pretty sure that we were going to go back to our original position, a flat out ban of TikTok.

Alas, and yet again, this was not to be. Ultimately, Mnuchin and his Greek chorus of Wall Street transactionalists would, as they so often did, wear the Boss down and ultimately win the TikTok war for Wall Street and the Chinese Communist Party—while losing it for America.

This late stage pulling of our TikTok punch further solidified the public's perception that the White House was not filled with serious policymakers seeking to bend the arc of history to the side of the working men and women of America. Wrote the *New York Times* in yet another opportunity Neville Mnuchin would hand to them to tweak our pulled-punch noses:

> *The saga of TikTok had everything: Ominous threats of surveillance. A forced fire sale. Threats of retaliation. Head-spinning deal terms that morphed by the hour. Dark horse bidders and a looming deadline. Now, as the dust settles on the weeks of drama over the social media app, investors and others are asking what it was all for.*
>
> *The answer? A cloud computing contract for the Silicon Valley business software company Oracle, a merchandising deal for Walmart and a claim of victory for President Trump.*[40]

Yet despite bad press clips like these, we still were not done pulling our punches. And the next punch Mnuchin and his bad company would pull would be one of the worst abominations imaginable. The afternoon this happened was, hands down, the saddest afternoon I would ever spend in the Situation Room during my entire four years in the Trump administration.

EIGHTEEN

A Slave Labor Debacle Debases the Situation Room

Fresh off their heated, "f**k"-encrusted shouting match in China, tensions and policy fissures between Donald Trump advisers Steve Mnuchin and Peter Navarro are at an all-time high.... Navarro has—according to multiple sources who spoke to The Daily Beast on the condition of anonymity—privately nicknamed Mnuchin "Neville Chamberlain" (in reference to the Conservative British prime minister famous for his foreign policy of appeasement toward Nazi Germany and Adolf Hitler) and likened the economic threat from China to that of fascist dictator Hitler.

—The *Daily Beast*, May 24, 2018[41]

Here's a funny story about this dust-up reported by the *Daily Beast*. It's a story that may help shed a useful spotlight on my four-year-long feud with Neville Mnuchin.

In May of 2018, Bob Lighthizer and I jumped on Steve Mnuchin's Treasury Department plane with a gaggle of National Security Council staffers and headed to Beijing for what would be our one and only round of major trade talks with the Chinese on their home turf.

This trip to the Far East immediately went south when Mnuchin *unilaterally* decided at breakfast just before the talks began that he would conduct one-on-one negotiations directly with China's chief negotiator, Vice Premier Liu He, rather than allow the rest of us to participate. Yep, we had just flown seven thousand miles only to have Stupid Stevie, rather than the Chinese, be the first to screw us.

Both Lighthizer and Terry Branstad, the ambassador to China, were predictably livid at Mnuchin, but I was the only one who bothered to speak up. In fact, I got right up in Steve's big-nosed ugly grill right outside the meeting hall and didn't let up until he agreed to back down and at least let Lighthizer into his stupid little negotiating party.

Mnuchin's gambit was indeed stupid. Through the eyes of the Chinese, we as a team lost considerable face, and the episode was a particular embarrassment to Lighthizer, the guy who was *supposed* to be our *real* chief negotiator.

The net result was that Mnuchin considerably weakened our negotiating position at the very beginning of what were already very sensitive negotiations.

That night, in a long dinner in which every course served seem to get weirder—to the point where I didn't even know what I was eating by the end—the Chinese purposely isolated Lighthizer. They did so by seating poor forlorn Bob alone in the middle of a huge table, with no one within ten feet of him on either side. Meanwhile, directly across from Bob at another huge table, our Communist hosts treated Mnuchin like an emperor, feting him with conversation and fawning all over him.

I wondered at the time whether I, with my cross-cultural training as a Peace Corps volunteer, was the only one in the banquet hall to pick up on this Chinese trick. Certainly Steve Mnuchin had no clue.

Now here's the funny part of the story: On the way home, somebody in the flight crew must have had a keen sense of history—or at least humor—because they showed the film *Darkest Hour*.

This glorious piece of cinema tells the tale of Winston Churchill's own dustup in the 1930s with Great Britain's prime minister Neville Chamberlain and Foreign Minister Lord Halifax. Churchill's fight comes as he is jockeying to become prime minister in the face of unrelenting Nazi aggression—which both Chamberlain and Halifax repeatedly appease.

After the movie was over, a number of us congregated in the aisles, and at one point, one of the National Security Council staff made the comparison between Trump battling the Chinese Communist Party and Churchill fighting the Nazis. When another staffer asked: "If Trump is Churchill, who is Neville Chamberlain and who is Lord Halifax in this administration?"

Of course, the hands-down, no question about it consensus was Mnuchin as Neville Chamberlain. There was, however, a split over Lord Halifax. Some folks thought it was Kushner, while at least to me, it was unquestionably Larry Kudlow.

At any rate, several weeks later, the *Daily Beast* would, as the lead-off quote to this chapter indicates, accuse little old me of christening Mnuchin as the "Neville Chamberlain" of our time, but I always like to give credit where credit is due. In this case, it was clearly a *group* decision made somewhere over the skies of Alaska on our way home to the DC Swamp.

After the Beasty story broke and the next time we were in the Oval Office, Mnuchin began to whine in front of the Boss about how I could possibly call poor Stevie "Neville Chamberlain." After all, it was the evil Chamberlain who had surrendered Europe to those far eviler Nazis who had killed so many of Stevie's Jewish ancestors.

All I could think of at the time—besides how weak Mnuchin looked in front of the president—was this. In fact, I didn't just think this. I said it right out loud to the Munchkin's face:

Hey, Neville, knowing what you know about what the Nazis did to the Jews, how is it that you don't give a flying puck about what the Chinese Communists are doing to two million Uighurs in the concentration camps of Xinjiang Province? Oh, and let's not forget about the ethnic cleansing in Tibet. What do you say about that Stevie?

Fast forward now to Thursday, September 10, 2020, and yet another showdown and throw down, this time in the White House Situation Room. On this day, Mnuchin, Lighthizer, Kudlow, and I along with several high-ranking officials from the Department of Homeland Security (DHS) march solemnly into the Sit Room, having been démarched by an overwrought Chief of Staff Mark Meadows.

Overwrought, by the way, was pretty much Mark's daily state of existence at the White House. Talk about being emotionally under-equipped and overwhelmed by a job.

In this case, the Chief's Chief Crybaby was needlessly trying to put the kibosh on a long overdue action by DHS against Communist China. This action was related to the proliferation of China's aforementioned Soviet-style *cum* Nazi concentration camps and slave labor factories in China's Xinjiang province. And when I say Soviet-style, I mean it literally—China's own gulags were largely constructed in the era of Mao Zedong using blueprints imported from the Soviet Union.

At any rate, I have made passing reference to Beijing's notorious gulags numerous times; but given the magnitude of what would be yet another Mark Meadows screwup, it may well be worth a little detail to lay the Adolf Eichmann-Josef Mengele predicate for this final install-ment of the saga of the Trump administration's pulled punches.

So let's start with the observation that since the days after Chinese Communist Party forces took Xinjiang in 1949 and Tibet in 1950 at the point of some very big guns, the CCP has conducted a widespread and persistent ethnic, cultural, religious, and genocidal cleansing of the Buddhist population in Tibet and the Uighurs in Xinjiang.

In this ongoing pogrom with Chinese characteristics, the CCP effectively bans most forms of religious worship. It has also destroyed large swathes of temples, mosques, and religious artifacts.

Then, there is this abomination: To quite literally breed the Tibetan and Uighur populations out of existence—and in a more subtle form of ethnic cleansing than a bullet to the head—Tibetan and Uighur women are exported to other parts of China not only to toil in factories. They are also forced to breed with so called "leftover" Han Chinese men who find Han Chinese women to be in short supply because of China's One Child Policy.

As for the Uighur and Tibetan men, they are forced to toil by the millions in slave labor hubs for the various kinds of commerce con-ducted in Tibet and Xinjiang—from cotton and tomato farming to the production of hair products and other light manufacturing.[42]

The "lucky" prisoners in these concentration camps work sixteen hours a day, seven days a week making baubles for export to Walmart and other big box retailers in the West. The *unluckiest* prisoners are those who, ironically, may be the healthiest and strongest.

These fine physical specimens, like their brethren in China's beleaguered Falun Gong community, often wind up first anesthetized while their organs and retinas are removed. After thus servicing the CCP's thriving organ trafficking scheme, these poor carved up souls are then cremated—often while still alive—with their ashes then scattered to the winds.[43]

The Curious Case of the Missing WRO

To say that people like Mnuchin, Kudlow, and Meadows, along with officials from the broader Trump administration like Kushner, should have acted to put a stop to this post-Auschwitz depravity right at the beginning of Trump's tenure is to also say that Barack Obama and Joe Biden should have done it *before* we Trump folks ever got there. But, I guess, with the kind of tough actions DHS was proposing that day in the Situation Room, it was a case of better late than never—although Chief of Staff Mark Meadows was about to violently disagree with even that.

So let's start that story with this excerpt from the press release that was eventually issued by the Department of Homeland Security after Meadows effectively gutted the DHS proposal:

> *U.S. Customs and Border Protection (CBP) issued **five** Withhold Release Orders (WRO) today on products from the People's Republic of China (PRC). The products subject to the WROs are produced with state-sponsored forced labor in the Xinjiang Uyghur Autonomous Region, where the Chinese government is engaged in systemic human rights abuses against the Uyghur people and other ethnic and religious minorities.*
>
> *"By taking this action, DHS is combating illegal and inhumane forced labor, a type of modern slavery, used to make goods that the Chinese government then tries to import into the United States. When China attempts to import these goods into our supply chains, it also disadvantages American workers and businesses," said Acting DHS Deputy Secretary Ken Cuccinelli.[44]* [emphasis added]

Here's the teaching point: What sometimes is left out of a press release is far more important than what is actually in it. What was left out was any mention of a *sixth* withhold release order.

After months of preparation, DHS Deputy Secretary Ken Cuccinelli and Commissioner Mark Morgan at Customs and Border Protection had indeed teed up a full six pack—not just five—of these WROs. These neat little hammers would empower CBP agents to block the import of *any* goods made in Communist China using forced labor in Xinjiang. However, over the weekend, Meadows had gotten wind of the pending DHS announcement and went into a full-blown, Al Haig, "I'm in charge" panic mode.

It still remains unclear to me why Meadows reacted so negatively to the idea of cracking down on concentration camps in China. Maybe it was a pointed call from Mnuchin. Maybe it was a missive from Meadows's erstwhile babysitter and real White House Chief of Staff Jared Kushner. But be that as it may, Meadows was hell-bent on stopping the DHS action.

And here is why Washington is sometimes so deliciously and leakfully evil. When Meadows called Cuccinelli and Morgan and told them to put a halt on their WROs, these gentlemen—and true patriots of the Trump movement—were incensed at this interference from the White House, and for two very good reasons.

First, the Department of Homeland Security had every right to exercise its authority in the matter. It really did *not* have to ask for the White House's permission.

Second, despite its autonomy in this matter but in deference to the White House, CBP had actually agreed to go through a full White House staff secretary process, and after weeks of delay, *it had received full approval.* So at that point, the coast for throwing that full roundhouse punch of six WRO orders should have been clear.

Neither of these reasons are the delicious part of the story, however. The delicious part is that somebody leaked to the anti-Trump rag *Politico* that Meadows was about to go weak on China yet again by blocking the WROs, and one of their reporters had called Meadows for comment. So when Meadows walked into the Situation Room, he was apoplectic at the leak.

Deliciously, that leak had backed Meadows into a political box where he could not just kill all of the WROs. He at least had to do *something* if he didn't want to look like a hardhearted Chinese Nazi himself.

Of course, understanding his dilemma, Meadows burst into the Sit Room that afternoon hotter than a counterfeit Chinese power strip. He then proceeded to rip Morgan and Cuccinelli two new ones for the leak.

Now, Mark Morgan, who is always a gentleman and one of my favorite patriots in America, might well put up with that kind of abuse from Meadows. But Ken Cuccinelli? Nope. Ken doesn't take that kind of crap from anybody. So there were rhetorical fireworks right at the outset, with Ken pushing back at Meadows *hard*!

In the ensuing discussion, Steve Mnuchin initially wanted to do nothing at all. As per his usual tactic, the Neville Chamberlain of our time—I never get tired of writing that—instead asked for a delay so that WROs could go back, as he whined, "properly through process."

At that point, I told Mnuchin in no uncertain terms that *all six* WROs had gone through a full process and been approved at the deputy level at *both* Treasury and USTR, and the NSC's Matt Pottinger—silent to that point—agreed as he had chaired the process.

Now at this point you might think I'm about to tell you that Cuccinelli and Morgan won this epic showdown; but *au contraire*. Meadows was the Chief, after all, and he decided that instead of approving all six of the WRO's like both Good Process and morality required, Meadows would agree to only five.

Ok. That that seems pretty good, doesn't it? Certainly, five of the six orders approves seems like way more than a glass half full.

But here was the very big Meadows-Mnuchin catch—and it was this catch that was conveniently left out of the DHS press release:

The one withhold release order that would be left off the list accounted for fully 80 percent of the cotton and cotton production that would be affected. That's right, 80 percent.

Of course, the press would light us up for yet another pulled punch. And here yet again, there was this high irony:

We as an administration took what was actually at least a semi-tough, five-of-six WRO action, yet because of the way we very publicly mishandled it, all our efforts did was make POTUS look weak on China yet again.

As a coda to all of this, I am at least pleased to report that Cuccinelli and Morgan dropped that sixth and last WRO on China after the election—and if you are curious, they did *not* ask for Mark Meadows's permission.

PART FIVE

That's the Way the Blue Wall Didn't Crumble

NINETEEN

The Iron MAGA Triangle of Populist Economic Nationalism

The man who has defied the expectations of political observers at every turn delivered his biggest surprise yet Tuesday night, beating Clinton by barreling through the so-called blue wall of states that had not been carried by a Republican in decades.... This clean sweep through the Rust Belt—netting 64 electoral votes, the exact number by which Mitt Romney fell short of the presidency four years ago— clinched the White House for Trump.

—*National Review*, November 9, 2016[1]

In 2016, we danced our way to victory by running on a Populist Economic Nationalist platform. Along our merry, jitterbugging way, the Democrats' vaunted Blue Wall of Michigan, Wisconsin, and Pennsylvania crumbled, Wall Street gasped, Hillaryites wept, and Donald J. Trump transformed the Republican Party of champagne, Davos, and Wall Street into the beer joints and State Fairs of Main Street.

If there ever were a case of "you should dance with the one that brung ya," our 2020 presidential election strategy certainly should have been it. Yet, by not doubling down *hard* on a Populist Economic Nationalist platform in the 2020 election aimed squarely at the Blue Wall, President Trump's campaign team engineered a strategic failure every bit as egregious as its failure to run on a credible Tough on China platform.

In 2020, we would lose all 46 Electoral College votes we had captured in 2016 in the Blue Wall states of Michigan (16), Pennsylvania (20), and Wisconsin (10). That would turn the Trump red tide into a wave of Biden blue and be the difference between having a people's lion versus a globalist puppet in the Oval Office.[2]

This strategic failure was a massive miscalculation that boiled down to one stark reality: all too often, we not only forgot *how* we had captured the White House, we forgot *who* we in Trump Land were supposed to be.

Economic Nationalism and the Trump Presidency

The seeds of Donald Trump's 2016 presidential candidacy together with the seeds of America's Populist Economic Nationalist movement were planted by three major, and highly destructive, seismic shifts in American economic history.

The first—a solid 9.0 on the free and unfair trade Richter scale—was the North American Free Trade Act signed by President Bill Clinton in 1994. NAFTA would not only jumpstart a massive offshoring of American factory jobs to the sweatshops and maquiladoras of Mexico, "SHAFTA," as it would be derisively called, would also catalyze North America's largest mass migration, one involving millions of Mexican campesinos.

The role of NAFTA in triggering successive waves of illegal immigration is generally far less understood than the job-crushing impact NAFTA would have on America's manufacturing base. The smack-talking Texas billionaire Ross Perot would describe this blow to American manufacturing as a "giant sucking sound" in his own 1992 presidential run.

Yet, Mexico would have its own version of Perot's giant sucking sound. As el Mexico let its own agricultural trade barriers down under NAFTA, America's highly efficient corn farmers would inundate Mexico with their fertile and literally dirt cheap exports.

While tortillas made with American corn became a few pesos cheaper in the mercados across Mexico after NAFTA kicked in—just like Made in Mexico automobiles were a little cheaper after NAFTA in the United States—millions of Mexican farmers would be kicked off their hardscrabble peasant plots right to the curb and forced to begin that long, winding, and dangerous journey to el Norte.

In a phenomenon known as "chain migration," these NAFTA refugees would, over time, be followed by millions more of their family members and relatives. With the help of often rapacious "coyotes" to facilitate this human traffic, this mass of humanity cum cheap labor would enter the United States and thereby help to *severely depress the wages of lower income Americans*, who disproportionately were blue collar Blacks and, not without irony, Hispanic-Americans.

Over time, these negative, illegal immigration effects on black and brown and blue-collar America would begin to drive a Deplorables wedge between the Democrat Party and several of its traditional bedrock constituencies.

Death By China's Seven Deadly Sins

The second seismic event that would help give rise to both a *President* Donald Trump and a unique brand of American Populist Economic Nationalism was Communist China's 2001 entry into the World Trade Organization. If NAFTA was a stiff jab to the nose of American factory workers, China's Seven Deadly Sins of economic aggression were machine gun bullets spraying across America's heartland.

This Seven Deadly Sins combo of cheap slave labor, pollution havens, state-owned enterprises, massive government subsidies, currency manipulation, and counterfeiting and piracy would put further downward pressure on American blue-collar wages even as it would lead to the loss of more than five million manufacturing jobs and the closure of more than 50,000 American factories—a disproportionate share of which were in the Blue Wall and Rust Belt states of the Midwest where presidential campaigns in the twenty-first century have come to live or die.

Adding insult to injury, the machinery and equipment from these closed American factories would often be exported to the factories of Beijing or Shanghai or Guangzhou. Here's how Democrat congressman Tim Ryan and Ohio furniture maker Jerry Treharn described this ultimate affront to worker dignity in my 2011 *Death by China* film:

Ryan: Some of the workers at companies, literally their last act at the factory was to unbolt the machine and load it up to be shipped off to China.

Treharn: I even talked to a fella down there. They wanted to send him over to China to teach the people how to run the machines that they were shipping over there. He was sixty-three years old. He said: "I only got two more years to go, and I can retire so I'm not going to bother doing it." He said: "Bad enough they took my job. Now they want me to show'em how to do it too."[3]

Volunteer Cannon Fodder

The third seismic event leading to the rise of a Deplorables-style American populism was the elimination of the so-called "draft" in 1973 in the waning days of a Vietnam War pockmarked by widespread anti-war protests. As a practical matter, replacing the draft with an all-volunteer military has meant that the sons and daughters of America's elites will never have to fight in any wars that these elites start. Instead, it is mostly the sons and occasional daughters of our working classes who today serve as cannon fodder for America's endless wars.

It is one thing to graduate from high school and join the American military and learn a trade that will serve you well in civilian life—the children of our middle- and upper-class elites rarely do that. It is quite another thing to be shipped out to a foreign war and be shipped back in a body bag—or come home with fewer limbs that you left with. The children of our elites never do that at all.

In the early days of the administration in 2017, I would sit with Steve Bannon in his small, cramped office in the West Wing and talk about these three seismic shifts and how they had helped build Donald J. Trump's rock-solid Deplorables base. And by the way, I believe I can speak for all of those in the Make America Great Again movement when I say we are eternally grateful to Hillary Clinton for that Deplorables moniker she spawned in a fit of elitist pique at a September 9, 2016, fundraiser.[4]

This Deplorable's moment was one of the greatest self-inflicted political wounds of all time. It was even head and shoulders above Hillary's monumental blunder in announcing on March 13, 2016, that she would shut down all of America's coal mines[5]—Trump would go on to win West Virginia in 2016 by forty-two points!

By the way, Hillary would later own her declaration of the war on coal as "the comment she most regrets,"[6] but if she had any political sense—which she doesn't—she would understand that the Deplorables gaffe was far more consequential.

Hillary's Deplorables are indeed the Blue Wall workers and "strivers" tossed from their factories by NAFTA and China. They are the blacks and browns in our inner cities struggling to compete against successive waves of illegal immigrant labor. And they are the parents of those children sent to dodge bullets and improvised explosive devices in the endless wars of Bush and Cheney and Obama.

Back in early 2017, when Steve was senior counselor to the president in the early days of the Trump administration, the walls of his office were ringed with MAGA white boards filled with the Bannonite Action, Action, Action we were planning to take on behalf of this Deplorable coalition. Through these sessions with Steve, I began to see Populist Economic Nationalism as an iron triangle.

Of Hillbillies and Harvard

The first leg of this MAGA triangle is Strengthen American Manufacturing. In Trump Land, this can be done through policies like hefty tariffs on China and Buy American, Hire American government procurement. It is our blue-collar manufacturing workers, many of whom are in the Blue Wall states, that benefit most from these policies—think here of mostly men with generally no more than a high school education.

For these Deplorables men, a job in an American factory may be their only real opportunity to earn a decent wage and raise a family behind that proverbial white picket fence. Lose that manufacturing job to a Mexican maquiladora or a Chinese sweatshop and you may well lose your wife, you most certainly will lose your home, and you may well take your own life through alcoholism, drug abuse, depression—or a hot shot of Chinese fentanyl.

Indeed, take that manufacturing job away, and it's a long bump down on the wage scale to the next best opportunity for a male factory worker without a college degree. It is a sharp and deeply uncomfortable descent for these men into a world where women are significantly less likely to marry them[7] and where more children will be born out of wedlock—children who, in turn, will have a statistically higher probability of growing up in poverty and perpetuating the cycle.

I vividly remember the time I circulated a memo about these so-called "socioeconomic impacts" of unfair trade within the White House in September of 2017. Some globalist inside the perimeter who wanted to stick a knife in me promptly leaked the CONFIDENTIAL memo to Damian Paletta at the *Washington Post*.[8] But the half-wit leaker unwittingly did me a favor.

Paletta and the *Post* included one of my charts in their hit piece—a beauty of a chart, if I do say so myself. This chart illustrated socioeconomic impacts ranging from higher abortion rates, lower fertility rates, increased single-parent households, lower marriage rates, and increased spousal abuse to rising mortality rates, higher incarceration rates, and increased homelessness.

So yes, I took about twenty-four hours of incoming rounds from all manner of fake news journalists who thought how silly it was for me to make such claims. Yet several days later (after I worked the phones a bit), there was a grudging admission out there in media land that I was spot on. There was sound academic research to substantiate every single claim in my chart, and it was research not from the University of Podunk but from Harvard and MIT and prime-grade think tanks like the National Bureau of Economic Research.[9]

Now here is one last key point: when a factory worker loses his or her job, this kind of job loss stone dropped in the middle of the economic pond sets in motion a wide range of ripple effects that can take down the entire community.

Here's how one of my great American manufacturing heroes, Richard McCormack, describes the "black holes" that are created by bad trade deals. Richard, by the way, did this particular riff in one take right off the top of his head when I filmed him for my *Death by China* movie in Washington, DC. It's an absolute thing of MAGA beauty. Says McCormack with eyes ablaze:

> *So when a large company decides to move its production off shore and it closes a factory in a city or a town in the United States, that*

basically leaves...it's like a black hole. Suddenly, that factory just disappears, and everything else goes down with it.

People who were supplying that plant with materials, equipment, maintenance services, even the accounting firms, design firms, R and D firms, and then all the other services around it like restaurants. What happens to them? They're doomed! They go down with it. They can't follow that company offshore to Shanghai![10]

Secure Borders Equals Rising Wages

The second leg of the Populist Economic Nationalist triangle is that of secure borders. In the Trump administration, this meant first and foremost building a smart and impregnable wall on our southern border. Does the chant "Build That Wall! Build That Wall!" ring a bell?

Here are some key facts worth noting: Historically, over 90 percent of illegal aliens crossing our southern border have come from Mexico and the three countries of the so-called Northern Triangle—Guatemala, El Salvador, and Honduras. Over 50 percent of these illegal aliens have less than an eighth grade education and only 25 percent are proficient in the English language.[11]

It follows that many of these poorly educated, English-illiterate, illegal aliens will compete in the very same labor markets as America's working poor and blue-collar working classes. The inevitable results are fewer job opportunities and lower wages for working-class Americans.

America's low-income blacks and Hispanics don't need PhDs in economics to understand these labor market pressures. At a visceral level, they understand that open borders are bad for them and secure borders will improve their lives.

It's not for nothing that in the 2020 election, Donald Trump significantly outperformed his 2016 vote totals in both the Black and Hispanic communities—and this was a pure MAGA Populist Economic Nationalist response. This excerpt from a *New York Times* post-election analysis says it all:

The Rio Grande Valley shifted decisively toward Mr. Trump, as heavily Hispanic areas along the border with Mexico...delivered enough votes to help cancel the impact of white voters in urban and suburban areas. Starr, a rural border county...had the biggest shift. Hillary Clinton won the county by 60 percentage points in 2016; Joseph R. Biden Jr. won it by a mere five.[12]

An End to Endless Wars

As for the third policy leg of the Populist Economic Nationalist triangle, there is the Deplorables' yearning for an end to America's endless wars. These wars are waged sometimes covertly and sometimes out in the shock-and-awe open.

They are wars fought in far-off hellholes that stretch from the Hindu Kush of Afghanistan and the Persian Gulf to the deserts of Iraq and the Horn of Africa. Mostly, they are wars that have been fought for so long that many Americans—particularly the elites far from the battle lines—have forgotten why these wars were started to begin with.

From the populist point of view, these endless wars are propagated by warmongers like Bush and Cheney. They are perpetuated by weaklings trying to look strong like Obama and Biden. They are not moral and necessary wars like World Wars I and II. Rather, they are futile and pernicious "plowshares into swords" wars that have drained trillions of dollars from the American economy to the benefit of a military-industrial complex and at the expense of modernizing our infrastructure, improving our schools, and lowering our taxes.

Just imagine what America would be like right now if that blood had not been spilled and those trillions of dollars of American treasure had not been squandered. Are you listening, George Bush, Dick Cheney, John Bolton, Paul Wolfowitz, Max Boot, Bill Kristol, and the ghosts of Don Rumsfeld and John McCain?

It is this kind of rebellious question that undergirds the third leg of Populist Economic Nationalism. It is this very same type of question that undergirds Deplorable support for Donald J. Trump and militates for the prompt withdrawal of American troops from foreign lands—from Libya, Somalia, and Syria to Baghdad and Kabul.

The Bannon Cavalry Arrives in 2016

Taken together, these three legs of the Populist Economic Nationalist Triangle—a rebirth of American manufacturing, stemming the tide of illegal immigration, and halting our endless wars—almost perfectly define the Trump Deplorable base. It's a very different kind of Rainbow

Coalition base that brings together working-class Americans of all colors who seek a good job at a decent wage and an end to being sacrificial lambs in America's globalist offshoring ventures and foreign war adventures.

No one understood this Trump Deplorables base and how best to appeal to it than Stephen K. Bannon in August of 2016. That's when he took over the reins of a Trump campaign heading for an almost certain stinging defeat.

With the clarity and relentlessness of George Patton's Third Army marching across Europe to take down the Third Reich, Steve Bannon helped Donald Trump drive the themes of Populist Economic Nationalism like Patton's Sherman tanks to rumble through and knock down the Democrats' Blue Wall states.

Yet with that 2016 victory, Bannon would last barely six months, and I would be left largely alone to fight the good Populist Economic Nationalist fight. Not surprisingly, over time, a large coterie of globalist elites within the Trump inner circle would continually try to push the Boss further and further away from his Populist Economic Nationalist roots.

By the time the 2020 rolled around, both President Trump's advisors and the Trump campaign had forgotten how important pushing MAGA policies like tariffs and Buy American, Hire American were to mobilizing and rallying our Deplorables troops and base. And that was the challenge I faced as I tried to push forward a wide range of Bannonite and MAGA actions in the months leading up to the November 3 election.

TWENTY

A Deplorable Basket of Buy American Executive Orders

We will follow two simple rules: Buy American and Hire American.

—President Donald J. Trump, Inauguration Speech,
January 20, 2017[13]

A key element of my strategic plan to populate the 2020 campaign with a strong MAGA message was a beautiful basket of Buy American, Hire American executive orders I had readied for the home stretch. These Action-Action-Action POTUS arrows were designed to add several exclamation points to the two most simple rules the Boss had set out in his 2017 Inauguration Speech. Yet, getting just about any of these Buy American executive orders signed before Election Day would turn out to be next to impossible—the Boss's two simple rules notwithstanding.

Nor was this an aberration. As the director of the White House Office of Trade and Manufacturing Policy, one of my primary missions was to strengthen and expand the federal government's Buy American, Hire American policies. Yet, for the four full years I would spend in the administration, I would encounter stiff opposition both within the White House perimeter and from many of the cabinet secretaries and their deputies that Donald J. Trump himself had appointed.

At the cabinet level, Defense Secretary Mad Dog Mattis, King Rex Tillerson at the State Department, and Elaine Chao's deputy Jeff Rosen at the Department of Transportation were particular bitter anti-Buy American pills to swallow.

Inside the White House perimeter, my biggest Buy American opposition invariably came from first Gary Cohn and then Larry Kudlow in their roles as the director of the National Economic Council. Cohn and Kudlow were child's play, however, compared to my epic throw downs with the Office of Management and Budget, first run by Mick Mulvaney as its director and then by Mulvaney's protege Russ Vought.

What all of these zealots had in common was an extreme free market ideology. So whenever I would try to move a Buy American executive order through the NEC and OMB bureaucracies, the draft would inevitably come back from the staff secretary process littered with snarky comments about how the order was going to increase the costs of government.

"No Shite, Sherlock," was always my first thought. Of course it's going to cost more to require that we Buy American. But it's also going to create more jobs and strengthen our manufacturing and defense industrial base.

My next thought was at least slightly more nuanced and went along the lines of: You free market zealots who never should have been allowed into a Trump White House just don't get it. If American companies are competing in a world of unfair trade where countries like China, China, and China unmercifully subsidize their manufactured products, it will be impossible for American manufacturers to compete.

Along with tools like tariffs, Buy American policies help offset this unfair trade by giving preference to American companies. And such policies do so within clear economic boundaries. To wit: *all Buy American statutes have very clear exemptions for both excessive costs and the possible scarcity of the item being procured.*

And how's this for nuance: for every dollar spent on Buy American government procurement, close to forty cents comes back to the government in the form of tax revenues.[14] Put that in your OMB pipe and smoke it.

More often than not, however, it would be me who would get smoked in the West Wing, and it would be on more than one morning

207

over the first three and a half years of the administration that I would wake up and ask myself: "Just what the hell is going on here?"

Yet, it would be during the last few months leading into Election Day that my chronic anger and frustration at the situation would morph into a sense of acute political urgency. This is because I knew that I had in my hot little hands a potent set of Buy American executive orders that could *truly move the political needle, particularly in Blue Wall country.*

One such order was designed to swiftly bring the United States Postal Service into conformance with our tough Buy American government procurement rules. My ulterior motive here—and it was pure politics given the Blue Wall stakes involved—was to make damn sure that when the USPS brain trust awarded a major pending $6 billion contract for a new fleet of almost two hundred thousand delivery vehicles, America's Postal Service would indeed Buy American.

By getting that executive order signed expeditiously, this would send the appropriate Buy American signal to the bureaucrats at USPS not to buy vehicles made in India or Turkey. Rather, they should favor a joint purely domestic bid from the Oshkosh Defense Company and the Ford Motor Company.

To be Blue Wall clear here, Oshkosh Defense—do not confuse it with the blue jean company—has a very large corporate headquarters and factory footprint in Wisconsin while Ford's humongous footprint in Michigan rivals that of the Abominable Snowman.

I personally visited the Oshkosh corporate mothership in Wisconsin twice. The first time was with the Secretary of the Navy Richard Spencer in 2019, and I was sad to see both the witty and urbane Spencer—and my access to his beautiful Pentagon Gulfstream jet—disappear when Rich was fired after exhibiting a wave of Never-Trump pique.

The second time I visited Oshkosh Defense was with the National Security Advisor Robert O'Brien in the weeks before the 2020 election. This was strictly a "no Hatch Act violation" policy trip—wink, wink. Never mind the major press conference Robert and I held that day touting the political virtues of President Trump's policies in creating great manufacturing jobs in Wisconsin.

And this may amuse you: with O'Brien at the wheel and me bouncing around in the back jump seat on a dare from O'Brien's deputy

Alex Gray, Robert drove one of Oshkosh's Joint Light Tactical Vehicles around its Afghanistan-lite mini-mountainous test course.

I am happy to report Brother O'Brien acquitted himself quite well. At one point, we barreled up an almost 40 degree incline in that heavily armored JLTV beast. It made a Humvee look like a little red wagon. Too much fun.

The sad MAGA post script here: this USPS Buy American executive order would indeed get signed, but on January 14, 2021, well after the election. It was a waste of some very good ammunition, and all because of Bad Personnel interacting with Bad Process and a feckless Chief of Staff Mark Meadows.

Chinese Drones at Twelve O'Clock

A second Buy American executive order I had ready to roll was a real beauty that would have cleared America's skies of made-in-China drones—at least the skies over government lands. This order was designed to prohibit the use of taxpayer dollars to procure Chinese drones at agencies like the Department of Interior, the Department of Justice, and the Department of Homeland Security.

It was insane that we had Chinese drones flying like swarms in the skies of America. It was insane because the Communist Chinese company known as DJI that makes most of these compact little flying spies has a clause right in its contract with its customers that it has the right to export all of the video footage collected by American users right back to servers on the Chinese mainland.[15]

That, in turn, means that if the Pentagon is flying DJI drones over our missile silos or the Department of Interior is flying drones over sensitive government lands, the Chinese Communist Party is going to get beautiful 4K footage of it to use for anything from precision missile strikes to the sabotage of our infrastructure.

Whoever thought it was a good idea to provide such high resolution footage of the American terrain to the People's Liberation Army courtesy of the US government and American taxpayers surely needs to get over more often to the Situation Room for classified briefings. Or maybe just read the frigging newspaper. It's not like the fact that the CCP is out to conquer the world is a state secret.

Quick story here: When I found out that the Department of Interior was using Communist Chinese drones in January 2020, I called up one of my favorite people in government, the Secretary of Interior David Bernhardt. He literally had those drones grounded by the end of the day.[16] God, I miss doing stuff like that.

By the way, like the Postal Service order, this particular executive order did indeed get signed. But again, it was weeks *after* the election. At least it got done.

Death by Kudlow for American PCBs

Still a third executive order I had queued up would have prevented the procurement of printed circuit boards from foreign sources. PCBs are the tiny little engines that drive virtually all of our electronics in both our commercial and military spaces, and this is an industry that has tremendous implications for both economic security and national security.

Absent such an executive order, it would be impossible for us to bring PCB manufacturing back onshore. Did I mention that America was the country that invented PCBs to begin with?

This particular printed circuit board order was based almost verbatim on an absolute beauty I had previously worked up with the Department of Energy to cut off the procurement of bulk power equipment from Communist China to the United States. POTUS signed the bulk power executive order on May 1, 2020—one of my rare China victories. Yet I must report here with deep regret that Joe Biden suspended this order in one of his first acts as president.[17]

Given the high national security stakes involved, the cancellation of this bulk power EO was just inexplicable stupidity—inexplicable, that is unless you believe that the "Biden crime family" really exists and is really and truly compromised by the Chinese Communist Party. Now that would be a helluva movie—Joe as the Godfather, Joe's brother James as the consigliere, and Hunter as an amalgam of the ineptness of Fredo and rashness of Sonny.

At any rate, some of my MAGA-friendly folks at the Pentagon loved that bulk power order so much they wanted to do a similar one for printed circuit boards. They knew that just too many of America's weapon systems were vulnerable to the Chinese PCBs that are all too often used to construct such systems.

Alas, this particular Chinese PCB order would die a prolonged death due to internal globalist opposition and never see the light of day or ink from the POTUS pen. Larry Kudlow not surprisingly would deliver the death blow.

Kudlow's snuffing of my Chinese PCB order was nothing, however, compared to the torture and systematic dismemberment of an executive order I had drafted early in the administration to restrict the offshoring of American jobs. This particular order would play Blue Wall Whale to my Moby Dick for four long years as I tried in vain to get it to the finish line.

Don't Call Me Ahab

In early 2017, a very angry POTUS called me over to the Oval and told me to write an executive order that would come down like a Zeus lightning bolt on any American multinational company that had the temerity to shut down a factory in the United States and offshore its production to Mexico, China, or to any other country in the big wide world not named the United States of America.

I had been summoned to the Oval after the Boss had been triggered by a company that had just announced it was closing its doors and moving its production to Mexico. This south-of-the-border offshoring was being done not just anywhere but in freaking Ohio where we could not possibly be reelected if we lost the Buckeye State.

The Boss's attitude as I walked into the Oval was: "How dare these sons of corporate bitches? Don't they understand that they are about to feel my full wrath?"

"That would not be so easy," thought I. My problem in crafting such an order was that I didn't really have any obvious sharp legal tools in the shed that could apply anything near the appropriate punishment—and thereby establish appropriate disincentives to such offshoring. So for an agonizing few days, I was in a quandary, worried that at any minute I would get a call from the Boss asking, "Where the hell is my executive order?"

To square this legal circle, I sought the help of one of my favorite people on the Democrat side of the fence—Lori Wallach of Public Citizen. Both Lori and Public Citizen began pounding President Trump early in the administration for continuing to allow the offshoring of American jobs by big US multinational companies despite promises on the campaign trail to stop it dead in its tracks.

In a particularly brutal statistics-based critique of our offshoring policies, here's what Wallach and Public Citizen had to say about our performance:

> [S]hortly after arriving in office, President Trump declared "Buy American, Hire American" as a guiding tenet of his presidency. Yet as we mark President Trump's first 100 days, the Trump Administration continues to reward—not punish—U.S. companies that offshore U.S. jobs.[18]

Here is what *really* what caught my eye when I continued reading Public Citizen's critique:

> [I]f President Trump is serious about delivering on his pledges to stop offshoring and create more manufacturing jobs in America, he could immediately invoke his executive authority over federal procurement decisions, one of the most effective tools at his disposal to help U.S. workers.[19]

After reading that passage, I immediately called Lori and simply said to her: "Do tell." And from that discussion was born a clever way to link, by executive order, the awarding of government procurement contracts to good versus bad offshoring behavior.

The central and simple idea embodied in the executive order was this: if a big multinational company wanted to offshore American jobs, we would make it a lot more difficult for that company to bid on, and win, government procurement contracts.

This was indeed a brilliant idea—thank you, Lori—because most of the multinational manufacturing companies in America who are guilty of the most egregious forms of offshoring *also have substantial US government contract work.*

For example, in any given year, companies from General Electric, Honeywell, and United Technologies to Dell, Ford, Textron, and IBM are awarded billions of dollars in government contracts. Yet, as the research of Public Citizen illustrated, these big, bad, salute-no-American-flag multinationals are also responsible for the offshoring of thousands of jobs annually.[20]

Here, then, was the yin and yang of my proposed order: On the yin side for offshoring, we would tack on a 20 percent price *disincentive.* So, for example, if a cost bid came in at $10 million, we would treat it as if it were a $12 million bid, thereby making it much more difficult for the company to win the bid.

On the good behavior yang side, we would use a price *incentive* to lower the sticker price of the bid by 20 percent if the company was *not* engaged in significant offshoring but rather embraced the MAGA ideal of Made in America production. So that same $10 million bid would be treated as if it were $8 million and thereby enhance the bidder's chance of winning.

Of course, I absolutely loved this offshoring executive order from the moment I drafted it—just as much as the globalists within the West Wing hated it from the moment I pitched to the president. That was indeed my perennial problem as this particular Moby Dick of an order *would sit gathering globalist dust for more than three years.*

Over that three-year period, first Gary Cohn and then Larry Kudlow at the National Economic Council did everything they could to block it. So, too, did Steve Mnuchin, Jared Kushner, Rob Porter, Derek Lyons, Chris Liddell, and every other globalist inside the West Wing.

Yet, in the summer of year four of the administration, during the months leading up to the election, I was able to breathe new life into this offshoring executive order. I was able to opportunistically do this during a chance conversation with the Boss when he was once again complaining about offshoring.

In that meeting, I explained to the Boss that I had this great offshoring order sitting in the dustbin in my office, and he told me to dust that puppy off. Yet, that was the bitch of it in the Trump White House: even if the Boss said "let's do this" on a Monday, by the following Monday, he might change his mind after a gaggle of globalists worked to convince him whatever "this" happened to be was a bad idea.

So once again, my offshoring Moby Dick got away. The order, meeting stiff resistance, died its one thousandth death. But call me Ishmael here, not Ahab—if you have a literary bent, you'll get my drift.

A Buy American WTO Nightmare

In the spirit of saving the worst abomination for last, one final Tear Down That Blue Wall Buy American executive order that got away from me would have had us withdraw from a trade deal the United

States had signed under the umbrella of POTUS's bête noire, the World Trade Organization (WTO).

This particular deal, known as the Agreement on Government Procurement (GPA) was a direct affront to the sacrosanct Trump concept of Buy American. It was also a direct assault on the strengthen American manufacturing leg of the iron triangle of Trump Populist Economic Nationalism. This is because under our Buy American rules, it is supposed to be domestic—not foreign—manufacturers that sell to the US government.

Yet, on January 1, 1995, the US government signed the WTO's GPA.[21] This exceedingly anti-Buy American trade deal thereby committed the United States to treating nearly fifty different countries—including every country in Europe—*as if they were American* for the purpose of bidding on US government procurement contracts.[22]

Yikes! Just think about that for a minute.

Under the World Trade Organization's Agreement on Government Procurement, countries like Germany, France, Great Britain, Singapore, and Turkey, are all now treated as America in the eyes of our procurement contract officers inside the US government.

That's not just insane. It was also a particular sacrilege inside an administration that featured a president who insisted—I remind you of this once again—that his two most "simple rules" of governing were "Buy American, Hire American."

What drove me and folks like Lori Wallach nuts about this WTO Buy American giveaway is that, at least according to the research of her organization Public Citizen, foreign countries received far more of America's government procurement dollars than American companies received from bidding on foreign projects.[23] Yep, this was just another case where American was getting fleeced in a one-sided trade agreement.

What galled me most about this whole situation is that the WTO's GPA was the easiest agreement imaginable to get out of. No fuss, no muss, no chance of foreign recriminations. *All our United States trade representative had to do was send the WTO a note of our withdrawal, and it would be a done deal in sixty days.*

If we had, in fact, undone that GPA deal, this would have been a powerful MAGA signal to the Blue Wall and a great boon for American manufacturers. And here was the real beauty of it all:

This Bannonite action stopped far short of the draconian step of leaving the WTO—that would have been far too disruptive right before the election. Yet, withdrawing from the WTO GPA nonetheless would have sent a very clear signal both to Geneva and to the American heartland that Donald J. Trump is not a man to be trifled with or fleeced in any trade deal.

These obvious political and policy benefits notwithstanding, the West Wing's confederacy of globalists would fight me tooth and nail on this proposed action right up to the bitter November 3 end. As this bad Moliere farce unfolded, I thought to myself: "If we can't even get this done, what the hell are we here for?"

* * *

In the next chapter, we will bring to a close our discussion of the iron MAGA triangle of Populist Economic Nationalism by showcasing the one major Buy American executive order that I *would* get signed exactly when, where, and in the way I wanted in the months leading up to the 2020 election.

This part of the story thereby provides an important capstone to our "Blue Wall Failed to Crumble" tale because it underlines the importance of both tariffs as a tool to defend America's blue-collar working classes and the very critical need to bring back to American shores the production of our essential medicines.

Writ large, the whirlwind Whirlpool event you are about to bear witness to also aptly showcases what could have, would have, and should have been our Populist Economic Nationalist strategy to tear down that Blue Wall.

TWENTY-ONE

The Last MAGA Tango in Clyde

*For eight years, Whirlpool begged the Obama-Biden adminis-
tration who did nothing to protect American workers from the
flagrant dumping of foreign washers, dryers into America. But
your cries for help fell on deaf ears. You didn't see any action.
They didn't act, they didn't care, and they never will.... In
defending your jobs here at Whirlpool, I was doing exactly what
I promised in June, 2016.*

—Trump Jobs Plan Speech, Whirlpool Corporation, August 6, 2020[24]

In the early 1980s, as I was in the midst of my PhD studies in economics
at Harvard University, temptation reared its seductive head. Professor
Murray Weidenbaum of Washington University in St. Louis invited me
to join him as a speechwriter in the White House where he had taken a
position as the chairman of the Council of Economic Advisers.

I had come to Murray's attention because of the work I had done on
a series of regulatory failures afflicting the electric utility industry, and
to say that I was intrigued, flattered, and yes, tempted by the offer would
be to understate the obvious. Yet I would decline that offer because I
feared that if I interrupted my doctoral studies, I might never make it
back to the banks of the Charles River to finish my PhD thesis.

I tell you this story because once I got to the White House—perhaps
because of that memory lingering in my mind—I began to develop
a hankering to have at least some hand in the Boss's speeches. In the

months leading up to the 2020 election, that hankering was in full bloom as it seemed to me that the Boss's rally speeches were in urgent need of a MAGA reboot. To that end, I hatched a plot to pitch directly to the president a major policy address on the theme of American manufacturing.

An Homage to Pittsburgh

Now I know that a Trump manufacturing speech doesn't sound all that original. But my special sauce in this venture was to make that major address an homage to the epic 2016 Pittsburgh Jobs Plan and its seven major campaign promises that we talked about in chapter four.

My idea for this new 2020 speech was to first remind folks how we had kept those promises and then unveil six new ones, each specifically aimed at wooing the Blue Wall states and thereby keeping them in the Trump column in 2020. And here was the best part of the plan I would hatch:

> The Boss would deliver this major policy address at a booming Whirlpool washing machine factory smack dab in the middle of the Rust Belt. This was a phoenix that had risen from the ashes of unfair trade by way of some big beautiful tariffs President Trump had slapped on the trade cheaters—and what better way to showcase our America First trade policy than at Whirlpool.

The battle over the Whirlpool tariffs had been one of my biggest fights early in the 2017 administration with the Gary Cohn-Steve Mnuchin-Rob Porter globalist faction of the West Wing. It had all started with a visit to my office by Sarah Bovim, a quintessential Washington, DC, lobbyist Swamp Creature.

Petite, attractive, intense, with a diamond ring on her hand almost as big as she is, Sarah had reached out to ask for my help in fending off a sustained mercantilist attack from both the Chinese and the Koreans. My only rule in listening to such Swamp Creatures was whether my help would create more jobs for blue collar Americans.

If not, I would send them briskly and abruptly on their way. But if the answer was yes—and this was the culture of my small office—I would move on the request in quintessential Trump Time, which is to say, as quickly as possible.

The Whirlpool case is fascinating because it illustrates just how difficult it is for American manufacturers to defend their factories and workers within the loose rules not just of the World Trade Organization, but also of the primary federal agency involved in the adjudication of trade disputes, the United States International Trade Commission (ITC).

Now you might think that a federal agency like the ITC would lean *towards* the side of American workers when adjudicating the many cases that come before it. But think again as this is yet another American agency that has been at least partly captured by American multinational companies that love to offshore American jobs.

This is an agency captured, too, oftentimes, by well-heeled *foreign* manufacturers. They assiduously leverage the large armies of American-born lobbyists camped along DC's infamous K Street corridor, which is less than a mile from the White House and a cannon shot from Capitol Hill.

My broader point here is that it is not always easy for companies like Whirlpool, which is a quintessential *domestic* manufacturer, to beat back trade cheaters even in the *American* court system.

In the Whirlpool case, its difficulties began when two of its Korean competitors—LG and Samsung—began dumping large quantities of subsidized washing machines into American markets from South Korea and Mexico. Whirlpool responded by filing its first anti-dumping case—and actually won that case in 2013. But here's the plot twist:

While the mercantilist Koreans were *supposed* to ante up countervailing duties per the court's ruling, both LG and Samsung chose to evade such duties. They did so by moving their production to Communist China in a scurrilous practice known as "country-hopping.

Beaten but unbowed, Whirlpool filed a second case, and in 2017, they were rewarded with a new anti-dumping order against LG and Samsung for the Made in Communist China washers. However, instead of paying the new tariffs, the Koreans just country-hopped again, moving their production to Vietnam and Thailand.

When I met with Sarah and her team, she was beside herself and Whirlpool's CEO Marc Bitzer was at his wit's end. This country-hopping and serial dumping was seemingly impossible to stop.

A Safeguard Solution

After more than considerable thought about Whirlpool's dilemma, my advice to the company was to file a different kind of case, a so-called "safeguard case." With a safeguard case, tariffs may be imposed if "an article is being imported in such increased quantities that it is a substantial cause of serious injury."

While a safeguard action had not been used since 2002, I believed it would quickly put an end to the problem of country hopping. This is because any tariffs imposed would apply *no matter which country the washing machines came from.*

Said I to Sarah, if they filed such a safeguard action, I promised I would do my best to try to move it quickly along. Together, we would get it done in Trump Time—yes, as fast as possible.

The case was indeed filed on May 31, 2017. In less than five months, on October 5, 2017, the United States International Trade Commission voted unanimously in favor of Whirlpool.[25] Yet, at that point, my fight on behalf of Whirlpool was only half over.

In the second phase of this battle, the ITC would recommend a level of tariffs, *but* they would only be imposed *if* President Trump agreed to them. Suffice it to say that I met stiff resistance from Gary Cohn as the director of the National Economic Council—and it was touch and go for several months.

Here is a small snippet of a typical interchange that Cohn and I would have in the Oval Office about the Whirlpool tariffs:

Cohn: Mr. President, you have to understand that if you put these tariffs on, that is going to raise prices and endanger our recovery.

Navarro: Boss, we ran on tariffs in 2016 and the frigging Koreans and Chinese are cheating like crazy. It's just off the charts. Your Trump tariffs are perfect for this situation.

The Boss: He's right (looking at Gary and pointing to me). We need to get on with it.

Cohn: But, sir, this is going to raise consumer prices.

The Boss: Can you believe this globalist? (Looking at me.)

Navarro: Unfortunately, I can, sir. He's your hire but he's been my problem.

At any rate, after numerous such go-rounds with Cohn over the ensuing months, the Boss would, on January 22, 2018, finally announce the imposition of what would be—a drumroll please—the very first tariffs of the Trump administration.

Yes, it took us a *full year* to cut to that tariff chase because of the gaggle of globalists in the White House. Yet, better late than never.

Morning Again in Blue Wall Country

Lest anyone believe that tariffs don't create jobs, come with me now as I reprise that beautiful factory tour we took of the Whirlpool factory in Clyde, Ohio, on August 6, 2020. All you really need to know about this factory is that Whirlpool's washing machines are now rolling off the assembly line at the astonishing rate of one every four seconds.

Touring this factory with the president was an absolutely beautiful Populist Economic Nationalist sight to behold. Within this 2.4-million-square-foot complex of buildings, there are literally miles of assembly lines that put together parts arriving from a supply chain spread across the Blue Wall states and beyond.

I confess to being nervous as the Boss went through the speech that I had drafted for him. What was unfunny was just about every bit of humor I had tried to interject into the remarks. Comedy is hard.

Still, it was a good speech and a great day for Populist Economic Nationalism. Here are my favorite lines—note the Boss's pitch to both the Blue Wall states and to local communities across the critical swing state of Ohio:

> Your company became a shining example from really a company that was down and out, it became a shining example of what tough trade policies and smart tariffs can bring to jobs and prosperity to communities like this one all over Ohio, Michigan, Wisconsin, Pennsylvania, and plenty of other states....[26]
>
> As a result [of the tariffs], Whirlpool's nine factories across the United States were soon thriving like never before. Investing in new products, new infrastructure and hundreds of new American jobs, and I just took a tour, and I actually wanted a couple of those machines for myself, but I just didn't know it was going to be appropriate to ask. But they are beautiful. That includes thousands of new jobs across the Ohio supply chain from right here in Clyde to Findlay, Ottawa, Greenville, and Marian.[27]

Twelve minutes into the speech, the Boss unveiled his six new promises for the 2020 campaign.

The Boss's "first and foremost" promise—was to "defeat the China Virus." Yes, I fought hard to make sure we put the word China in the same breath as virus. I also fought hard to make this the "foremost" promise because I was ever so mindful that we were failing miserably at a strategic level in addressing the politics of our pandemic problem.

The second promise was a nice modern-day riff on FDR's "nothing to fear but fear itself" designed to place a comforting hand on the shoulders of America's unemployed. Said the Boss: "We will arise from the current adversity…and we will be more prosperous and more resilient than ever."

The third promise was really the sweet spot of the day for me and the real ringing of the bell for Populist Economic Nationalism. Here, in a clear policy fusion of fighting the pandemic and strengthening our manufacturing base, the Boss promised to:

> [T]urn America into the premier medical manufacturer, pharmacy, and drugstore of the world. As we've seen in this pandemic, the United States must produce essential equipment, supplies, and pharmaceuticals for ourselves. We cannot rely on China and other nations across the globe that could one day deny us products in a time of need. We can't do it.… We have to be smart."[28]

And, with another drumroll please, POTUS announced that, to immediately begin fulfilling that third promise, he had just "signed a new executive order to ensure that when it comes to essential medicines, we will buy American." Huzzah and hosannas! As POTUS noted:

> The executive order will require that US government agencies purchase all essential medicines that we need from American sources. The executive order will also sweep away unnecessary regulatory barriers to domestic pharmaceutical production, and support advanced manufacturing processes that will keep our drug prices low and allow American companies to compete on the world's stage.[29]

In my world, it doesn't get much better than that. This was an executive order that had taken me *six long months* to get to the finish line when it could have—and should have—been done in less than a week. But as it would turn out, the timing was at least second best to perfect.

With the benefit of hindsight, I now realize that this glorious Whirl-pool event was a battle decisively won but also a Blue Wall war lost. Sadly, with fully ninety critical days left before Election Day, this would be the Boss's last major policy address focusing on the critical Blue Wall Must Crumble theme. This would also be the last major executive order the Boss would sign to substantially move forward our Populist Economic Nationalist agenda.

And that's the way the Blue Wall did *not* crumble.

Yet, there is are at least one important coda to this dearth of major MAGA- and manufacturing-themed events that would contribute to the quite needless loss of a key battleground state. This event, which I had proposed, fully staffed, and tentatively scheduled, involved a beautiful MAGA enterprise known as the Commercial Metals Company.

Losing Arizona

President Trump had not only protected the Commercial Metals Company with steel tariffs to facilitate its resurrection. CMC was also booming because much of the rebar that the company was making was going right into building the president's border wall.

The specific event I had in mind, drafted up by one of my staffers Joanna Miller, was an Air Force One fly-in to a brand-new $300 million CMC micro steel mill in Mesa, Arizona. This expansion represented a thousand new jobs at the mill and would bring in annually half a billion dollars of new economic activity to this critical battleground state,[30] all by the grace of God, Donald J. Trump, and a little targeted help from my Office of Trade and Manufacturing Policy.

In effect, then, we had perfect "twofer" event that would highlight both our tough trade and tariff policies along with our equally tough immigration policies. Moreover, it would do so in an increasingly hotly contested battleground state. As an added bonus, the event would even have great political optics in the form of a dynamic female CEO in Barbara Smith.

Regrettably, Hope Hicks, the White House event wrangler, just would not go there. Or more precisely, Hope Hicks just would not let POTUS go there. She just turned her nose up at the event like it was brisket at a caviar party.

Given that we lost Arizona by less than eleven thousand votes, this one particularly hurts in hindsight. You can't fix politically tone deaf no matter how pretty it looks.

PART SIX

The Hillary Clinton Campaign on Quaaludes

TWENTY-TWO

From Trump Force One to Hillary's Hindenburg

The bad news for President Donald Trump: He may well lose reelection later this year. The good news for his top campaign staff: They will wind up really rich either way.

—S.V. Date, *Huffington Post*, May 7, 2020[1]

If you spend $800 million and you're 10 points behind, I think you've got to answer the question "What was the game plan?" said Ed Rollins, a veteran Republican strategist who runs a small pro-Trump super PAC, and who accused Mr. Parscale of spending "like a drunken sailor. "I think a lot of money was spent when voters weren't paying attention."[2]

—*New York Times*, September 7, 2020

Twenty people on an airplane. Fifty more in the Trump Tower War Room. A few money guys raising a few bucks. And all the free press the starry-eyed mainstream media couldn't wait to give us. That was the ethos, strategy, and organizational culture of the come-from-behind, close-the-deal Trump 2016 campaign.

On a daily basis, Candidate Trump would limo out to LaGuardia airport in the late morning, hop on his 757 Boeing "Trump Force One" jet, fly a few hours away to some flyover state, give a rousing rally speech in some beat up hockey rink or basketball arena, maybe host a quick fundraiser at a local country club or quasi-mansion, and then hop back on that plane and always be home and tucked into his own bed in Trump Tower by that night.

Likewise on a daily basis, Candidate Trump thickly spread himself across all of the corporate media, which at that point clearly viewed him as a novelty rather than an existential threat. It would be phone calls with left-wing celebrities like Morning Joe Scarborough and his wife Mika on MSNBC. Evening hits on right-wing Fox News with Sean Hannity or Lou Dobbs. And anything else DJT could get in between to rack up what is the most valuable commodity for any political candidate—"free," or as they say in the trade, "earned" media.

Of those twenty people on an airplane supporting the Boss, the razor sharp Dan Scavino had already ensconced himself as in-resident Tweet Meister, Keith Schiller and Johnny McEntee—two of the greatest and most competent guys you will ever meet—weighed in as the Boss's body men, and Stephen Miller served as speechwriter.

On a daily basis, Stephen would dress up the basic stump speech in all its fresh and local coloring glory, and it went something like this:

- Fly into Des Moines, and the Boss would remind the crowd of how China had literally tried to steal Iowa's seed corn, with such a reminder thereby reinforcing Trump's Tough on China theme.

- Drop into Flint, Michigan, and Candidate Trump would wax eloquent about how globalization was killing the auto industry.

- Pop into Miami, and the Boss would surely sneak away for a couple of daylight hours to visit his Doral Golf Club. But then he would light up the night—and a massive local Cuban-American community—with attacks on Fidel Castro and warnings about the dangers of socialism.

It was a big, beautiful barnstorming formula that only Donald J. Trump could pull off. In 2016, he literally was the P. T. Barnum of politics, and there was no question that a Trump rally was the greatest show on political earth.

Of course, after Trump won the Republican nomination, the cable networks loved to cover the rallies live because they knew it would be great for ratings—and that was surely a great earned media bonanza for the Donald.

A Beautiful Muscle Car Political Machine

Back at the mothership—Trump Tower in Manhattan—there were about fifty of us supporting the Trump flying circus in the War Room on the fourteenth floor, with many of us like me there as a freebie on a volunteer basis.

The Trump Tower War Room was the perfect embodiment of an organizational culture in which all aspects of the campaign were perfectly integrated into each other in support of the candidate. What we had on that single fourteenth floor was one small, slick, sleek and oh-so-beautiful Shelby Cobra muscle car of a political campaign machine.

- While the money guys and lawyers were all upstairs, we had a communications team organized into two hard-nosed SEAL teams evenly divided between proactive messaging and rapid response.
- We had a small policy shop punching well above its weight grinding out a never-ending stream of position papers.
- We had the master strategist in Steve Bannon,
- A take-no-prisoners deputy campaign manager in Dave Bossie, and, praise the Lord and political gods,
- Jared Kushner and Steve Mnuchin mostly stayed out of the way.

Most of all, at least most of the time, we just had a heck of a lot of fun. And when I say "most of the time," my most enduring unfun memory of the 2016 campaign relates to the notorious Billy Bush scandal. When the Never-Trump *Washington Post* broke this "October Surprise," virtually everybody in the War Room stopped what they were doing and gravitated towards the TV screens. After listening to no small amount of "woe is me" whining from this gaggle of worker bees, I gave the one and only direct order that I would ever give in that War Room.

In a loud and measured voice, I told everybody to get their asses back to work. Said I: "We've got this."

And have it, we did. We had that 2016 election because we had a great candidate with a great message with a lean organization with a wealth of free media and a brilliant strategy and strategist. In other words, we had everything we would *not* have during the 2020 campaign.

No Money, No Message, Big Problem

For every one thing the Trump campaign did right in 2016, we did at least ten things wrong in 2020. At the top of what would be a very long and tawdry laundry list of "what not to dos" was the appointment of Brad Parscale as the official campaign manager and Jared Kushner as the *de facto* campaign manager.

Putting Parscale in charge of what would be the biggest, and historically most consequential, presidential election in history was like promoting a journeyman NFL placekicker to starting quarterback in the Super Bowl. It was the ultimate mismatch in skill sets.

During the 2016 campaign, Parscale was a specialist in digital media, and he was reasonably good at what he did—ergo the placekicker analogy. However, Parscale knew virtually nothing—no pun intended—about managing a political campaign. He knew even less about running a presidential race that was certainly going to be one of the most contentious and complex in history.

The fact that I never saw Parscale once in the War Room at Trump Tower in my entire stint on the 2016 campaign speaks volumes about just how very specialized Brad's role in the campaign was—and at six feet and eight inches, Brad is impossible to miss.

In fact, during the 2016 campaign, Parscale mostly hung out in San Antonio, Texas, behind a computer figuring out innovative ways to game Facebook and Twitter. Said Parscale on *60 Minutes* in a thinly disguised attempt to claim credit for the Trump 2016 win:

> *I understood early that Facebook was how Donald Trump was going to win. Twitter is how he talked to the people.... Facebook was the method—it was the highway in which his car drove on.*[3]

In this ill-fated burst of braggadocio, Parscale would go on to reveal that employees from Facebook, Google, and Twitter were all actually embedded in the Trump campaign, effectively working to defeat Hillary Clinton. Parscale's big social media reveal, however, in and of itself reveals how politically naïve small-thinking Big Brad is.

Revenge of the Social Media Oligarchs

The abiding fact of the matter here is that Parscale's revelations would set off a firestorm in Silicon Valley as the Left would rain down a hailstorm of criticism on the likes of Twitter, Facebook, and Google. Following Newton's third law of motion as applied to politics, this hailstorm would provoke an equal and opposite reaction that would cost us dearly during the 2020 campaign cycle.

To wit: Pummeled and provoked as they were, Twitter's CEO Jack Dorsey, Mark Zuckerberg at Facebook, and Google's CEO Sundar Pichai would all be out to exact their revenge—and get back into the good graces of the Left. And they would do so by kicking the living bejesus out of Donald Trump in 2020 using their deep pockets and the enormous and abusive censoring, de-platforming, and cancelling powers of their social media oligarchies.

> *Zuckerberg alone would spend more than half a billion dollars to defeat Trump.*[4] *With his precise targeting in key Democrat strongholds like Milwaukee and Detroit, Zuckerberg would wind up spending more than the Trump campaign in the battleground states where the election outcome would be determined—and much of those Zuckerbucks went to boost the number of illegally cast absentee ballots.*

For his part, Jack Dorsey would shadow ban, throttle down, and purge Trump surrogates from the Twitter traffic. Eventually, Dorsey would cut off the Twitter account of the most powerful man on the planet.

Dorsey's gambit was arguably the biggest F-U in American political history. This was all the more so because Dorsey's cancellation of Trump revealed the impotence of the most powerful politician on the planet: the Boss and the White House simply had no legal tools to police Silicon Valley's Far-Left-Leaning, Virtue-Signaling Social Media House of Cancel Culture Cards.

Meanwhile, Google would engage in all manner of search engine suppression. Like both Facebook and Twitter, Google would also aggressively de-platform Trump and Trump supporters on its YouTube platform, effectively cutting off the messaging oxygen needed to keep the Trump base and swing voters vibrant and alive.

And yes, it should not be lost on anyone that even as Zuckerberg, Dorsey, and Pichai were de-platforming Republicans, Deplorables, and others in Trump Land, everyone from the Death to America Ayatollahs of Iran to the purveyors of counterfeits and kiddie porn would go uncensored on Facebook, Twitter, and Google.

And so I do indeed lay much of this "Revenge of the Social Media Oligarchs" fiasco at the feet of Brad Parscale. For his stupidity alone in poking the social media bear, he never should have gotten the job as campaign manager in 2020.

Management by Zoom Is Not Management at All

The biggest problem with Brad Parscale as campaign manager was not so much that he didn't know what the Hades he was doing. It was that he was rarely at the Trump campaign headquarters in Arlington, Virginia, to try to do anything at all.

Just as in 2016 when Parscale would spend most of his time in sunny San Antonio, Brad would, in 2020, spend most of his time in sunny Fort Lauderdale, Florida. In truth, for an introvert and computer geek like Brad who hated cold weather, the pandemic was a gift from the Chinese Communist Party Virus gods.

Indeed, masks, social distancing, and economic lockdowns all became perfect excuses for Parscale never to fly into the Washington Swamp. Instead, "management by Zoom conference" became the perfect tool for someone who, by temperament, preferred the cold comfort of a computer monitor over warm face-to-face human contact.

There was also the matter of how Parscale was making himself singularly *nouveau riche* off the backs of Trump donors. And to this point, here is a little peek behind the political curtain for any of you newbies who don't know how campaign consulting *really* works:

For every political consultant in it for the money rather than the mission, the fastest way to wealth is neither through a monthly stipend nor even a winning bonus. It's getting a piece of the advertising and marketing action.

To this end, Parscale would funnel to himself millions of dollars of commissions through his various reelection companies to pay for what would eventually become a quite *nouveau riche* portfolio of three posh Miami condos and six other properties; luxury wheels that ranged from a Ferrari and Range Rover to a BMW X6; and that favorite Fort Lauderdale accessory, a nearly half-a-million-dollar yacht.[5]

Of course, Parscale wasn't the only one siphoning big bucks into his bank account off the backs of small Trump donors. Remember Katie Walsh? I told you earlier about how this Cruella got fired as the deputy chief of staff to Reince Priebus because of her alleged rampant leaking.

Yet here we have a case of "no bad deed goes unrewarded." Parscale would funnel nearly $1 million to Walsh's firms.[6]

Clown Prince of the Universe

With Brad Parscale mostly in Florida knocking back another cool one at poolside, reeling in another amberjack on his boat, or raking ever more lucrative commissions, that left Jared Kushner to fill the campaign manager vacuum at the Arlington, Virginia, headquarters. But here's the thing:

The job of a campaign manager is a full-time, 24/7 job. Whether your candidate is running for state legislature, Congress, the Senate, or president, if you are doing anything else but managing that damn campaign, you are not doing your job.

That stark reality posed a dilemma for Kushner. That's because his real full-time job was at the White House playing, what the 1980s iconic author Tom Wolfe used to call a "Master of the Universe." Within the West Wing, Kushner simply had all of his eight fingers and two thumbs in every possible pie—China, the pandemic, peace in the Middle East, get out of jail free cards, you name it.

Here's an albeit tongue-in-cheek sample day at the West Wing in the life of the Clown Prince:

- First thing in the morning, back channel his Chinese Communist Party handlers and Wall Street's unregistered foreign agents on the latest in trade negotiations and thereby weaken the bargaining position of United State Trade Representative Bob Lighthizer.

- Midmorning, back channel his counterpart in Saudi Arabia, Crown Prince Mohammed bin Salman, to help MBS evade any responsibility for the murder of Jamal Khashoggi and thereby send Secretary of State Mike Pompeo into yet another paroxysm of rage at the meddling of the Boy Wonder.

- At noon, back channel Israeli prime minister Bibi Netanyahu on the latest in Mideast peace talks and thereby keep National Security Advisor Robert O'Brien like a mushroom in the dark heaped in Jared's excrement (which at least doesn't stink—or so we were told).

- Midafternoon, meet with his extended staff on the latest developments in mismanaging the pandemic and see what else they can screw up.

- At sunset, call the vice president's chief of staff, Marc Short, and see what data they can manipulate to make it look like the pandemic is getting better; and

- Afterwards, drop into the Oval Office for what would be the fifth time that day to see the Boss and tell him how great his polls look.

By the way, Kushner would endlessly peddle this "the polls look great" piddling stream of piss-poor judgement to whoever would listen, and it would be this single piece of utter Kushner bull ship that would contribute so much to the inertia and lack of urgency within both the West Wing and campaign headquarters.

In fact, there were two main pollsters on the campaign during the Parscale-Kushner reign of error—John McLaughlin from New York and Tony Fabrizio of Florida. Capable though each was, these two gentlemen could not have been more different.

On the one hand, John McLaughlin exhibited both a good "bedside manner" with POTUS and a willingness to bend with the rose-colored Kushner winds. Not surprisingly, his polling data tended more towards the glass is half full side of the median voter.

On the other hand, Tony Fabrizio is a "zero sugar" pollster who wastes no time on flattery and just sticks it to you if you are indeed getting stuck. For example, if you're down by five, you're getting crushed by women, and you are getting your head handed to you by college-educated men, Tony is going to tell you *exactly* that.

From this tale of two pollsters, you will not be surprised to learn that Jared Kushner would regularly rip Fabrizio—a guy with more than twenty-five years of experience—telling Tony he had "no idea how to poll." The standard Kushner line to Fabrizio was: "Tony, your numbers are off by five points every time because you don't understand the hidden Trump voter."

Now there is certainly *something* to the theory of the "hidden Trump voter." The idea behind this theory goes something like this:

> *Many people inclined to vote for Trump in the sanctity and secrecy of the ballot box were in no way inclined to actually admit that to their friends and relatives, much less to a pollster—and for good reason. In the virtue-signaling world we have come to be cancelled in, revealing that you are a Trump voter often can end badly.*

To this point, some of my favorite clothes in my closet are the shirts and jackets and hats I have with the Trump logo on them. Yet, dating back to the 2016 campaign, I have never worn such Trump gear out in public for the simple reason it would materially increase the probability that someone would either scream at me or, in the worst case, try to punch me right in the proboscis.

Here, I vividly remember the October 2016 night one of our Trump War Room worker bees came back from a New York bar with a bloodied and broken nose. Someone had simply walked up to him and sucker-punched him without so much as a word—all for the sin of wearing Trump garb.

At any rate, I do buy into the idea of the hidden Trump voter. But there's no way in Hades, Kushner's lament notwithstanding, that a pollster as good as Tony Fabrizio does not make the appropriate adjustments in his data sampling and interviewing techniques to account for this hidden Trump voter problem.

Now here's the bigger point—and Jared's bigger lie: Whenever Kushner would brief POTUS on the internal polling, he would always plus up Tony Fabrizio's results by five points. So if Tony's polls said the Boss was down by four in Michigan, by the time the information got to his desk via Kushner, POTUS would be up by one.

It wasn't just the Boss being bamboozled by Kushner's "everything's going great" spin. Oftentimes, we would hear about the internal polling during our trade team meetings with the Boss in the Oval. So even as I was trying to make the case that we faced a very tough race and we were getting killed on the pandemic and we had to get Tough on China and we had to get back to our Populist Economic Nationalist roots,

Mnuchin and Kudlow would point to Jared's internal polling to make their case we were going to win in a landslide.

And that, of course, was the game Mnuchin, Kudlow, and Kushner were all playing. Stand pat. Don't rock the China boat. And we are going to sail to victory.

Every time this kind of rhetoric splattered the walls of the Oval Office, I felt like I was back in the court of Louis XIV listening to all of the sycophants telling the king how wonderful everything was—the filth and chaos and violence in the streets a few blocks from the King's palace notwithstanding.

You Will Never Come into the Oval Again

In March of 2020, Corey Lewandowski and Dave Bossie came within a whisker of putting an end to this toxic Kushner rosy poll game. After months of Kushner's bull ship, the Boss called Corey to ask him how he thought things were *really* going so Corey suggested he and Dave Bossie come see the Boss and have a frank discussion about what the *real* polling data looked like.

Let's hear it now straight, no chaser, from Corey as to how that meeting went:

> So Dave Bossie and I go into the Oval, and we take the RealClear-Politics publicly available tracking polls with us. As we sit down in front of President Trump, I say, 'Sir, here are the real numbers. These are not our numbers, Sir. They're not Tony's numbers. And they're not John's numbers.
>
> What you have here is a compilation of ABC, NBC, CBS, CNN, and Fox News. They do a running total, and they give you your margins. According to the average of these numbers, we are getting our clock cleaned.
>
> As soon as I show the Boss these numbers, it's like alarm bells go off in his head. He tells me, "Corey, we're going to lose based on those numbers." Then, as Dave and I sit there, he starts calling state directors. He says, "Hey, how am I doing in Ohio? How am I doing in Florida?" And so on. Finally, I think to myself: "He is finally getting it."
>
> The next day I fly home to New Hampshire, and Jared Kushner calls me that night and says, "If you ever do that again, I will ban you from the White House." I say: "Do what?" And he says, "I've been

spending all day trying to stop what the f**k you're doing. You have no right to come in and tell the president this information."

So I say, "Hey Jared…if you're so afraid of presenting the president the publicly available polling data, then maybe we need to re-look at what we're doing." And he says, "If you guys keep this up, I will make sure you and Bossie never get into the White House."

Jared simply didn't want me and Dave in there telling Trump the plain truth, which was: "Your campaign is in disarray. You have no f**king plan. You're going to lose, and you've got literally two thousand people on payroll right now, and that's what Hillary Clinton had. It's not Trump Force One. It's the f**king Hindenburg."

Then I say, "And by the way, Jared, the lowest level staffers are making ten to twelve thousand dollars a month! How do you justify paying salaries like that? A hundred and twenty grand for people with no experience!

Between the campaign and the Super PAC, Trump 2020 has become a dumping ground for anybody who couldn't hack it in the White House.

Memo to the Boss: This issue of a bloated, overpaid, and underexperienced staff that Corey raised in his particularly incisive rant was also a pet peeve of mine. We went from a total of around eight hundred low-paid staff and volunteers in the 2016 campaign to more than two thousand in 2020, many making obscene sums for a political campaign.

The practical result was a monthly overhead nut *in the millions of dollars*. And know this: millions of dollars will buy you a ton of TV and radio ads in the media markets of Arizona, Georgia, Michigan, Pennsylvania, and Wisconsin in the final weeks before a presidential Election Day.

Instead, when cash push came to campaign overhead shove, the Trump campaign—the most well-funded in history—had to pull its expenditures on ads. That's right, the highest funded campaign in presidential history had to pull ads in key battleground states because it was out of cash. Thank you, Brad Parscale and Jared Kushner.

Here is how the *Los Angeles Times* rubbed salt into this particular self-inflicted wound:

[J]ust two weeks out from the election, some campaign aides privately acknowledge they are facing difficult spending decisions at a time

when Democratic nominee Joe Biden has flooded the airwaves with advertising.[7]

Yes, in the critical weeks leading into the November 3 Election Day, the Biden campaign would outspend the Trump campaign by about $75 million.[8]

Of Silos and Fiefdoms

In the bitter end, the practical result of a missing-in-action and profligate Brad Parscale and a Clown Kushner Prince huddled in the West Wing was to create an organizational culture and structure that was the absolute antithesis of the Trump 2016 effort. Remember here, that in 2016, everybody on that campaign of any consequence aside from the state directors spread out across the country were all working shoulder to shoulder, elbow to elbow, and hand in glove every day in the War Room at Trump Tower.

In sharp contrast, in 2020, campaign structure devolved into a series of silos and fiefdoms that, as a matter of organizational culture, effectively set their own priorities and interacted rarely with the other silos.

One of my key takeaways from my whole experience with the 2020 campaign is something I had actually learned long ago: In a campaign, it is not how much money you raise. Nor is it how much you spend.

In many cases, it's not even about *how* you spend your money. Instead, the most important thing of all when it comes to money is *when* you spend it.

I did indeed learn this lesson the hardest of ways and from personal experience. In fact, I would likely have "Mayor of San Diego" on my resume right now if I had spent what money I did spend in that 1992 campaign towards the end of the race rather than at the beginning and in the middle.

The paradox of the 2020 Trump presidential campaign was just that. The most well-funded presidential campaign in history ran out of money when it was most needed because it spent money when it was least needed.

The poster child for the profligate ways of Brad Parscale and Jared Kushner was the ten million dollars burned on a sixty-second Super

Bowl ad before Donald J. Trump even had a Democrat challenger.[9] To put this in perspective, one of the very few staunch supporters of Trump in Silicon Valley, Peter Thiel, would write a $250,000 check to the Trump joint fundraising committee.[10] Imagine how Thiel felt when he realized that his hard-earned dough was used to pay for less than two seconds of that Super Bowl ad.

My favorite synopsis of all this Parscale-Kushner conspicuous political consumption is captured in the following simian analogy offered up by Republican political consultant Mike Murphy:

> *They spent their money on unnecessary overhead, lifestyles-of-the-rich-and-famous activity by the campaign staff and vanity ads way too early.... You could literally have 10 monkeys with flamethrowers go after the money, and they wouldn't have burned through it as stupidly.*[11]

TWENTY-THREE

The Bannon Cavalry Rides into a Kushner Ditch

White House senior adviser Jared Kushner on [Fox and Friends]
expressed optimism that…by June…"a lot of the country should
be back to normal, and the hope is that by July the country's
really rocking again."

—The Hill, April 29, 2020[12]

There was a big meeting out in the Hamptons with Steve
[Bannon] and big money donors like Keith Frankel, Bernie
Marcus, and Ron Lauder. The donors all want Kushner and
Brad Parscale out the door. Don Jr. and Kimberly Guilfoyle feel
the same way. This could be really interesting. It may also be our
last chance for victory.

—Navarro Journal Entry, Thursday, June 25, 2020

In being so wrong about the pandemic, Jared Pangloss Kushner woke
up a sleeping and restive big Trump donor base that, up to that
point, had kept hoping, despite abundant evidence to the contrary, that
Kushner and the Trump campaign would, at some point, get its ship
together. Within days of Kushner's "back to normal" bumble on *Fox
and Friends*, a group of these big donors led by Home Depot founder
Bernie Marcus would begin a "Draft Steve Bannon" movement. This

movement would steadily gather steam over the months of May and June with a steady barrage of late-night phone calls to Donald J. Trump in the East Wing.

Quick aside: If somebody needed to get ahold of the Boss and I thought it was a good idea, I always told them to call the East Wing residence through the main switchboard between nine and eleven at night. If, instead, they called during the day, they would be routed through Molly Michael or Nick Luna in the Outer Oval.

In that scenario, it was a near certainty the call would be intercepted by the chief of staff—Kelly, Mulvaney, or Meadows, they all did it. Personally, I hated when these misguided martinets walled off the Boss from people he *really* needed to talk to, but that was one of the systemic problems in a West Wing that would often prevent, as Corey Lewandowski might say, "Trump from being Trump."

At any rate, Home Depot founder Bernie Marcus is as pure a form of a billionaire with the common touch as billionaires go. At more than 90 years old, and as a man who worked his way up from the very bottom of society, Bernie is that rare individual in big donor politics who wants nothing other than success for the American people, particularly those blue-collar Americans who are proud to say they are part of the Trump Deplorable base.

For months leading into the Kushner's "virus gone by July" gaffe, Bernie's own private polling operation was showing the Boss was sinking ever deeper into a morass of pandemic-despair, weak-on-China jitters, and just outright campaign mismanagement. When Kushner predicted the pandemic would be history by summer, Marcus crossed his own kind of Rubicon and was ready to make a move.

I was well aware of the possible coup d'état being planned out in the Hamptons. Steve Bannon and I had talked about making such a change in the White House as far back as March when it had become increasingly obvious that, absent a change in campaign leadership, we were doomed.

As for my part in the coup d'état, I was going to be the inside West Wing guy for Steve while he ran the campaign from the Arlington, Virginia, headquarters. At that point, Steve was well aware of all of the Action-Action-Action executive orders I had teed up. He was also totally in sync with my read of the situation that the only way to win was by running on the twin platforms of Tough on China and Populist Economic Nationalism.

Despite my hope for a change at the top, I knew it would be a long shot. But with Bernie Marcus now on board—a man that the Boss has the deepest of respect for—those long odds at least got a little shorter. Yet, there were the three big obstacles in the way:

First, Steve Bannon would never agree to take over the campaign unless Jared Kushner stepped down, out, and completely out of the picture. He told me as much on more than one occasion while we had sat at his dining room table at the Breitbart Embassy near the Supreme Court where Steve both lives and livestreams his *War Room: Pandemic* show.

Second, Kushner himself would never go quietly into that good night. Just a few weeks earlier, Kushner had sent a veiled threat my way for even daring to appear on Steve's *War Room* show. Clearly, Jared wanted to, as he succinctly put it to me, "crush Bannon like a bug."

Third, any Draft Bannon movement would also have to face the residual anger of the Boss. POTUS was still about a 4 on a scale of 1–10 pissed at Steve for taking what the Boss saw as too much credit for the 2016 win.

Truth be told here, Donald J. Trump was the only Republican who could have beaten Hillary Clinton. Yet, it is also true that he could not have done that without Stephen K. Bannon coming in towards the end of the campaign and righting the Kushner ship.

The even bigger truth here is that the combination of the Boss and Bannon as an unstoppable force in politics has rarely ever been matched in American political history. If this campaign variation on *Butch Cassidy and the Sundance Kid* had been able to ride again, it would have been a sight to behold.

My trepidations notwithstanding, Bernie Marcus and his small group of very big donors still thought they might have just enough leverage with the Boss to bring Bannon back into the fold. And I was ready to help in any way I could.

The situation would soon come to a head. As indicated by my journal entry leading off this chapter, Steve Bannon met with Bernie Marcus and several other big donors out in the Hamptons on Thursday, June 25, to plot the next move.

Bernie would fly into the DC Swamp that Saturday on his Gulfstream jet with his assistant Steven Hantler. There, Bernie would have a private dinner meeting with the Boss to make his coup d'état pitch.

Shabbat Shalom and Sayonara

The timing of the Marcus-POTUS meet was in and of itself strategic: Whenever DJT wanted to meet with somebody beyond the prying eyes of Kushner, he always scheduled the meet on Saturday. Saturday is the Jewish Shabbat or Sabbath, and the Boss knew Kushner would be home, offline, and off the grid.

When Bernie arrived at the White House at dusk, I was working over at my office in the EEOB. So I met Bernie and Steven Hantler at security and escorted them over to the East Wing.

As we sat in the East Wing's beautiful Yellow Oval Room, you could hear the hordes of protesters restive and ready to rumble outside the White House perimeter. In fact, by that late June, Washington, DC, was a war zone like perhaps no other time in its history.[13]

As usual, the Boss was running late, so Bernie, Hantler, and I were able to spend almost an hour talking through the whole Draft Bannon scenario.

The plan was simple. Bernie had to let the Boss know in no uncertain terms that he was going to lose the election unless he handed the helm over to a more experienced operative. Bannon was the only guy at this dangerously late date who could pull this particular rabbit out of the hat. And Steve was good to go, but only if the Boss was good to have Kushner gone.

Just as an historical note here, this planned Bernie Marcus coup had more than a touch of déjà vu to it. In fact, a similar scenario had played out in August of 2016 when another billionaire, Robert Mercer, had recruited Steve to take over the then stumbling Trump campaign, again with a bumbling Kushner at the *de facto* helm.[14]

In that 2016 case, the coup succeeded, and Steve was able to work his magic. In this 2020 case, I'd like to be able to tell you that the Marcus meeting with the Boss went well, that Kushner once again went gently into that good political night, that the Steve Bannon cavalry rode to the rescue, and that we won the election. But I'm not writing a novel here. I'm simply reporting history.

What actually happened is even more tragic than it actually had to be. In this case, the Boss readily agreed with Bernie that Jared had to be replaced with Steve. He also indicated to Bernie that there would be "family troubles" if Trump himself had to deliver the bad news to his son-in-law and father of his grandchildren. So rather than being shot himself, the Boss asked Bernie to be the messenger.

Of course, Bernie accepted the mission—albeit grudgingly. So the next morning Steven Hantler dutifully set up a phone call between Bernie and Jared for five o'clock that Sunday afternoon.

In what was the ultimate insult, the young whippersnapper Jared Kushner stood up the old sage Bernie Marcus for that Sunday appointment. When they finally talked a few days later, Jared told Bernie in no uncertain terms that things were fine with the campaign, there was no way he was stepping down, and, in effect, Bernie Marcus and his big moneybags could go pound sand.

And that was that. And the rest is a catastrophic strategic failure history.

PART SEVEN

Playing Checkers in a Speed Chess World

TWENTY-FOUR

Stimulus Interruptus and the Trump MAGA Trillion

It will take years and smart policies to overcome a stagflation trap. Absent a well-crafted [stimulus and] relief package, expect small business bankruptcies to increase dramatically along with evictions and foreclosures. This situation is dire, and we are moving to fall off an economic cliff absent action.

—Navarro Memorandum to Chief of Staff Mark Meadows, September 29, 2020[1]

O f the all the strategic failures that would help take down the White House of Trump, the abject failure to successfully negotiate a Phase IV Stimulus and Relief Bill with the US Congress *before* Election Day was easily the most avoidable.

Passage of such a Phase IV bill *prior* to Election Day would not only have provided an urgently needed boost to the American economy and the flagging pandemic fortunes of many American workers, families, and small businesses. It would have illustrated President Trump's ability to forge a strong bipartisan consensus.

Oh, and let's not forget this not-so-little political nugget: those Trump-signed government checks arriving in the mail from the US Treasury for America's beleaguered working classes would have surely been repaid in kindness at the ballot box.

247

This particular strategic failure must be laid squarely at the feet of the president's lead negotiators—Chief of Staff Mark Meadows and Treasury Secretary Steve Mnuchin. Yet, as we shall see in the next chapter, National Economic Council Director Larry Kudlow must also be implicated. Kudlow's repeated "don't worry, be happy" comments about an alleged "strong V-shaped recovery" both to the media and in senior staff meetings would contribute mightily to the lack of any sense of urgency and thereby undermine the negotiations.

Shouting Fire in a Deaf White House

Over the course of my four years in the Trump administration, nothing would frustrate me more as an economist than the inability of the Meadows-Mnuchin negotiating team to move briskly forward on passage of a well-targeted Phase IV Stimulus and Relief package. My degree of frustration was firmly rooted in one of the few things I can say I do very well, which is to look accurately into America's macroeconomic future.

I'm not sure exactly why I can do this. Certainly my Harvard training as a PhD economist has a good bit to do with it. I did, after all, learn at the knees of macroeconomic giants like Martin Feldstein and Dale Jorgenson.

Yet, as I would frequently tell my MBA students at the University of California-Irvine, the understanding of economics is a lot like playing music. Anyone can play *some* music through hard work. But absent a healthy dollop of innate talent, there's no way you are ever going to wind up at Carnegie Hall—practice, practice, practice notwithstanding.

Now, here is the irony: While my father was a professional musician, I don't have a lick of musical talent. Goats with cans around their necks sound better than me with a guitar in my hand. Thanks, Pops. Yet, when it comes to gazing into the macroeconomic crystal ball, I have been far more right than wrong even in the boldest of my predictions.

For example, in my first book published in 1985 while at Harvard University, I predicted in *The Dimming of America* that we would face widespread electricity shortages by the year 2000. I made this prediction based on my data-driven observation that the electric utility industry had all but stopped building coal and nuclear power plants because of burdensome regulations. Therefore, it was only a matter of time before demand outstripped supply and the lights went out, and I certainly hit that blackout nail on the head when such shortages ravaged what was by then my home state of California in the early 2000s.

This was no one-trick crystal ball forecast either. In a series of speeches to groups that included California realtors and credit union executives, I correctly predicted the 2006 collapse of the housing bubble. In my *Savvy Macrowave Investor* newsletter, I also warned in November 2007 of what would soon be a horrific stock market crash. That single prediction saved many of my subscribers literally millions of dollars.

There is also my 2006 *Coming China Wars* book prediction that Communist China would likely trigger a viral pandemic that would kill millions, and more broadly, my numerous warnings about a rising and increasingly militaristic China—warnings that today look like they are straight out of a Pentagon or State Department report.

And let's not forget that I was one of the first to state unequivocally that the Chinese Communist Party virus almost certainly came from the Wuhan Institute of Virology. Branded as a conspiracy theorist then, I yet again have been proven right.

I am telling you all this now because, as I watched the China-spawned pandemic begin to rip and roar through the American economy from my perch in the White House, I saw a new and very dark stagflationary economic future coming at us like a bullet train out of Shanghai. And this wasn't my first apocalyptic vision or rodeo.

Shortly after Osama bin Laden's terrorists bombed the Twin Towers on 9/11, I got a phone call from Peter Passell, who I had first met in the 1980s when he was a member of the editorial board of the *New York Times*. As the now editor of the *Milken Institute Review*, Passell wanted me to write an article about the likely long-term macroeconomic impacts of 9/11.

Deeply troubled as I was by the radical Islam terrorist assault that had just rained down upon America, it was a project I immediately threw myself into. Indeed, I was grateful for the opportunity because I saw the publication of such an article as a way I might make a tangible contribution to my country.

The central conclusion of the article I would write—prescient in its own way—was that the long-term costs of 9/11 would dwarf those of the costs of that actual day. I based this conclusion on what would likely be profound structural economic adjustments triggered by 9/11.

It was not just that we would have to dramatically bolster the security of our transportation networks following the attack. There would also likely be a significant escalation of the war on terror, with all its attendant costs—although even I could not predict the stupidity of the Bush-Cheney-Rumsfeld-Wolfowitz quartet in tying us up in the trillion dollar tar babies of Iraq and Afghanistan.

My 9/11 article's conclusion more than twenty years ago might just as well apply to an assessment of the structural economic impacts of the pandemic today. Wrote I:

> *The full picture has yet to be painted. The ultimate economic cost of the tragedy will turn on how successfully policymakers cope with new challenges…. The stakes here are simply breathtaking.*[2]

A Pandemic Rubik's Cube

In seeking to parse the likely macroeconomic impacts of the pandemic, I immediately saw that the structural economic adjustments facing us would be far more complex even than those following 9/11. In this pandemic version of a macroeconomic Rubik's cube, it became immediately evident to me that the virus from Communist China would hit our major metropolitan areas like a neutron bomb. This is because the virus likely would spread far more easily in high density urban areas.

In such a scenario, the practical result would be to severely undermine the three major pillars of urban life: high-rise commercial office buildings, mass transit, and sports and entertainment districts.

As I write this, much of white-collar employment has indeed fled to digitally enabled home offices in the suburbs even as the occupancy rates in commercial office buildings have plummeted in cities from New York and Chicago to Los Angeles.[3] Meanwhile, many of the janitors, waiters, beauticians, and other service sector workers who are part of the urban economic ecosystem have been kicked to the unemployment curb.

These "service sector refugees," as I have called them, have neither the skill sets nor mobility to fill job openings in other sectors of the economy. So we now have one of the mothers of all labor market distortions in which millions of people are unemployed in the midst of millions more job openings.[4]

And that's just one example of one of the worst kinds of structural economic adjustments of the pandemic I saw coming. And I knew that there would be many more.

So it was that in early May of 2020, I began working feverishly with Tyler Goodspeed, the acting chairman of the Council of Economic Advisers, on likely macroeconomic outcomes and scenarios and possible policy responses.

The Right Faux Brit for the Job

Tyler Goodspeed was born in New Hampshire and is as red-blooded an American as they come. However, you would never guess that by looking at or speaking with him. Instead, your first impression—it was certainly mine—might be that of an English émigré, particularly with Tyler's past academic affiliations with Oxford and King's College London.

Dapper and always immaculately dressed, with a long-distance runner's light-on-his-feet physique, Tyler is living proof of the Duchess of Windsor's dictum that "you can never be too thin."

From the moment I met Tyler, I liked him, and we forged a strong bond over the last seven months of the administration. This was in part based on the fact that we seemed to be the only two people in the White House deeply worried about the trajectory of the economy. But that bond was also forged over our mutual trials and tribulations with Tyler's boss and acting chairman of the Council of Economic Advisers at the time, Tomas Philipson.

As to how Tyler would eventually replace Philipson on June 23, 2020, it's a not-so-funny story that almost led to Philipson infecting the president of the United States with a deadly virus from China. I'll spare you the risqué details of what was an unconscionable act by Philipson, but, as a practical matter, the far more objectionable part about this particular martinet was his dogmatic attachment to the globalist, free market, anti-tariff tenets of that bastion of free marketeers, the University of Chicago.

Here, in Tomas Philipson, was just another Bad Personnel misfit in the Trump administration who was constantly throwing grenades into whatever efforts Trade Representative Bob Lighthizer, National Security Advisor Robert O'Brien, and I were trying to advance on the fair trade and Tough on China fronts.

In the Oval Office, I knew Philipson's days were numbered when, after a particularly contentious argument that involved Philipson interrupting the president not once but several times, POTUS looked Philipson in the eye and said: "You are a very mean person."

Philipson would be gone within days. So I lobbied Meadows hard for Tyler as the new Council of Economic Advisers chairman even as I put in a very good word for the lad with the Boss.

The Trump Two Trillion

My first big project with Tyler Goodspeed began in earnest on July 18, 2020, and it actually came at Chief of Staff Meadows's request. A beyond frustrated POTUS had told Meadows in no uncertain terms to get moving on a Phase IV Stimulus and Relief bill. As media report after media report would reveal,[5] this was a bill clearly stalled in the Bermuda Triangle of House Speaker Nancy Pelosi, Senate Minority Leader Chuck Schumer, and Senate Majority Leader Mitch McConnell.

On the left wing, Pelosi and Schumer were pimping a big blimp of a *$3 trillion* smorgasbord. Stripped of the "gotta help struggling families" rhetoric, the Pelosi-Schumer lollapalooza was mostly a mega-bailout of Deep Blue states like New York, Illinois, and California—all wrapped up in a not-so-cleverly disguised *faux* COVID relief package.

On the right wing, the silk stocking heir to Marie Antoinette, Mitch McConnell, had drawn a red line in the sand at *$1 trillion*. No bread for America's working classes? Let them eat my Kentucky bourbon cake.

If McConnell wanted to reinforce the public perception of the Republican Party as a hardhearted tool of the corporate elites, he was doing a helluva job, and Pelosi and Schumer never got tired of reminding the media of that.

Surveying this Capitol Hill *Keystone Kops* checkers board, the Boss told Meadows—again, in no uncertain terms—to split the $1 trillion versus $3 trillion difference with a $2 trillion package. The Boss did so under the Huey Long theory—about which I heard POTUS wax eloquent on more than one occasion in the Oval Office—that "no political candidate ever lost an election by spending too much money."

A Payroll Tax Cut Contretemps

The day after our July 18 meeting with Meadows, Tyler and I hand-delivered him our plan in the form of a memo entitled "Stage Four Proposal: Bring Home American Manufacturing."

This missive to Meadows involved a clear division of labor between Tyler and me.

The first trillion dollars of the package—what I would call the "Trump MAGA Trillion"—would be dedicated, in large part, to what was clearly in my policy wheelhouse: the onshoring of good-paying American manufacturing jobs so as to shore up what was emerging as the pandemic-induced structural rot in our economy.

To eliminate that rot, for example, we could build up our blue-collar manufacturing base and couple that with some job retraining. This structural adjustment alone could move a lot of those service sector urban refugees I previously referenced to good-paying manufacturing jobs.

The second trillion dollars of the package was right in Tyler's wheelhouse. It was a double shot of artfully designed macroeconomic stimulus at a critically needed time.

This part of the Trump package proposed further extending unemployment benefits, cutting a second stimulus check for American families, and topping up the Paycheck Protection Program, a loan program targeted at small businesses. But, per the Boss's direction, my strong suggestion, and his own instincts, Tyler also included a payroll tax cut.

The intense internal debate that would erupt over the payroll tax cut within the White House would be yet another example of Bad Personnel and Bad Process leading to Bad Politics. As a strong proponent of that payroll tax cut, I would have more than one knock-down drag-out fight with Steve Mnuchin over a measure that both Tyler and I saw as an absolute no-brainer.

On the worker side, a payroll tax cut was equivalent to an immediate wage hike of more than 7 percent.[6] By putting more cash in the pockets of workers, we would achieve a greater consumption stimulus—while taking very good care of the Trump working classes.

On the employer side, businesses, particularly small businesses, would be better able to manage their cash flow—and therefore less likely to lay off any employees. Notch another win for the Trump Deplorables.

According to Tyler's econometric modeling, an immediate Trump payroll tax cut would increase America's gross domestic product by a full 2 percent in 2020 alone while lowering the unemployment rate by as much as 1.8 percent. What's not to love about that?

Unfortunately, with Mnuchin, it was apparently quite a bit. Stevie was just dead set against that payroll tax cut, and he wouldn't—or couldn't—even clearly articulate why.

After one particularly brutal Oval Office showdown between Mnuchin and me, the Boss gave Secretary Stevie a very strong and crystal clear command to negotiate a payroll tax cut as part of *any* package up on Capitol Hill. The Boss's directive went something like this:

The Boss: Get it done, Steve.

Mnuchin: Yes, sir.

The Boss: I mean it, Steve. I want that payroll tax cut and I want that two trillion dollar package. Get it done now. I mean it.

Mnuchin: Yes, sir.

Upon hearing that, I should have been happy for what looked to be an apparent victory. Yet, call me a cynic, all I did when I watched the Boss' directive to Mnuchin was roll my eyes.

I rolled my eyes because here's pretty much all you need to know about Steve Mnuchin: In the presence of the Boss, Steve was always the quintessential "Yes Man." Outside the Oval Office, however, this munchkin was far more of a "Say Yes, Do No" kind of most willful Bad Personnel denizen of the West Wing that one might ever conjure up.

Predictably, as soon as Mnuchin got up to Capitol Hill, he immediately folded on the Boss's payroll tax cut proposal. Said one news account: "When pressed...about why the Trump administration caved on the payroll tax cut so quickly, Mnuchin responded that 'it was very clear that the Democrats were not going to give us a payroll tax cut.'"[7]

Back at the Oval, after Mnuchin's quickest surrender in Capitol Hill history, the president was predictably PISSED! When called to account, Mnuchin would whine:

Nancy and Chuck and Mitch didn't like the payroll tax cut so we had to drop it from the negotiations.

All I had to say in the Oval when the topic came up was: "More weak-ass shit from Mnuchin." Yes, that's exactly how I talked about Mnuchin to the Boss and anybody else who would listen by that point in the administration. Steve was just weak-ass, shiny, whiny, Wall Street, Goldman Sachs, on the spectrum, off the Trump reservation stink-to-high-heaven manure.

Which begs the question as to why Mnuchin would be allowed to lead the negotiations on the Phase IV deal to begin with. In this case, POTUS saw Mnuchin—a not-so-closeted liberal Democrat—as one of the few people in the administration who appeared to get along with the Democrats' lead negotiator, Nancy "The Pill" Pelosi. Of course, others of us in the West Wing—I was not alone on this one—believed that the only reason why Stevie got along so well with Pelosi was because of his obsequious tendency to let Nancy have her way with him.

A Perverse Mnuchin-Pelosi Incentive

Arguably the second worst Mnuchin surrender to Pelosi would come in the Phase III CARES Act passed on March 27, 2020. During those negotiations, Mnuchin meekly acceded to Pelosi's demand for a one-size-fits-all $600-per-week unemployment compensation benefit for laid-off workers, and here was the problem:

While this one-size-fits-all payment may well have represented a decent lost wages offset in high-cost-of-living states like Chuck Schumer's New York and Nancy Pelosi's California, it was at least a prince's ransom in low-cost-of-living states like Alabama, Arkansas, and Mississippi.[8] The practical effect of this "perverse incentive," as we say in economics, was this:

> It was far more rational for millions of American workers in low-cost-of-living states to kick back and collect a far bigger $600 government check in the safety of their homes than work for a much smaller paycheck while exposing themselves to the virus.

To say that this perverse Mnuchin-Pelosi incentive created a significant drag on the economy by distorting our labor markets, disrupting our supply chains, and spawning significant stagflationary pressures is to understate the obvious.

As for the "Trump MAGA Trillion" portion of the Phase IV package I would design, my goal was not just to create more jobs for Americans by onshoring production. I also sought to dramatically reduce our dependence on foreign imports of our essential medicines and personal protective equipment (PPE).

My Buy American, Hire American vision was hardly orthogonal to earlier phases of the congressional pandemic response. These previous packages had contained billions of dollars for both the Department of Health and Human Services (HHS) and the Pentagon to use for the onshoring of our PPE and essential medicines production.

With those earlier funds available, I had worked particularly productively with HHS Deputy Secretary Bob Kadlec to allocate them to a wide variety of domestic manufacturing projects. These projects had indeed significantly boosted our domestic PPE and pharmaceutical production—while lighting a Roman candle underneath Operation Warp Speed.

In a similar vein, the proposals I developed in conjunction with Kadlec for the new Trump MAGA Trillion package included $7.5 billion for the domestic production of masks, face shields, and gowns and another $6 billion for manufacturing our essential medicines.

Bob and I also included $3.5 billion for the construction of a Kadlec favorite—a Domestic Pandemic Response Complex and Advanced Technology Center. It would "feature an annual drug substance capacity of 1.5 billion doses, with the ability to finish and fill up to 1.4 billion doses." Just very good MAGA stuff.

As a nice Tough on China twist, my favorite line item in the memo that Tyler Goodspeed and I sent to Mark Meadows was a $70 billion set of incentives to bring American factories home from China. This particular gut punch to Beijing was an homage to a similar 220 billion yen package Japan had already implemented with considerable success.[9]

To qualify for these funds, all an American multinational enterprise had to do was liquidate its plants, property, and equipment in China and invest an equal amount in the good old US of A. And note here:

Eligibility for the program was not limited to the medical industry. In other words, this was a "Get Out of China Free" card for *any* American manufacturer yearning to come back home.

A Puerto Rico Big Pharma Renaissance

My second favorite line item in the Trump Trillion is likewise worth mentioning because of its important political implications. This was a $10 billion tax break to reestablish the pharmaceutical industry in Puerto Rico.

When President Bill Clinton let a previous tax break lapse, Big Pharma had fled the island like it was being chased by a large navy of tax collectors. And mostly Big Pharma fled not back to the American mainland but rather to the sweatshops of Asia and tax havens like Ireland.

I had been working hard since Hurricanes Irma and Maria had flattened large portions of Puerto Rico back in 2017 to get the Puerto Rican economy back on its feet. In this case, a tax break clearly targeted at workers rather than at the Big Pharma corporations themselves would be a great way to create the maximum amount of new jobs while lifting real wages on the impoverished island.

And here was the fortuitous political twist: more than a million Puerto Ricans live in Florida, and that number had swelled dramatically after Irma and Maria hit. Whenever we at the White House could provide good news for Puerto Rico, that augured better news at the ballot box in the Sunshine State.

Drowning in a Mighty Sea of Coronavirus

Beyond such political considerations, the most strategic Trump MAGA Trillion appropriation was a $21 billion allotment for domestically produced "active pharmaceutical ingredients" and so-called "starting materials." To understand the national security implications of this gambit, a quick lesson in Drug Manufacturing 101 might be useful.

To manufacture finished dosage form medicines—from pills like Lipitor to injectables like insulin—you have to start with, yes, "starting materials." These are the raw chemical building blocks of modern pharmaceutical manufacturing.

From such starting materials, you can then produce the APIs—the active pharmaceutical ingredients. Just like at the paint store where you start with basic white and mix in colors, it is the palette of various APIs that can be used to mix up your finished dosage form medicines.

Now, as bad as our foreign dependencies are for finished dosage form medicines, the situation is *even worse* for starting materials and API—and much of that dependency is with Communist China.

This is no small strategic matter: At one point during the pandemic, China's state-run Xinhua News Agency threatened to plunge America into a "mighty sea of coronavirus"[10] by cutting off our supplies of PPE and medicines. Yes, chew on that one for a bit the next time you buy a product made in China.

Faced with the specter of such ongoing blackmail, I saw it as extremely critical that we quickly begin producing starting materials and API in large quantities *on home soil*. If only Trump apostates like Larry Kudlow had seen it the same way. And that is the next part of our stimulus interruptus, checkers in a chess world story.

TWENTY FIVE

V-Shaped Kudlow Nonsense in a K-Shaped World

[White House economic advisor Larry] Kudlow claims US is in "a strong V-shaped recovery" despite Wall Street selloff. NEC director doubts recovery depends on "so-called second stimulus package."

—Fox News, September 21, 2020[11]

Even as Tyler Goodspeed and I were working with Mark Meadows to try and move POTUS's $2 trillion package, National Economic Council Director Larry Kudlow was doing everything in his considerable powers to put the brakes on any Phase IV bill. His repeated comments about a V-shaped, rocket ship of an economic recovery were emblematic of his mindset. Such an alleged V-shaped recovery made it totally unnecessary in Kudlow's mind to engage in any further stimulus.

For months, Kudlow had been preaching this false gospel of a V-shaped recovery when, in fact, this recovery resembled far more of an anemic K-shape. In this K-shaped recovery, only *some* sectors of our economy were recovering smartly.

These booming sectors included, sadly, alcoholic beverages; curiously, bicycle production; and most intuitively, telemedicine. And in this economist's alphabet soup, these and other buoyant and growing sectors were evidenced by the upward sloping portion of the letter K.

On the other hand, plummeting sectors of the economy—think, for example, the airlines, cruise ships, the oil patch, restaurants, commercial office buildings, and brick-and-mortar retail—were all being hammered by the pandemic and heading straight into a ditch. Of course, this carnage was evident in the downward sloping portion of the letter K.

Now here's the broader point and buried lede:

The problem with Kudlow preaching his V-shaped nonsense in a K-shaped world was that it created a false sense of security at the same time that it significantly undermined any public perception of the real urgency of passing an additional stimulus and relief package.

It's not for nothing that both Tyler and I found Larry's rose-colored, V-shaped rhetoric on TV, at senior staff meetings, and in the Oval Office to be frustrating and counterproductive.

Here, it must be said that of the five worst days I had during my four years serving in the Trump administration, the day I heard that Larry Kudlow had been hired to replace Gary Cohn as NEC director was certainly one of those days. It was March 14, 2018, to be exact, and beware of anything that close to the Ides of March.

Frankly, I was astonished that the globalist Kudlow had been hired for the most powerful policy position in a putatively nationalist White House. I was astonished because I had been all-too-familiar with Larry's anti-Trump rants during the 2016 campaign. Just consider this little poison pill in the Never-Trump *National Review*, and you will quickly get my drift:

Given the recent rise of presidential candidate Donald Trump, we should all be thankful that stocks haven't plunged. Trump's agenda of trade protectionism, dollar devaluation, and immigrant deportation is completely anti-growth. It's like Fortress America in an economy that is completely globalized and where the U.S. must compete in the worldwide race for capital and labor. Trump's policies don't fit.[12]

Even after Trump was elected, Larry continued his globalist harangues, particularly after POTUS began implementing tariffs on both steel and aluminum as well as China. So I thought that based on Larry's Never-Trump history—other candidates for administration positions had been vetoed for much less—Kudlow would *never* be allowed to join the administration.

I thought this to be particularly true after the president's crash and burn experience with the traitor in our midst, Gary Cohn. Surely one Wall Street globalist and obnoxious airhead as NEC director was enough for a first presidential term. Silly me.

It Is Really Hard to Be That Wrong That Often

In light of Kudlow's star-crossed love affair with a V-shaped recovery that didn't exist, I should also note that Larry had a well-established and long-standing reputation as one of the worst economic forecasters to ever walk the streets of New York and pontificate on such matters.

For example, while I was warning of a catastrophic collapse in the housing market in 2005, Kudlow was calling people like me "bubbleheads who expect housing-price crashes in Las Vegas or Naples, Florida, to bring down the consumer, the rest of the economy, and the entire stock market."[13] Of course, that's exactly what happened. Score one for the bubbleheads.

And then there is also this: while I was warning my investment newsletter subscribers in November of 2007 to cash out of the market, Kudlow was confidently declaring:

> There's no recession coming. The pessimistas were wrong. It's not going to happen. At a bare minimum, we are looking at Goldilocks 2.0. (And that's a minimum). Goldilocks is alive and well. The Bush boom is alive and well. It's finishing up its sixth consecutive year with more to come. Yes, it's still the greatest story never told.[14]

Not content to be that spectacularly wrong once the recession hit, Kudlow would then triple down with pearls of wisdom like these:

- **Kudlow–February 2008:** "Lay off the panic button…the economy will be rebounding sometime this summer, if not sooner. We are in a slow patch. That's all."[15]
- **Kudlow–July 2008:** "We are in a mental recession, not an actual recession."[16]
- **Kudlow–August 2008:** "With the U.S. dollar up and oil down and businesses investing, I think [the] Goldilocks [economy] is back in business."[17]

Of course, several weeks later, Lehman Brothers in particular went spectacularly *out* of business and almost took the entire financial sector with it.[18]

Here's the obvious question for historians: Just how can you be that wrong that often and wind up as the top economic cop in the White House? And why would anybody on Wall Street or Main Street—much less in the White House—ever take a Larry Kudlow V-shaped recovery forecast seriously after Larry's well-publicized serial screw ups?

The answer to the first question is very simple. POTUS loved Larry, and he loved him for one simple reason. Despite his reputation for almost always being wrong in his predictions, no one could give pleasure to the stock market better than the golden-throated Kudlow.

With a voice made ever more deep and resonant by his chain-smoking—the easiest way to find Larry at the White House was to go to the canopy outside the West Wing where he would often catch a smoke—Larry was the fluffer of all time when it came to getting on television and getting the Dow Jones Industrial Average up.

In one story the president loved to tell—it pained me every time I had to listen to it—Larry had done a star turn on Fox Business and moved the Dow up five hundred points. Of course, in order to move the Dow up like that, Larry often had to undermine our entire China negotiating strategy.

Here, the scenario was always the same. Our US trade representative Bob Lighthizer would take a hard line in the Communist China negotiations, and the markets would fall. The next day, Larry would get on the tube and start freelancing about how our side might be willing to lift the tariffs or get back to the bargaining table if only China were willing to do this or that or whatever it was Larry could come up with that day.

Of course, the markets would rally on Kudlow's rosy scenario. And of course, Larry's gambit would also significantly weaken Lighthizer's negotiating position with the Chinese.

In a perfect world, the Boss would have hired Larry as the director of the Office of Communications rather than the National Economic Council. Just let Larry do a weekly White House TV show, interview the Boss once a month, and, in between, Larry could go out to the cameras on the North Lawn of the White House and pimp the latest economic data.

Instead, the Boss put the anti-tariff, open border Kudlow Fox in charge of the White House trade policy henhouse. This was not just a headache for me. It was a full-blown, two-year migraine for Lighthizer and the Trump trade agenda.

The problems Bob and I would have beating back Larry's anti-tariff gambits would be further complicated by the fact that Larry's second-in-command, Andrew Olmem, was a holdover from the Gary Cohn regime. Olmem, a DC lobbyist, was a one-man wrecking crew when it came to getting in the way of Trump trade policy.

With Larry in poor health much of the time he served—first a heart attack and then hip surgery—and with Larry often spending long Friday-through-Monday weekends at his home in Connecticut, Olmem became the *de facto* NEC director. That gave Olmem and his junior globalist henchman, Francis Brooke, wide latitude to do all manner of mischief.

In my *In Trump Time* memoir, I explained how Larry's role as a "virus denier" on TV and in other public appearances would make it very difficult for the administration to appear credible on the issue of taking the virus seriously. Kudlow would, in fact, be one of the key reasons why our approval rating on the pandemic was so abysmal in the months leading up to the 2020 election.

Yet, in the case of his strident V-shaped recovery opposition to the Phase IV Stimulus and Relief Package, Larry Kudlow may ultimately have done even more damage to POTUS.

I think Kudlow committed his economic malpractice *not* because he truly believed things were really V-shaped and rosy. Rather, it was because Larry always wanted to be the celebrity economist to go on television and see the market go up as he sermonized on his own press gaggling version of the Mount. The abiding truth here is this:

If Larry went on, say, Fox Business with Stuart Varney or CNBC's *Squawk Box* with Andrew, Becky, and Joe and he rang any kind of K-shaped recovery alarm bells, the market might well have gone dead red down, and Larry simply didn't want that bearish cross to bear.

So, ever wanting to bask in the glow of the Boss's praise for driving up the Trump market, Kudlow was like a little terrier with a V-shaped toy in his mouth. He simply wouldn't let go of that toy no matter what the data said.

At times, when I saw him on TV or had to listen to him in senior staff meetings, I wanted to at least figuratively smack Larry right in his big, fat, full-of-bull market mouth.

Instead, Tyler and I simply held our tongues and worked behind the scenes to push Mark Meadows towards a quick and workable $2 trillion resolution with Congress per the Boss's wish and command.

Phase IV Negotiations at a Turtle's Pace

Unfortunately, the Mnuchin-Meadows Phase IV negotiations would drag on in the back rooms of Capitol Hill throughout the summer and into the fall. As Election Day moved ever closer, the Boss vacillated between anger and frustration even as I believed it was time to significantly up the White House ante.

Here is a shortened and annotated version of the email I sent to Meadows on the morning of September 29. This was a day after yet another of Larry Kudlow's rose-colored rants in the senior staff meeting and a week after Kudlow went on Fox's *America's Newsroom* and dumped on the prospects of a Phase IV deal. And note in this memo my prescient reference to the stagflation that we are now so firmly in the grip of—as I have said, for whatever reason, I'm a pretty damn good forecaster. So here we go:

From: Peter Navarro

Sent: Tuesday, September 29, 2020 10:31 AM

To: Mark Meadows

Subject: Phase IV Imperative

Chief,

Here's how I view the [Phase IV] chessboard in a few easy bullets:

- *We are in the midst of a profound structural change in our economy as people adapt to the virus, with workers in industries like services, entertainment, transport, and energy stranded [This is what economists call "structural unemployment."]*

- *The "natural rate of unemployment," which is the lowest rate we can go without sparking inflation is likely to double or more from*

3.5% to 6–7% [because of this structural unemployment] and we will see that in the numbers along with a fall in the labor force participation rate as discouraged workers leave the workforce.

- *Productivity is likely to fall in the new more virtual economy and increase stagflationary pressures as growth sinks to 1% to 1.5%. It will take years and smart policies to overcome a stagflation trap. ["Stagflation" is when you have simultaneous recession and inflation—the worst of all economic worlds as any stimulus only exacerbates inflation and any attempts to control inflation only exacerbate the recession.]*

- *Absent a well-crafted relief package, expect small business bankruptcies to increase dramatically along with evictions and foreclosures. This situation is dire and we are moving to fall off an economic cliff absent action.*

- *Central to recovery will be Made in the USA which is why any Phase IV deal must have substantial funds to bring our jobs onshore. The line items Tyler and I suggested [in our July 19 memo] remain OPERATIVE....*

Your humble forecaster,

Navarro

What Meadows and Mnuchin, along with Pelosi, Schumer, and McConnell, could not seem to wrap their heads around was this: once a small business fails, it likely isn't coming back, and as we would lose more and more small businesses because of a lack of a Phase IV package, the effects were going to ripple out far and wide across our great land.

A mere four months later, in January of 2021, Joe Biden's new treasury secretary and former Federal Reserve chair Janet Yellen would accurately describe this new American carnage I was highlighting and forecasting as "longer-term scarring."[19]

Leverage Has No Leverage

So it was that a little more than a month to go before Election Day, I was absolutely fed up with Mark Meadows as one of our negotiators, and the problem I saw was one of pure hubris on Meadows's part.

As a legend at least in his own mind, Meadows had told the Secret Service to refer to him as "Leverage" for his codename. This had been Mark's nickname on Capitol Hill during his one brief and shining moment when Meadows played an outsized role in toppling John Boehner as the Republican Speaker of the House.[20] Although Meadows would never again have that level of success, he maintained the delusion that somehow he was a master of the Capitol Hill universe.

> In Mark's universe, he thought he could cut deals every bit as quickly and smartly as Donald Trump ever did in Manhattan or LBJ ever did in the DC Swamp. As a result of this delusion, Mark was simply spending too much time in the back rooms of Capitol Hill seeking accommodation with people he could not read properly and who had no intention of accommodating anybody or anything from the Trump White House.

Indeed, by this critical juncture a month out from Election Day, it was crystal clear that Nancy Pelosi and Chuck Schumer simply did not want to give POTUS a Phase IV win that might help his reelection effort—small businesses and American workers be damned. At the same time, Senate Majority Leader Mitch "The Turtle" McConnell, was simply too hard-shelled and penurious to move off his $1 trillion bid.

In my view, the only way we could get to the president's $2 trillion MAGA compromise was to flush the negotiations out. Yep, flush them out into the open like an Oklahoma bird dog flushing out a covey of bobwhite quail. My flusher would be something that I would dub "speed chess."

When Bobby Fischer Met Nancy Pelosi

Speed chess, also known as fast chess or blitz chess, is when you play on the clock, with each chess player given the same allotment of minutes to make his or her moves. In this context, my idea was to forget about any backroom, wheeler-dealer, Meadows bull ship. Instead, the White House itself would do *all* its negotiating out in the open and with the best disinfectant, sunshine.

As our opening gambit, Meadows, on behalf of the president, would announce the speed chess plan loudly and clearly from the "sticks." This is the bank of microphones out in front of the West Wing at the White House.

Mark's message to Congress—and the American public—would simply be this: President Donald J. Trump *demands* an immediate deal, and our commander in chief is willing to split the difference between the Democrats' $3 trillion Cadillac bailout for the Blue States and Mitch McConnell's inadequate Marie Antoinette $1 trillion penury package.

Meadows would then describe the speed chess proposal at the same time he would assure the American people that a great Trump deal could be done *in a mere three days.* Here's how the speed chess proposal was designed to hit that three-day mark:

- On day one, the lead negotiators for each side would agree on all of the expenditures they could agree upon. This was certainly a quick and easy thing to do as each side had common elements in their proposals that collectively added up to sums in the range of $1 trillion.

In a mockup proposal Tyler Goodspeed and I had sent to Meadows on August 19, we had identified at least eight areas of bipartisan agreement that would surely be uncontroversial. Easy peasy.

- On day two, the two sides would divvy up the remaining $1 trillion or so of the $2 trillion Trump package in a speed chess format.

To wit: Each side would take turns putting forward the expenditures they wanted, and they would do so in $100 billion increments. As in speed chess (and other activities like the NFL draft), this taking of partisan turns would be done under a strict time clock, and as with the first stage, each of the five turns for each side could be completed within a single day.

- On day three, the Stimulus and Relief package would go to the floors of the House and Senate for passage with a promise from POTUS that he would pressure all Republicans to support it.

Now, in order for this speed chess proposal to go smoothly and quickly, there was one other critical element. To wit: *both* sides had to agree that *neither* would cross the other's political redlines with any proposed expenditures.

For example, the Democrats would not throw funding for Planned Parenthood in the face of the Republicans. At the same time, the Republicans would *not* try to slip in funding for Second Amendment activities or charter schools.

Of course, if the Democrats wanted to use their $500 billion of discretionary expenditures on a Cadillac bailout of the Deep Blue States, so be it; at least the voters would know that it was the Democrat preferences and not the Republicans.

And by the way, this speed chess gambit had absolutely *no* political downside. By taking the negotiations out of the back rooms of Congress and putting them in front of the American people, POTUS would be expressing his strong empathy for all those facing unemployment, eviction, or foreclosure.

By doing so, the Boss would be sending the strongest of signals to all of those voters soon to be heading to the ballot box that he not only understood their pain; he was doing everything he could to salve their wounds.

If speed chess worked, it would be a strong statement of President Trump's leadership in forging a bipartisan consensus. And those big, beautiful checks from the Treasury Department, maybe even with the Trump name on them, would start rolling into mailboxes, often side by side with absentee and mail-in ballots.

On the other hand, if the clown show on Capitol Hill with a collective RealClearPolitics job approval rating somewhere south of 75 percent[21] refused to play ball—or more specifically refused to play speed chess—the American public would *not* blame POTUS. They would instead hold accountable Nancy Pelosi, Chuck Schumer, Mitch McConnell, and the rest of that Confederacy of Dunces that otherwise goes by the name of the US Congress.

So both Tyler Goodspeed and I saw speed chess as a beautiful strategy both economically and politically. Yet Mark Meadows, the consummate checkers player, could never quite pull the speed chess trigger.

Try as I might, in multiple urgings to him to get his derriere out to the sticks and bring it on, Mark "Leverage" Meadows was just more comfortable in the back rooms up on Capitol Hill where he had cut his political teeth and where he had had one brief shining John Boehner moment of Andy Warhol fame.

In the bitterest of strategic failure ends, Mark Meadows and Steve Mnuchin, with a big assist from Larry Kudlow, simply never got a Phase IV deal done that the commander in chief wanted and that might have well turned the 2020 election.

PART EIGHT

Ink By the Barrel, Cable By the Mile

TWENTY-SIX

The Inglorious Never-Trump Media Bastards

So, with printer's ink, by the barrel, the new comer was cried down.[1]

—John F. Steward, *The Reaper*, 1931

Boy, the media in this country suck. Don't they?

—Mark Levin, February 17, 2021[2]

Strategic Failure #5 may well be the most surprising failure that would lead to the fall of the White House of Trump. This was the chronic and pernicious inability of the White House communications team to fight back against the information warfare of the so-called "mainstream media." This Never-Trump media would run fake news circles around us, thereby dominating each day's news cycle and leaving the Boss to bellow, howl, and lash out across the Twittersphere on an almost daily basis.

As we explore this strategic failure, there is only one rule: *no whining.* Instead, let's take it as a given that throughout President Trump's four years in office, and particularly in the critical months leading up to the November 3, 2020, election, an overwhelming majority of the media were virulently Orange Man Bad anti-Trump and hell-bent on his defeat.

To say, think, or insist otherwise is to simply ignore this critical abiding truth: we have reached a sad, sordid, and very dangerous inflection point in American history where the preponderance of our print and TV journalists are Left-leaning, often rabidly partisan, and absolutely fearless in their "political ends justify the journalistic means" propagandist approach to covering what used to be called the news.

Today, that "news" is, as President Trump has so often charged, often *fake* news. It is nothing more than propaganda cleverly and deceitfully packaged by earnest, blow-dried, hair-dyed talking heads who would desperately have you believe they traffic in facts rather than the gutter trash that passes for truth.

All the Fake News Fit Enough to Print

The *Oxford University* Press defines propaganda as "information, especially of a biased or misleading nature, used to promote or publicize a particular political cause or point of view."[3]

The *Encyclopaedia Britannica*, on the other hand, prefers "dissemination of information—facts, arguments, rumours, half-truths, or lies—to influence public opinion"[4] while *Merriam-Webster* cites "the spreading of ideas, information, or rumor for the purpose of helping or injuring an institution, a cause, or a person."[5]

My favorite definition of propaganda, however, is this by Oxford Reference: "Persuasive mass communication that filters and frames the issues of the day in a way that strongly favours particular interests.... Also, the intentional manipulation of public opinion through lies, half-truths, and the selective re-telling of history."[6]

Now, if collectively these definitions don't fit the Never-Trump mainstream media, then I don't know what does.

Just what exactly do I mean when I reference the "mainstream media"? These are the major newspapers, television networks, and cable TV channels from which nearly half of America gets its daily news.[7] And within this mainstream media—let's call it interchangeably as I have done in this book the "corporate media"—the bulk of the major players generally drive straight down the left side of the ideological street.

In the print world, the most prominent big left-wing dogs include, by circulation and political influence, the *New York Times, Washington*

Post, and *USA Today*. As a countervailing force on the Right, you have the second and fourth largest newspapers by circulation, the *Wall Street Journal* and the *New York Post* along with the fast-charging *Epoch Times*.

While both the *WSJ* and Big Apple *Post* are owned by Rupert Murdoch, the *Post* is far more pro-Trump and Main Street MAGA than its more highfalutin Wall Street cousin. By the way, if I had to read only one newspaper in the world, it would be the *New York Post*, if for no other reason than its incredibly entertaining "Headless Body in Topless Bar" headlines. And the *Epoch Times* is now a regular part of my daily scan-the-news routine, particularly for international news.

As for the TV world, the mainstream media's big left-wing megaphones include—and sadly so—all three major broadcast networks, ABC, CBS, and NBC along with the Public Broadcasting Service (PBS). From the golden days of giants like Walter Cronkite, Huntley and Brinkley, and Edward R. Murrow—and legends like Robert MacNeil and Jim Lehrer—our major networks have descended into a fool's gold age of woke pearl clutchers.

Of course, this Never-Trump media TV universe also includes two of the top three cable news channels, CNN and MSNBC.

To refer collectively to these left-wing newspapers and television networks as part of the "mainstream" media is therefore really a misnomer. This media is mainstream only in the sense that it delivers much of its content to Main Street Middle America.

To put this another way, there is nothing really "mainstream" about a relatively small cadre of Left-leaning journalists numbering no more than in the thousands who have little in common with the *hundreds of millions* of Americans who stand squarely in the political center of this country.

As to where this political center lays across the ideological spectrum, we are for better, and I think *not* worse, *a moderately right-of-center country*. And that is the paradox of our times, that Left-leaning media cadres are effectively serving as primary content deliverers for a far more centrist America.

Just how did American journalism wind up in this ideological paradox? The answer begins in a brief microwave history of the precipitous decline of America's print media in the digital age.

Death By Internet

In the golden age of print journalism, which occupied much of American history right into the 1990s, newspapers were king. And there were glorious rags on both sides of the ideological aisle that would duke it out across this grand land.

For example, the left-wing Che Guevaras of the *New York Times* and *Washington Post* would do righteous battle against the right-wing Attila the Huns of the Hearst papers and publications like the *New York Herald Tribune* (once famously cancelled by JFK at the White House).

In this golden age of print journalism, Americans loved to pick up paper newspapers and stretch them out on the kitchen table, peruse them on their porcelain thrones, or fold them up subway-style to read on their daily commutes. Even in bad times, advertising revenues stayed relatively good, and newspapers thrived.

Once the internet arrived, however, and news came digitally and in real time—rather than delayed on its circuitous route to your doorstep—a lot of folks just canceled their subscriptions, and print newspapers began dropping like flies.

Between 2004 and 2019, more than two thousand papers[8] with daily circulations totaling several hundred thousand or more each would go belly up. These newspapers ranged from the *Seattle-Post Intelligencer* and *Honolulu Star-Bulletin* to the *Tampa Tribune, Albuquerque Tribune,* and *Green Bay News Chronicle.*

And here's even worse news for the cause of good investigative journalism: those relatively few newspapers that did remain invariably slashed their budgets and staffs to the point where relatively little real investigative journalism would or could get done. As a canary in this particular coal mine, the *Ithaca Journal* of upstate New York once employed an editorial staff of more than twenty people. It would shrink to a pale shadow of its former self with just two full-time reporters.[9]

Over time, the scourge of the internet left newspapers to compete with other forms of information delivery, first with news aggregators and, eventually, with a wave of social media platforms. In the wake of such technological disruption, many of today's so-called "print journalists" have become nothing more than Facebook and Twitter pirates who wake up every day praying to God or the God of Relativism that this will be their day they go viral.

In this new social media age, rather than do the hard work of investigative journalism, today's so-called reporters devote far more of their time dredging the Swamp for gossip, engaging in punditry, and often getting bamboozled by a bevy of anonymous sources with agendas sharply divergent from the pursuit of truth. Think, here, highly talented reporters like Maggie Haberman of the *New York Times*, Jonathan Swan of *Axios*, and Josh Dawsey of the *Washington Post* who have nonetheless gone the way of all gossip flesh.

The end result: Today we live in a world where the editors and reporters of America's big three national newspapers—the *New York Times*, the *Washington Post*, and *USA Today*—like to think (and often pontificate) that they still engage in what passes for true investigative journalism. However, each of these three papers is the palest of shadows of its former self.

Across these diminished rags, and the broader diaspora of pilot fish political publications like *Axios*, *Politico*, the *Daily Beast*, and the once mighty Drudge Report, I can count on my right hand the number of left-wing print journalists who actually do their homework and report "without fear or favor," as the old saying goes—and sorry, David Lynch, Daniel Lippman, and Shawn Donnan, you are not on the list. The rest, in my judgment, are just old grifters with no consciences and new millennials without any sense of history trying to make a dishonest dime on the back of Donald Trump's blue-collar America.

On the TV side, I can count on my left hand a similar number of journalists who transcend their celebrity and actually do some real journalism and investigative work—and sorry, John Berman, Rachel Maddow, Joe Scarborough, Margaret Brennan, Jake Tapper, Chuck Todd, and David Gergen, you're not on my list either.

A Bezos Rascal in Alfalfa Land

To be clear here, there's nothing new about the *New York Times* and *Washington Post* being unabashedly liberal and supportive of the Democrat Party. After all, it was the "Gray Lady" *Times* with its Pentagon Papers and the "Democracy Dies in the Washington Swamp Dark" *Post* with its Watergate coverage that helped take down Republican Richard Nixon.

However, with the *Washington Post* in particular, things have gotten a lot more complicated politically since the paper was bought by Amazon founder Jeff Bezos. That further complication comes in the form of the many tentacles of the Amazon-Bezos octopus that are now reaching into the coffers of the American government.

One such tentacle is trying to corner the market on online government procurement services. Another is scooping up lucrative contracts for offerings such as cloud service computing.

The billionaire Bezos has also joined up with other social media oligarchs like Facebook's Mark Zuckerberg, Twitter's Jack Dorsey, and Google's Sundar Pichai to silence Republican and conservative voices on the internet through tools such as de-platforming, search suppression, shadow banning, and denial of cloud services. For example, Amazon Web Services at one point delivered what was reported as a "killing blow" to the conservative Twitter alternative Parler by suspending its account.[10]

With Amazon, there is also the fact—and I was the tip of the spear on this—that the Trump administration, as part of its Tough on China policy agenda, aggressively began to crack down on the trafficking of Chinese counterfeit goods through e-commerce platforms like Amazon.

Here, I vividly remember the night of January 26, 2019, when, at the annual Alfalfa Club dinner, I bumped into Bezos and his new paramour. It was a chance meeting for the ages.

By way of background, this Alfalfa Club dinner is the yearly gathering of the swampiest A-list cast of the swampiest creatures in the Washington lobbying firmament. As to why a lumpen proletariat Deplorable like me was there, that's a story for another day.

Suffice it to say that I told Bezos, quite frankly, that the growth rate of counterfeiting over his crown jewel e-commerce Amazon platform was moving at a pace far faster than the growth rate of the budget and resources Amazon was using to police such counterfeiting. As the problem was spiraling out of control, Americans were being defrauded by the millions, and every single day, thousands of Americans were being put in harm's way by Amazon's lack of safe e-commerce practices.

And note here, I wasn't just talking statistical smack. I informed Jeff Bezos that evening that under my direction, the White House had been running a joint operation with Customs and Border Protection dubbed Operation Mega Flex. Every month, CBP was opening thousands of additional packages from Communist China, and the bulk of them came into America via e-commerce platforms like Amazon, Alibaba, and eBay—now there is a trifecta of thieves in the dark web night if I have ever seen one.

Said I that night at the Alfalfa Club to Jeff Bezos:

The 'hit rates' we are getting from Operation Mega Flex for contraband and counterfeits from China are off the charts. Over the nine months that we have been conducting the operation, we have been averaging rates well above 10 percent. We're finding deadly counterfeit products, including counterfeit prescription drugs like Lipitor and Viagra. We're also finding deadly contraband ranging from opioids and gun silencers to smuggled pork products infested with swine flu. And much of it is coming over e-Commerce platforms like Amazon.

As Bezos smiled at me politely, I explained just how crazy it is for Amazon shoppers to face a one-in-ten chance of getting ripped off and possibly harmed or killed by products from Communist China, and I asked for Bezos's help—sincerely and respectfully.

That night, Jeff Bezos seemed equally sincere with that earnest grin of his, but what would follow over the next couple of days was anything but. Bezos's promise to meet with me personally quickly devolved into a comic farce the next day when I tried to arrange such a meeting through Amazon's chief lobbyist Jay Carney.

Carney, by the way, is a former Obama high-ranking official who is now cashing in with Amazon. He told me that "Jeff" would not be able to meet. However, he, "Jay," would be happy to sit down and chat.

Irked, I told Carney I was not really interested in meeting with a lobbyist and proceeded to publicly call out Amazon and Bezos during my next television appearance. All I got from that was a passive aggressive Instagram post from none other than "Jeff" himself.[11] He denied that he had ever agreed to meet with me to begin with.

"Oh really," thought I. That blatant lie was all I had to know about who Jeff Bezos *truly* is. He is yet another billionaire like Jeff Zuckerberg and Bill Gates and George Soros who got to where he got by caring simply about himself and his bottom line rather than the American people. Call me naïve, but I expected more from someone who should be thinking at this stage in his rich life more about *our* nation and *our* people rather than *his* profits.

Of course, once I started going after Bezos, *WaPo* quickly turned up the "hit piece" heat on me. At the same time, any possible access I might have to their op-ed page as a White House official was brutally and swiftly severed.

Indeed, shortly after that blow-up, I had an op-ed that had been accepted and fully cleared by the op-ed editor Michael Duffy. Yet, lo and behold, the next thing I knew Duffy said the *Post* was *not* going to be printing it. So much for the claim from the *Washington cum Amazon Post* that the paper operates independently from Jeff Bezos.

McPaper's Fauci Apologist

Allow me now to make a brief and similar comment on McPaper—*USA Today*—as it further helps underscore the lack of independence in today's Never-Trump media. On July 14, 2020, Bill Sternberg, the editorial page editor of McPaper, invited me as a White House official to pen a piece about my bête noire Tony Fauci.

This was an op-ed that almost got me fired. Yes, in a rookie mistake for which there was no excuse, I failed to run the op-ed through the review process within the White House.

In my defense, everything I said in the op-ed I had already said on television several times. Moreover, the text of the op-ed had been posted in a press release almost verbatim so this never should have been the tempest in the teapot that it became.

Still, I got my ass handed to me by Chief of Staff Mark Meadows and I even got a bit of a spanking from the president publicly, who said: "He shouldn't have done it." Well, maybe. But maybe not.

The op-ed itself was a scathing indictment of Fauci's flip-flopping scurrilous ways and everything in it was factually accurate.[12] Yet McPaper's Sternberg would publicly apologize for publishing something that "did not meet *USA Today*'s fact-checking standards."

This was of course utter nonsense. To repeat: Everything in the op-ed was pure fact. Zero Pinocchios. Fauci foibles straight, no chaser.

To me, Sternberg's public self-shaming was the big reveal about *USA Today* itself being just another journalistic tool of America's left wing and growing cancel culture.

The Wall Not Main Street, Journal

Now you might think that at least Donald J. Trump had the putatively conservative *Wall Street Journal* on his side during the 2020 campaign. You might think that. But you would really be wrong.

- The *Wall Street Journal* is just that—the *Wall Street, Globalist, Offshore Our Supply Chains, Silk Stocking, Multinational Corporation, Party of Davos, RINO Journal.*

- What the *WSJ* is decidedly *not* is the *Main Street, Make America Great Again, Populist Economic Nationalist, Pro-Trump Journal.*

Indeed, the *WSJ*'s core ideology is the same as that of the traditional free trade, open borders, endless wars Mitch McConnell-Pat Toomey-Chuck Grassley-Mitt Romney-Ben Sasse RINO wing of the US Senate and Republican Party prior to the coming of Donald J. Trump. That would be the same traditional RINO wing of the Grand Old Party of Davos that tried to make life miserable first for Candidate Trump in 2016, then for President Trump for four long years, and now for ex-President Trump, who they rightly fear is the odds-on favorite for the 2024 Republican nomination.

By the way, if I had a dime for every time the *WSJ*'s editorial page editor Paul Gigot trashed me and Bob Lighthizer during the four years of the Trump administration, I would have a shipload of dimes.

In fact, I was the *WSJ* whipping boy for at least two editorials predicting I personally would be responsible for a recessionary implosion of the American economy because of my alleged wild-eyed trade policies. Here's an excerpt from an August 11, 2019, lead editorial in which the *WSJ* waves the bloody tariff shirt:

> *Multiple reports out of the White House last week say President Trump overruled all of his economic advisers other than Peter Navarro when he decided to impose new tariffs on China. Global and American economic conditions have been heading south ever since, so perhaps we should call this the Trump-Navarro trade-policy slowdown.*[13]

I suspect that that when the Navarro Recession never hit, Gigot was deeply disappointed. Instead, we would have the best economy in modern history—and the Trump, dare I say Navarro, tariffs were a big part of the reason.

As for the remaining midsized state and regional papers—from the *Bangor Daily News* and *Cleveland Plain Dealer* to the *Los Angeles Times* and *Philadelphia Inquirer*—many are likewise Left-leaning and were eager to thump Trump during the 2020 cycle.

I remember very clearly during the last few crucial weeks of the campaign trying to get some very legitimate news into the *Bangor Daily News*. In one case, POTUS had managed to pull several lobsters out of his policy hat to help one of Maine's leading industries—POTUS would dub me the "Lobster King" for my yeoman efforts in this regard. Yet, it was extremely difficult to get favorable coverage out of Bangor, this despite the fact that the Maine lobster industry itself was over the moon about what the White House had pulled off.

Why Print Media Bias Matters

Now here is why, at the most subtle level, the Never-Trump bias of the print media is so important in the world of American politics. Lazy and understaffed fools that they tend to be, many of the cable TV producers at networks like CNN and MSNBC and Fox rely almost exclusively on the print media to supply them with the news that they will be choosing from to shape the so-called "daily news cycle"—at least the fake daily news cycle they want to propagate.

I'll get to that bit of fake daily news cycle sleight-of-hand in the next chapter—the concept of the daily news cycle is one of the most important in electoral politics. But first, let's do an equally brief history of the leftist shift over time first of CNN and eventually MSNBC. And let's do so within the context of this question:

> *Do broadcast and cable shows that purport to deliver the news have any obligation to report such news in, to use the half ironic and always comic tagline of Fox, a "fair and balanced way"? Or, in a free society where the First Amendment is first in our Bill of Rights for a very good reason, are these news shows free to package their propaganda any which way they want within the loose guise of news?*

This is certainly not a question we will answer definitively in this book—I think you know where I stand. However, it is nonetheless a critical question for us to have a national dialogue about given the sorry place our Fourth Estate has arrived at.

That sorry place is simply a cable news universe that is split right down the middle between the rabid leftists at CNN and MSNBC and what used to be the rabid conservatives at Fox News who have become, shall we say, more complex and subtle in their older age. Before going to that particular Never-Trump Fox conundrum, let's, however, do a quick three-act play about the tragic devolution of cable TV news into two partisan warring camps.

In act one—circa 1980—Ted Turner seized upon technological change in the broadcasting industry to found the Cable News Network (CNN). Conservative though he might have been, Turner played it straight down the fair and balanced middle from the get-go, and through a brilliant fusion of technology and innovation, Turner built a global empire that became the envy of the journalism world.

It was a good sixteen-year run while it lasted, but then in 1996, in act two, along came Roger Ailes and the ideological beast and behemoth of Fox News. The pugilistic and always pugnacious Ailes approached cable TV like a no-holds-barred political campaign.

Ailes believed that viewers wanted their news packaged in the comfort of their own ideological beliefs, he correctly foresaw that the largest demographic in the country to be captured in terms of bang for the ad revenue bucks leaned Republican and conservative, and he carved out a media empire with the help of a very deep-pocketed Rupert Murdoch at Fox News by relentlessly and skillfully targeting that demographic.

For CNN, it was like Mr. Rogers getting tossed into the ring with Muhammad Ali. Within a few short years, CNN not only got knocked to the ground. It was almost tossed out of that very same ring.

By the way, my favorite Roger Ailes quote is this: "Truth is whatever people believe."[14] Nuff said.

In act three—circa July, 2016—after hemorrhaging large chunks of its audience, CNN decided to take what was Left over by Roger Ailes—pun intended—by taking a very hard Left and becoming the anti-Fox network and the mouthpiece of liberals and the Democrat party. As for MSNBC, it would pursue a similar strategy, albeit with a small detour.

During that detour, MSNBC would have an ever-so-brief flirtation with the conservative side of the TV audience spectrum. At one point—yes, this should surprise you—MSNBC featured a lineup of conservative beacons like Ann Coulter, Laura Ingraham, Alan Keyes,

Tucker Carlson, and Pat Buchanan. However, after a ratings decline, MSNBC went full bore Left—out with the Lauras and Tuckers and in with the Keith Olbermanns and Chris Matthewses and, eventually, that supercharged Goddess of Spin, Rachel Maddow.

> *At that point—with Fox the voice of the Right and CNN and MSNBC the voice of the Left—all hope was lost for nonpartisan investigative journalism. Instead, it was polarization game-on in the political arena. It was also game-over for real, nonpartisan investigative journalism on cable TV.*

Roger Rolls Over in His Grave

At least prior to the coming of Donald J. Trump, this polarization in the cable news cosmos was at a fairly stable equilibrium. Fox could promote conservative views and values and support Republican politicians. CNN and MSNBC, with roughly the same amount of viewers as Fox *combined*, could champion progressive and liberal causes for Democrats. So somehow, this all seemed fair and balanced, at least in the broader aggregate.

The problem Donald Trump faced in 2020, however, is that, with Roger Ailes first MeToo hashtagged and then dead and gone, at least part of the Fox tools in the putatively Republican shed went sideways on Trump and disturbed that Left-Right, Democrat-Republican equilibrium.

Some of that Fox talent was overtly hostile—Shep Smith, Chris Wallace, Neil Cavuto, Charles Gasparino, Juan Williams, and always Karl Rove, just to name a few. Others like John Roberts, Brian Kilmeade, and Bret Baier would take more subtle passive-aggressive shots at Trump over the course of the campaign—but they would be shots nonetheless.

> *If Roger Ailes had been around, these off-the-reservation Indians would have been out on their asses in a New York minute with hot pokers up said asses. But with Ailes himself out the door in July of 2016 and then in the cold, hard, ground less than a year later, the anti-Trump inmates in what should have been a pro-Trump Fox asylum were free to roam.*
>
> *When President Trump fought back and publicly criticized Fox as an institution or singled out specific anchors or reporters—rather than*

privately back-channel Rupert and ask for relief—the Fox top brass, many Never-Trumpers in their own right, simply doubled down on Fox's anti-Trumpism. As the schism grew, the chasm widened.

Here, it must be said that no amount of support from Trump stalwarts like Lou Dobbs, Sean Hannity, Tucker Carlson, and Laura Ingraham could completely offset the significant damage others in the Fox orbit were doing to Trump, and given the transformation of Fox from a hard Trump drive to an uncertain floppy disk, no amount of rival conservative networks like Newsmax or OANN or Real America's Voice could make up for the loss of a unified Fox News behind President Trump in 2020.

The Full Pompeo

During that 2020 presidential election cycle, it wasn't just the cable news networks that were piling on and pummeling us in our White House bunker. Every Sunday morning, we faced the Orange Man Bad firing squad of Margaret Brennan hosting CBS's *Face the Nation*, George Stephanopoulos or Martha Raddatz at ABC, and Chuck Todd at NBC's *Meet the Press*, along, of course, with Jake Tapper at CNN, and Chris Wallace at Fox.

During the first three years of the administration, despite the poor treatment we usually got from the hosts, these Sunday shows were coveted appearances that each of the various White House senior staff and cabinet officials would jockey for. If there was a really big issue in a given week, one of our top officials might even go on all five shows—inside the West Wing, we called that the "Full Pompeo" because our secretary of state Mike commonly got that nod.

Once the virus hit, however, during the election year, there were not a lot of the usual suspects fighting to defend the president. Mick Mulvaney, Mark Meadows, Steve Mnuchin, and Larry Kudlow were all mostly missing in action. They just didn't want to take the heat because all the Sunday show hosts wanted to talk about was the virus, virus, virus and how we were screwing it up. Meanwhile, Saint Fauci would stand in front of a microphone and a camera any time he got a chance and rip us every which way but Sunday—and whenever he could *on* Sunday.

And, of course, the lead in to the Sunday shows was NBC's anti-Trump *Saturday Night Live*. The relentless skewering of the president by the unfortunately straight-shooting Alec Baldwin juxtaposed against the kid-glove treatment of bumbling Joe Biden by Jim Carrey was the least funny thing I found on television.

All in all, it was a sorry Never-Trump media spectacle to behold, and they would kick our butts on an almost daily basis during what we shall now see was the daily battle to determine who would dominate the daily news cycle. Spoiler alert: it wasn't us.

TWENTY-SEVEN

Dominate the News Cycle
or Be Dominated

What is truth?

—Pontius Pilate

*This is a president who…is acting erratically and desperately,
and we need to not normalize that…. I think we need to lean
into that.*[15]

—Jeff Zucker, President, CNN

Just parse that Zucker moment for a minute. That's the president of
what was once the most respected cable news channel in the world
caught red- and left-wing-handed on a secret tape by Project Veritas
plotting to overthrow that other president—yeah, that guy in the White
House who actually got elected.

This is what we were up against *writ large* with the Never-Trump
media. Its mission was to defeat Donald J. Trump by whatever means
necessary—short (perhaps) of committing a felony. And, in many ways,
the now ex-president Jeff Zucker and CNN were the tips of this poisonous, spinning-out-of-control spear.

Tell Us What You Really Think

That the Never-Trump media was on a lethal mission to take down and
take out the president in 2020 should not be in dispute.

Consider this zinger, for example, from the *New York Times* editorial board: "Mr. Trump doesn't care if you think he's corrupt, incompetent and self-centered. He just wants you to think everyone else is just as bad...."[16]

In endorsing Joe Biden, *USA Today*'s editorial board went full character assassination, citing "Trump's unbounded narcissism" and his "ducking responsibility for his actions, spewing streams of invective at his critics, trafficking in racial fearmongering, governing more as the leader of the Red States than of the United States, and relentlessly attacking the free press."[17] Ouch.

And here's how the *Washington Post* led off its endorsement of Joe Biden with arguably the lowest bar set in presidential election history: "In order to expel the worst president of modern times, many voters might be willing to vote for almost anybody."[18]

Note, here, how these serfs on the Jeff Bezos plantation snuck in that qualifier of "modern" times. Through my lens of history, and taking the longer view, there are surely worst presidents in less than modern times—James Buchanan, who helped trigger the Civil War; Warren G. Harding, renowned for corrupt scandals like Teapot Dome; or Herbert Hoover, father of America's Great Depression. Not to mention Millard "Fugitive Slave Act" Fillmore or Franklin "Bleeding Kansas" Pierce.

But if the Bezos propaganda machine wants to limit its assessment of Donald Trump to modern times, are you really telling me that Jimmy Carter with his stagflation and double-digit "misery index," Bill Clinton with his signing of NAFTA and shoehorning Communist China into the World Trade Organization, Richard Nixon with his Watergate scandal, or Barack Obama with his stagnant wages and serial fumbles on foreign policy were better presidents than a POTUS 45 who created the strongest economy in the aforementioned modern times, finally stood up to the Chinese Communist Party, and delivered at least a quasi-vaccine in one third the time it normally takes?

My broader point is simply this: During the 2020 election cycle, these media propagandists wore their Never-Trump biases on their collective editorialist sleeves. Here, the idea that there is some Chinese wall between the editorial side and news side of today's modern times newspapers and news stations has long ago gone the way of all flesh.

The Daily Spin

The core information warfare strategy of the Never-Trump media was as simple as it was relentless and cynical: dominate the daily news cycle and thereby drive *down* President Trump's favorability and job approval ratings and drive *up* those ratings for Joe Biden.

The daily news cycle is simply and collectively the lead story or stories that will be incessantly featured that day. It's the front page stuff you see in papers like the *New York Times* and *Washington Post*. On cable TV news, it is collectively the major stories that inhabit the so-called A- and B-block segments that comprise the first half of any given news hour.

Here, it is axiomatic that every day of a president's political life, it's a battle over this news cycle. If it's favorable to a president, that's a very good day. If not, it's going to be a very long day of defense—never a good position to be in.

Of course, the single most important responsibility of any White House communications team is to win the daily battle over the news cycle, and sadly, in what would be Strategic Failure #5, the Trump White House would fail miserably at doing so.

To execute its "Dominate the Daily News Cycle" game plan, the Never-Trump media used a complex and synergistic set of five basic "daily spin" tactics.

1. Selectively screen the news for stories that enhance the anti-Trump and pro-Biden narratives and push these to the top of the news cycle.
2. Deemphasize or ignore any stories that enhance the pro-Trump narrative or shine a harsh light on Sleepy Joe. This was the fake-news lie of omission.
3. In league with the Democrat Party, parrot, and perhaps help craft, the talking points related to the daily anti-Trump, pro-Biden narrative.
4. Use "echo chamber" in-house experts and other anti-Trump surrogates to relentlessly drive the daily news cycle and its collateral daily spin narratives.
5. Deeply freeze out pro-Trump voices from the White House or the Trump campaign while diminishing, harassing, or simply discrediting any pro-Trump surrogates if they appear on set.

Under the onslaught of the Never-Trump media's negative press, President Trump's overall job approval rating would plummet from a high of 52 percent[19] at the start of the pandemic in February 2020 to as low as 38 percent[20] in the final months before the election. At the same time, President Trump's favorability rating would swoon from a high of 48 percent in January of 2020[21] to 42 percent[22] by the eve of the election.

In baseball terms, this was like falling below the Mendoza Line. That's when a batter's average drops below 200. Drop below that Mendoza Line and pretty soon you are out of the "the show"—or, in this case, the White House.

Twisted Policy Twists

To attack the president's personal character—and therefore his favorability rating—the Never-Trump media used any story that helped portray Trump as a liar, a racist, a cheat (usually a tax cheat), a homophobe, or a heartless, horny, misogynistic philanderer. These were surefire, favorability-rating killers.

At a purely policy level, driving down the president's job approval rating was far more tricky. This was because a broad swath of America supported many Trump policies. Thus, in the daily fake news cycle, there would have to be these kinds of twisted policy twists:

- The highly popular Trump stance of secure borders would become synonymous with "kids in cages;"
- Standing up to Communist China by raising tariffs simply raised American consumer prices and hurt the poor;
- Deregulation was just a nasty synonym for environmental degradation;
- Peace on the Korean Peninsula was really coddling up to dictators;
- Increased defense spending on "guns" was criminal in an age of crumbling "butter" in the forms of broken infrastructure, broken down schools, and lead-tainted water;
- Withdrawing troops from endless wars in the Middle East would simply lead to more terrorism on home soil; and
- Any discussion of healthcare would always have to end with "Trump wants to do away with pre-existing conditions"—an issue that polled negatively off the charts.[23]

Of course, once Joe Biden won the Democrat primary, anything that could reinforce the idea that Biden was experienced, empathetic, and a friend of the working class would, in turn, reinforce the anti-Trump narrative.

As for Sleepy Joe himself, while he was gaffe-prone, these gaffes were just as we had observed throughout his whole career. In the Never-Trump media, they were simply harmless and endearing foibles—certainly not any sign of advancing age, much less senility or dementia. And large cadres of Orange Man Bad quasi-journalists spun all this like whirling daily news cycle dervishes.

The News Cycle Deconstructed

Now you might think at this point that the daily news cycle "is what it is." After all, every day there's a set of actual breaking stories inside America and from around the world. Surely there must be widespread agreement in newsrooms on what the most important story of the day is.

In my White House experience, that generalization was only true on the thankfully rare days that there was some kind of natural disaster or major life-threatening national or global event in progress—a hurricane off the coast of Florida, a tsunami bearing down on Japan, India and China on the brink of nuclear war, and so on.

Such catastrophes would get CNN in particular off POTUS's back as this was the network that made its original bones covering these many forms of chaos and pathos. In fact, CNN still has much of its institutional memory and resources to pull off such coverage quite well.

My broader point is that on most days, and absent some global or national disaster, the Never-Trump media had a surfeit of Pontius Pilate discretion about what actually should dominate any given daily news cycle. And that's where the tactics of the Never-Trump media came into play during the 2020 election cycle with such a vengeance.

For CNN and MSNBC in particular, the best daily news cycle was one that prominently featured—and screamed if it could—any carnage associated with the pandemic. In this spirit of "if it bleeds, it leads," bad virus news and big body counts were always far and away the best anti-Trump topics of A-block choice to lead with.

That said, racism was a close second. Here, for the Never-Trump media, the tragic death of George Floyd was like hitting the jackpot of all jackpots of Trump's a racist spin.

Of course, comments by or about white supremacists were always icing on the "systemic racism" cake. And make no mistake about this. Words matter. And it doesn't have to be a lot of words.

In fact, it can be just two words like those the Boss let slip about the white supremacist group known as the "Proud Boys." During POTUS's first September 29 debate with Joe Biden, the Boss urged this fringe group to "stand back." In doing so, the Boss put two good words into the plus column.

However, in the same breath, POTUS also added the direction to "stand by." Taken literally, this "stand by" directive could easily be interpreted to imply the use of vigilante force by the Proud Boys if things began to spiral out of control.

Boy, did the Never-Trump media have a field day[24] with that.

The Grim Reaper Meets Burn Baby Burn

Of course, other "let's beat up Trump" topics that would jump to the top of the list included the Russia Hoax, POTUS's tax returns, impeachment, and, for a brief shining moment, the mass protests that followed in the wake of the George Floyd murder.

I say "brief shining moment" because the whole subject of the protests got quickly confusing, at least for CNN and MSNBC and its incessantly self-righteous anchors and commentators. While both of these networks initially gave the George Floyd protests wall-to-wall coverage, those protests quickly morphed into an orgy of arson and looting.

In just a few short whiplash weeks, America seemed to go from the equivalent of Woodstock in August of 1969 to the violence just four months later of the Hells Angels-infested episode otherwise known to my generation as the Altamont Speedway Free Festival debacle. As this Woodstock to Altamont transformation took place before their very left-wing eyes, the anchors and reporters at CNN and MSNBC were collectively caught off guard and flat footed.

As directives began to rain down from the corporate suites of Zucker Land and MSNBC/Comcast, these "see no leftist evil" networks began to sharply curtail and sanitize their protest coverage even as both CNN and MSNBC doubled down on coverage of the pandemic and its body count. Indeed, as Fox News reveled in the sight of burning police stations, looted jewelry stores, and whacked-out Antifa autonomous zones in the People's Republic of Seattle, such footage was comically nowhere to be viewed on CNN or MSNBC.

On the most violent of such days, it was as if Joe Scarborough and Mika Brzezinski on MSNBC and John Berman and Alisyn Camerota of CNN all came down with a bad case of morning lockjaw.

Nor was it a happy day for CNN and MSNBC when that virtuous crusader against systematic racism otherwise known as Black Lives Matter was outed as a bunch of raving Marxists[25] who wanted to dismantle the bedrock of Americana—the American nuclear family.

As the Never-Trump media moonwalked backwards faster than Michael Jackson from all this Antifa-BLM anarchy, it was indeed often as comical as it was jarring to me to flip channels back and forth between CNN and MSNBC versus Fox.

It was like a daily spin horse race offering no better proof of the main thesis of this chapter, namely, that the Never-Trump media were out to get the president and their primary weapon was the domination and control of the daily news cycle. The broader abiding reminder and truth here is this: For the Never-Trump media, what to feature in the daily news cycle was very much a discretionary matter. As to how this Never-Trump media exercised this discretion, let's drill down now more deeply into their five main tactics introduced at the beginning of this chapter.

With tactic one, the Never-Trump media would selectively screen breaking news for any big stories that would enhance the anti-Trump or pro-Biden narratives. As previously noted, the most highly coveted stories to emphasize included any bad news about the pandemic— rising infection rates, rising hospitalizations, spikes in the body count, shortages of personal protective equipment, any dissension in the ranks between the White House and the healthcare bureaucracy, and all things Saint Fauci.

The Never-Trump media understood early on—regrettably, even before the Boss's closest advisors understood this—that the pandemic would be the president's Achilles' heel in the 2020 election.

As a lies-of-omission corollary, tactic two involved producers deemphasizing or ignoring any stories that might enhance the pro-Trump narrative. They similarly underplayed or ignored any stories that might shine a harsh or less than charitable light on Sleepy Joe Biden—with Hunter Biden's "laptop from hell" at the top of the pyramid of all that was ignored.

Here, the implicit CNN and MSNBC motto was this: "Never give a sucker or Donald John Trump an even break—and always put your forgiving finger on the scale for Sleepy Joe."

Stories that the Never-Trump media assiduously shunned because they might help Orange Man Bad included any evidence of a robust economic recovery, declining infection rates, proof that opening up the economy had no more effect on infection rates than severe lockdowns, and especially any possibility that Trump might deliver a vaccine before Election Day.

Yes indeed: Let's not give any hope to the poor and huddled masses of American voters yearning to be gainfully employed and free of a deadly pandemic.

And by the way, there was also this platinum rule: never blame Communist China for the pandemic because to do so would be to absolve Donald Trump of any such blame.

Nowhere was this lies-of-omission phenomenon more evident than when Israeli prime minister Benjamin Netanyahu and the foreign ministers of the United Arab Emirates and Bahrain came to the White House on September 15, 2020, to sign the so-called "Abraham Accords." This was the first peace treaty between Israel and any Arab countries since Israel's normalization of relations with Jordan in 1994.

For the American media in normal times, this should have been a very, very, very big—the Boss would say *huge*—foreign policy achievement. It was an achievement custom made for the A-block of every major cable and broadcast news show and should have been placed above the fold on the front page of every major newspaper. So of course, there was barely any coverage in the mainstream media. Not with President Trump standing to gain a gob of good press right after the Labor Day kickoff of the final home stretch to Election Day.

Comedy or farce, call it what ye will, this particular lie of omission took a page right out of Dante's Inferno—"abandon all hope for good journalism, all ye biased hacks who enter the newsrooms of CNN and MSNBC."

Lemmings Singing from the Same Sheet of Spin

In tactic three, during the 2020 cycle, cable news producers, hosts, in-house experts, and friendly surrogates would quickly develop key talking points for the stories of the day, with the implicit daily spin directive being: *everyone shall sing in perfect harmony from the same sheet of Never-Trump music.*

At times, the lemming-like spin would boil over into the hilarious. On this comedic note, one of my great pleasures during the campaign was watching folks like Sean Hannity and Tucker Carlson create skewering montages whereby a baker's dozen of personalities on CNN or MSNBC would all mouth the exact same talking points. Verbatim. One. After the other. After the other.

And it was a huge bonus when a Hannity or Tucker montage comingled Democrat politicians mouthing the very same talking points as the CNN or MSNBC personalities. Such rapid-fire montages thereby underscored not just the incestuous and collusive relationship between the globalist political class and the Corporate Never-Media but also the shared mission of defeating one Donald John Trump.

Tactic four was joined at the hip with tactic three: It involved the coterie of in-house echo chamber contributors and external surrogates that every cable news channel employs. It would be this choir of Never-Trump sopranos that would collectively help drive the daily fake news cycle.

From the same sheet of spin, these contributors and surrogates would mindlessly parrot whatever talking points were propagated by cable show anchors and the so-called news "packages" put together by the CNN and MSNBC reporters.

On shows like MSNBC's *Morning Joe*, for example, this echo chamber featured pompous windbags like globalist extraordinaire Richard Haass, legal expert and Zoom porn star Jeffrey Toobin, and the once obese poverty pimp turned skinny poverty pimp otherwise known as the "Reverend" Al Sharpton.

By the way, I liked the fat Al Sharpton from the 1980s a whole lot better than Skinny Al. That portly, "hate those crackers" version of Al Sharpton was a lot more honest, albeit in his own dishonest way.

At the Dawn of Cancel Culture

The fifth and final tactic in the daily spin cycle was the "freezeout." Particularly in the last few months of the 2020 campaign, both CNN and MSNBC began to sharply limit the appearances of any surrogates from the campaign or the White House who might forcefully and credibly present the president's point of view, and this particular tactic would hit me right between the eyes.

Time after time, Roma Daravi or Emily Weeks on the White House communications team would pitch me to producers across the Never-Trump media diaspora. The non-response: emails never answered, voicemails never acknowledged, and a whole lot of crickets. In fact, the only administration official these networks would ever take at the drop of the hat was Saint Fauci—which never ended well for us.

In this freezeout, the one TV personality I found the most disappointing—a true case of woman bites dog—was Judy Woodruff, anchor of the *PBS NewsHour*. The *NewsHour* is one of the longest running and most prestigious news shows in American history—I myself began watching it as far back as 1983 when it was the *MacNeil/Lehrer NewsHour*. It was just top-shelf, first-class journalism, at least back in the day.

Not so anymore with Woodruff at the helm, a gaggle of Never-Trump producers managing content, and a steady stream of left-wing analysts and insufferable commentators like Mark Shields and David Brooks—all courtesy of the US taxpayer.

By the way, it's long past time to shut that government spigot off to PBS and its radio sister, National Public Radio. If they want to play partisan politics like CNN and MSNBC, that is certainly their right and choice. But under such circumstances, they need to go out and raise their own money from their left-wing base. MAGA folks like me have no interest in paying for crap like that. Just saying.

And by the by the way, if you want to know who the *real* Judy Woodruff is behind that sweet, grandmotherly countenance, just watch her ask the first question in the October 5, 1988, vice presidential debate between Republican Dan Quayle and Democrat Lloyd Bentsen. At that time, Dame Judy was in full blossom in her blonde and beautiful youth, and she was already deeply into the process of sharply elbowing her way into what, at the time, was very much a man's world. Good for her.

Of course, to make her mark in that vice presidential debate, the not-so-good Ms. Woodruff first faked a hard punch to Quayle's nose and then kicked him somewhere south of his belt buckle with this opening question:

> Senator, you have been criticized, as we all know, for your decision to stay out of the Vietnam War, for your poor academic record. But more troubling to some are some of the comments that have been made by people in your own party. Just last week former Secretary of State Haig said that your pick was the dumbest call George Bush could have made. Your leader in the Senate, Bob Dole, said that a better quali-fied person could have been chosen. Other Republicans have been far more critical in private. Why do you think that you have not made a more substantial impression on some of these people who have been able to observe you up close?[26]

It simply does not get more brutal than that. And you have to wonder if Dan Quayle had been a Democrat whether Woodruff would have even gone there. Bias is as bias does.

More than forty years later, as the now the wizened face of public television news, Woodruff repeatedly refused to put any White House spokespersons on her show during the final months of the campaign.

As it was told to me by the comms team, Poor Judy was in a freeze-eout pique over the fact that President Trump had not agreed to be interviewed by her. Whined Woodruff and her producer: "I'm the only TV anchor the president has not agreed to be interviewed by."

My own theory is that PBS simply did not want to give us any air-time. Either way, Judy's show became the *PBS Fake News* and *Freezeout Hour* right along with CNN and MSNBC, the Sunday news shows, and all the broadcast networks.

In the end, the information war waged against President Trump by the Never-Trump media was yet one more nail in the 2020 elec-tion coffin lined with far too many strategic failures. As we shall see in the next chapter, which will bring our discussion of Strategic Fail-ure #5 to a close, the root of all this evil was a mediocre White House

communications team and a not-so-merry band of Trump media surrogates simply not up to the job of Trumpian domination of the daily
news cycle.

TWENTY-EIGHT

A White House Confederacy of Media Dunces

If you aren't on TV, you can't be in this administration.

—President Donald John Trump, Oval Office, June 22nd, 2020

[Chief of Staff Mark] Meadows gets slaughtered on CNN by Jake Tapper. Marc Short and four other members of Vice Presidents Pence's staff get COVID. This couldn't happen at a worse time as it emphasizes the coronavirus theme and how we have mishandled it even as it threatens to take Pence off the campaign trail.... Only [National Security Advisor Robert] O'Brien on Face the Nation has a good [outing].... No money [left] for get out the vote. No money for advertising. No money for lawyers to contest what is likely to be a contested election.

—Navarro Journal Entry, October 24, 2020

To dominate the daily news cycle, any presidential administration has at its disposal at least four distinct pools of talent.

- First and foremost, there is the White House press secretary;
- Second in importance and potential impact is the White House chief of staff;

- Within the perimeter of the White House, there should also be key senior officials ready, willing, and able to serve as TV surrogates; and

- Fourth, there should likewise be a very deep bench of media-hardened and well-seasoned cabinet secretaries.

Unfortunately, in the Trump White House, we would not hit cleanly on one of these four cylinders.

A Parade of Mediocre Press Secretaries

Like an orchestra conductor, the White House press secretary should lead on a daily basis a beautiful symphony of pro-administration talking points designed to define, shape, and ultimately dominate the daily news cycle. To pull off such a feat, however, any press secretary must possess a keen intellect, be a quick study, have the ability to equally quickly throw counter punches, and do all of this in a witty and urbane fashion.

Press secretaries who fit this description historically include the truly debonair Pierre Salinger for John F. Kennedy; the wise-as-an owl Bill Moyers for Lyndon Johnson; the straight- and plain-speaking James Brady for Ronald Reagan; the Aaron Sorkin-inspiration Dee Dee Myers and Q-factor-off-the-charts George Stephanopoulos for Bill Clinton; and the elegant street fighter Dana Perino and erudite streetfighter Ari Fleischer for George W. Bush.

Compare any one of these historical figures with Trump's Sean Spicer, Sarah Huckabee Sanders, Stephanie Grisham, and Kayleigh McEnany, and none ever completely measured up.

Spicer was a hot head on a cool medium with all the pugnaciousness of his Boss and none of the Trump charm.

Spicey literally blew it on day one of the administration with his hyperbolic over-estimate of the Trump Inauguration Day crowd. Melissa McCarthy would stick both a fork and a knife into Spicey the minute she played Sean androgynously on *Saturday Night Live*.

Spicer would last just 211 days—a New York minute by press secretary standards.

By sharp contrast, Sarah Sanders, the second Trump press secretary, would endure for almost two years. Ironically, Sanders had virtually no ability to counterpunch when Never-Trump media emissaries like CNN's Jim Acosta and Kaitlan Collins or ABC's Jonathan Karl would throw repeated leftist hooks at her glass jaw. I say "ironically" because Sanders worked for the greatest counterpuncher in presidential history in Donald Trump.

Trump's third White House press secretary, Stephanie Grisham, would go down in history as the only press secretary to *never hold a regular White House news briefing*—this over the course of her *nine* months in office. "You can't win the news cycle if you won't play," might be the definitive gambler's slogan here for Grisham. But nobody—including the Boss—ever wanted to gamble on putting Stephanie on the podium.

As for the Trump White House cleanup hitter, Kayleigh McEnany, she never had the *gravitas* to make any of her talking points stick—and talking points was all she really had when she went to the podium. So when Kayleigh got hit with a tough question, she was often like a deer in the headlights.

Let me drill down just a minute on that *gravitas* problem: You take a Bill Moyers or Ari Fleischer or Dana Perino, and they clearly had both the intellect and training to understand the nuances of the policies they might be sent out to the podium to defend. Absent those qualities, any press secretary is going to get eaten alive.

A Motley Crue of Chiefs

As a second pool of talent to draw from in the daily battle to dominate the news cycle, the White House also has at its disposal its chief of staff. Chiefs who have excelled in this dimension include Lyndon Baines Johnson's Kenneth O'Donnell, Jimmy Carter's Hamilton Jordan, Ronald Reagan's Fabulous Baker Boys—James and Howard—Leon Panetta for Bill Clinton, and Rahm Emanuel for Barack Obama.

Once again, if we compare any one of these historical figures to the four Trump chiefs of staff, we again come up wanting. As we discussed earlier in this book, the first chief Reince Priebus was just the wrong, small, and inexperienced man for a very big job.

As for Chief #2, John Kelly, from a media perspective, this was like recruiting a trucker to drive a Formula One car. Or maybe like using a chainsaw for open heart surgery.

With his thick Boston accent, a smile always missing in action, and "I don't suffer fools from the media gladly" tattoos stuck on both his forehead and sleeves, Kelly was brutally and simply incapable of messaging *anything* to the press.

Fortunately, Kelly didn't try to "meet the press" very often, but during the 519 days that Kelly served as chief of staff—I painfully counted every one of them—we sure could have used somebody in that office to help us dominate the daily news cycle.

That somebody certainly was not Mick Mulvaney—Trump's third chief of staff. Or should I say "acting" chief of staff.

That "acting" part of his title was a little dig that the Boss liked to stick into Mick so he never got comfortable in the job. The more Mick begged, the more permanent his "acting chief" status would become.

From a media messaging perspective, the problem with Mulvaney was that God blessed this smug Mick with an overabundance of both arrogance and hubris. It would be these character traits—as they say, "a man's character determines his fate"—that would lead to one of the worst press conferences ever held by a chief of staff.

On October 17, 2019, Mulvaney would shoot both himself in the foot *and* POTUS in the chest with fateful remarks that instantly gave new life to an impeachment that the Boss was desperately trying to avoid. Wrote one newspaper:

> *The hastily announced White House news conference was supposed to be a full-throated defense of President Trump's controversial decision to host next year's Group of Seven summit at his private golf club in Florida. By the time it was over, acting chief of staff Mick Mulvaney had made much more explosive news—adding to Trump's impeachment troubles and calling into question his ability to lead the White House staff in a time of crisis.... And Mulvaney's situation was made worse, some Republicans said, by his decision to attempt to retract his remarks hours later in a bellicose written statement blaming the media reporting his remarks.*

Yikes. That single press conference was the beginning of the end for Mulvaney even as it underscored yet again the inability of the White House to dominate the news cycle.

I would like to tell you that, at least with Mark Meadows, the "fourth time was a charm." However, Meadows himself would earn the dubious distinction of being ranked as the "worst chief of staff in history" by the reigning scholar on the subject, Chris Whipple.[27]

To this I will again say my three favorite words I learned from the Washington Swamp: "I don't disagree." Although it's probably more of a dead heat between Meadows, Mulvaney, and Kelly.

Note to Reince: I think you would have turned out to be the best of the bunch if the Boss had only given you a bit more time to prove yourself.

As still a third pool of talent a White House communications team can draw upon in its efforts to dominate the daily news cycle, there will always be a large stable of senior advisors within the West Wing.

Given that the post of senior advisor to an American president represents the pinnacle of achievement, it is most often the case that a president will be surrounded by tough, smart, and typically media-savvy individuals for whom walking out to Pebble Beach for a media interview is certainly not their first rodeo.

By the way, "Pebble Beach" is the nickname of the set of media tents lined up along the Northwest wall of the White House between the White House itself and the Eisenhower Executive Office Building. For me, Pebble Beach was love at first sight because for years back in California I had had to schlep miles upon miles to satellite studios when I started doing regular TV hits on CNBC and Fox Business and occasionally CNN.

At the White House, the ability to simply cross the street from my office and step into a tent with beautiful lighting and crisp sound to do my TV hits was a pure delight. It was a pure delight, except, of course, in the dead of winter when it was 20 degrees or when the lawnmowers were going full bore on a 100-degree July day.

At any rate, particularly during the worst days of the pandemic, there were few senior advisors capable of walking out to Pebble Beach and doing anything but sticking their feet—yes both feet—into their mouths.

While Senior Counselor Kellyanne Conway would have been a very useful asset, she resigned for family reasons just a few days before Labor Day. That was an unexpected and harsh blow to the Trump reelection effort as Labor Day marks the traditional kickoff of the home stretch for any presidential race and having Kellyanne suddenly out of the picture was a real setback.

By the way, Kellyanne was one of my favorites at the White House. She called me the "unbroken thread" for the fact that I was one of only three senior White House officials who managed to survive all the way from the campaign to the end of the administration. When her thread was unexpectedly broken, it was indeed a loss.

As for the *one* senior White House official who likely could have made the most difference in the media, at *least* on the trade issue, there was the Greta Garbo of the West Wing—United States Trade Representative Robert E. Lighthizer. The few times Bob was on TV—including big shows like *Face the Nation*—he knocked it out of the park.

On TV, Lighthizer never flapped. He always had a very calm demeanor, he was in absolute command of the facts, and whenever challenged, Bob would quickly put any anchor or reporter in their place and do so with either grace or like a cat gently playing with a mouse.

His impressive media skill set notwithstanding, Bob Lighthizer absolutely refused to go on television, particularly during those last months before Election Day when we needed him most. Bob just would not do it. No way. No how. Not good. Shame on Bob.

In sharp contrast, the one guy who *was* always willing to go on TV and who actually was very good—National Security Advisor Robert O'Brien—was one of the few assets we had. I liken Robert to the political equivalent of Jimmy Stewart for our times.

With an impish charm, a head of full and wavy hair to die for, and a surfs-up, California optimism, Robert could pivot and spin his way out of any trap that might be set for him even as he advanced our message of the day. The problem, however, was that Robert's domain was limited primarily to national security when what we really needed to be campaigning on—and dominating the news cycle about—was the economy and trade issues. So as good as Robert was, his contributions would be limited down the home stretch.

Cabinet of Clowns Redux

As a final pool of talent to draw upon in the unending quest of any White House to dominate the daily news cycle, there should be a very deep bench of seasoned, media-savvy masters of their cabinet universes. As with the post of senior advisor to the president of the United States, a cabinet secretary position likewise represents the pinnacle of achievement.

Given that fact, you should normally expect a murderer's row of highly polished media killers in the cabinet secretary pool. Regrettably, this was just not so in Trump Land.

Ever the media hound, Treasury Secretary Steve Mnuchin got the most airtime. It was *never* a good thing.

On TV, Mnuchin spoke like a robot, often with an uncomfortable nervous tic around the corners of his mouth. To most viewers, he was just an uncomfortable cross between cringeworthy and a Wall Street hack with yawning lack of credibility. Here, both Mnuchin and Larry Kudlow had great difficulty connecting whenever they went beyond the friendly globalist confines of the Fox and CNBC business networks.

In the heat of the pandemic, there was also the always punctilious Secretary of Health and Human Services Alex Azar. A former Big Pharma top executive, Azar had a nasty habit of distancing himself from the Boss at the first hint of trouble. So, on net, Azar usually did far more media harm to the Boss than good—even as he would burnish his own credentials.

Of course, we had the very same distancing and "diss the Boss" problem with other high-ranking officials across the healthcare bureaucracies. FDA Commissioner Steve Hahn, Centers for Disease Control Director Robert Redfield, and National Institutes of Health head Francis Collins would each throw POTUS under the bus even faster than Azar—as would other key officials like the insufferably pompous Brett Giroir and of course, the king of stepping on White House messaging, Saint Fauci.

The short and long of all of this is that mediocrity reigned across the four main talent pools any White House Communications Team usually draws upon to perform the most important task in its job description: dominate the daily news cycle in strong support of the president.

Because of this endemic mediocrity, it was far more often the case that the Never-Trump media would do the dominating and thereby successfully drive down President Donald Trump's favorability and job approval ratings.

This strategic failure was all so unnecessary—as was so much of what went on in the Trump White House that would drag the Boss down.

TWENTY-NINE

Fauci, Russia, and the Ghost of Bush v. Gore

The Biden administration's strategy to universally vaccinate in the middle of the pandemic is bad science and badly needs a reboot. This strategy will likely prolong the most dangerous phase of the worst pandemic since 1918 and almost assuredly cause more harm than good—even as it undermines faith in the entire public health system.

—Dr. Robert Malone and Peter Navarro, *The Washington Times*, August 5, 2021[28]

Very sobering news after a phone call with Reince Priebus. The absentee voting is absolutely off the charts. At this point, there are as many absentee ballots already cast as there were entire votes cast during the 2016 election.... This does not bode well if the Democrats have been running a stealth get-out-the-vote operation with all the money they have, which is highly likely. Did we get caught sleeping?... The candidate himself is doing everything possible in the home stretch but the absentee ballots are already cast, and he's talking to a dwindling audience.... From now to Election Day, the Boss will hit 13 stops. He is tireless, but much of the damage...has been done.

—Navarro Journal Entry, October 30, 2020

The overarching lesson of this book has been that Bad Personnel inevitably leads to Bad Policies and Bad Politics. My broad mission in illustrating this critical principle of the exercise of effective presidential power has been twofold:

First, in advance of the 2024 presidential election and a likely Trump candidacy, I have sought to explain the essence of Trumpism, the MAGA movement, and Populist Economic Nationalism.

Second, I have also sought to provide a definitive insider's account of Five Strategic Failures that helped lead to the fall of the White House of Trump in 2020.

I firmly believe that if President Trump had avoided even a few of these failures, he would be sitting in the Oval Office today and America would be both far more safe and certainly more prosperous. Yet, as we bring this book towards its close, I would be remiss in not at least briefly acknowledging three additional strategic failures that no doubt also moved the political needle towards Joe Biden.

Fauci's Bloody Lie of Omission

Strategic Failure #6 speaks to the way the White House would handle—and often mishandle—the Made in China pandemic. I have not gone into depth in this book about this particular failure because I covered it extensively in my *In Trump Time* memoir. Suffice it to say here that we in the Trump administration did a far better job actually defending America against the virus then we did explaining what we were doing and how we were achieving that result.

As documented in *In Trump Time*, unsung heroes with names like Paul Mango, John Polowczyk, Bob Kadlec, and Katie Arrington did incredible work making sure that Americans had all of the masks, goggles, gowns, and other personal protective equipment our country and its first responders needed.

Miraculously, President Trump would ensure that every American who needed a ventilator had a ventilator, and the Boss was likewise able to get a suite of at least "quasi-vaccines" developed in one-third of the time it normally takes.

Regrettably, the Boss's vaccine miracle would turn out to be very much a mixed blessing. This is because the Biden regime's forced vaccination mandates and authoritarian implementation of those mandates would do considerable damage to our children, our combat readiness, our workforce, our supply chains, our democracy and freedoms, and, most ironically, to our public health.

To be clear here, and for all the reasons I have written about elsewhere with Dr. Robert Malone[29]—see the quote leading off this chapter—those vaccines should only have been used voluntarily and limited to those at most risk from the virus, principally senior citizens and people with significant co-morbidities.

That said, the one thing missing from my *In Trump Time* book relates directly to Strategic Failure #6 and what must be considered the biggest Lie of Omission ever committed by a high-ranking US government official. This biggest of lies would come from the lips of a man who, throughout the pandemic, was put up on a pedestal by both the Never-Trump media and the Democrat Party. I am talking, of course, about Dr. Anthony Fauci.

As you may recall from *In Trump Time*, I first met Fauci on January 28, 2020, in the iconic White House Situation Room. I had been sent there by the Boss to convince the nascent White House Coronavirus Task Force[30] to support President Trump's travel ban on China.

My primary antagonist that day—besides the hapless Mick Mulvaney who chaired the meeting—would be none other than Tony Fauci. I had never met the man before that day, and when I walked into the Sit Room, I had no idea Fauci was regarded in at least some quarters as a living legend.

Without such prior knowledge, I simply took the measure of the man based on what would be a very contentious showdown. I would come away from that clash with the quite unsettling belief that Fauci thought he was a lot smarter than he was and—call it one of my premonitions—Fauci was almost certainly going to hurt both President Trump and this nation. As it would turn out, I would be right on both counts.

At any rate, Fauci had gone on record just a few days earlier insisting that the virus from Communist China was, in his words, "a very, very low risk," and therefore nothing to worry about.[31] Perhaps not surprisingly, when Fauci strode into the Sit Room that day, he was adamantly against slapping a travel ban on Communist China, insisting repeatedly that "travel bans don't work."

At least on that day, I would beat back Fauci's resistance to the travel ban, and President Trump would wind up saving millions of American lives with his early, quick, and decisive action.

But here is the real Fauci Lie of Omission point: We now know that when Fauci walked into the Situation Room at literally the dawn of the pandemic on January 28, 2020, Fauci likely *already knew* at least six stunning facts that would make Fauci himself complicit in the looming pandemic. These facts included:

1. The SARS-CoV-2 virus almost certainly did not come from nature;
2. China's virus almost certainly came from the Wuhan Institute of Virology;
3. The Wuhan Institute of Virology had received substantial funding from Fauci and his bureaucracy within the National Institutes of Health (NIH);
4. Fauci's NIH funding had been specifically used in Wuhan to conduct so-called "gain-of-function experiments" that can transform harmless bat viruses into human killers like COVID-19;
5. SARS-CoV-2 was in all probability genetically engineered using Fauci's gain-of-function technologies; and
6. The Wuhan lab doubled as a bioweapons lab for the People's Liberation Army. Therefore, the virus itself may have been intentionally designed as a bioweapon.

At this critical time, Fauci was also acutely aware that he, himself, along with National Institutes of Health Director Francis Collins, had gone behind the back of the Trump White House to lift the ban on gain-of-function experiments in 2017. That ban had been imposed by the Obama administration in 2014 after a series of dangerous accidents that should have warded Fauci off from the dangerous game of God he was playing. Instead, after the ban was lifted, Fauci promptly began funding additional gain-of-function experiments at the Wuhan lab, experiments that likely led directly or indirectly to the pandemic.[32]

Put all these facts together and Tony Fauci had, on the day he walked into the Situation Room on January 28, 2020, both a moral and ethical obligation as well as a duty to his country to disclose all these facts both to the president and the White House Coronavirus Task Force.

Instead of coming clean, the not-so-good Doctor Fauci would engineer an elaborate cover-up designed to advance a "virus from nature" theory and thereby hide his own possible role as the godfather of the pandemic.

Fauci would engineer this cover-up with the help of a corrupt bureaucratic cutout named Peter Daszak of the EcoHealth Alliance and a group of scientists, including Kristian Andersen, Robert Garry, and Michael Farzan. These cover-up artists had received substantial NIH funding through the largess of Tony Fauci prior to the pandemic; once that cover-up was executed, these scientists would receive tens of millions of dollars more in hush money grant funding.[33] How these highly educated elites look themselves in the mirror I simply cannot comprehend.

Now here is why Fauci's Lie of Omission and subsequent cover-up was so despicable and damaging to the Boss's reelection prospects:

If Fauci had simply come clean, President Trump would have demanded that President Xi Jinping and the Chinese Communist Party immediately reveal the truth about the virus and, most importantly, release the original genome of the virus that had been genetically engineered.

I cannot overstate how important this single act of transparency on the part of Communist China would have been. The quasi-vaccines that have been developed by corrupt Big Pharma companies like Pfizer to fight the Wuhan virus have turned out to be both primitive and dangerous instruments. These mRNA quasi-vaccines are not true and safe vaccines like those for smallpox and polio but, as Dr. Malone and I have explained, merely leaky and non-durable gene-therapy technologies with a wide range of very dangerous side effects—which, by the way, Pfizer and the FDA were well aware of but have hid from the American public.

If, on the other hand, with the benefit of the original genome, we had known from the beginning what we were up against, our vaccine strategy would have been far more complex, effective, and safe. Millions of lives around the world could have been saved. Our economy would not be in such great distress. Communist China would not be using the pandemic so effectively to advance its military and geopolitical interests. We would have already reached herd immunity, and the pandemic would likely effectively be over.

Strangle the Fauci Baby in its Crib

One other pertinent detail that I left out about Fauci in my *In Trump Time* book is also well worth mentioning within the context of Strategic Failure #6. To wit: I urged President Trump to fire Fauci right after my January 28 contretemps with him in the Situation Room, and I would urge the Boss to fire Fauci on at least one other occasion.

I do not blame the Boss for not taking my advice. After all, I was just his trade and economic advisor, and on the other side of the "fire Fauci" fence, Fauci had the entire healthcare bureaucracy behind him.

Indeed, whenever there was any talk about President Trump's discontent with Fauci and a possible firing, the Boss would hear from the likes of Francis Collins at NIH, Doctor Robert Redfield at the Centers for Disease Control, Stephen Hahn at the FDA, and Secretary Alex Azar of the Department of Health and Human Services. Each would always provide a full-throated defense of that evil little Lie of Omission beast otherwise known as Fauci.

Of course, the other major obstacle to firing Fauci was the weak-kneed Acting Chief of Staff Mick Mulvaney and no shortage of pearl clutchers on the White House communications team. They feared firing Fauci would be a public relations disaster—and no doubt it would have been a major story, at least for a few days.

That said, my view—and I told the Boss so—was Churchillian: We needed to strangle that Fauci baby in his crib before he gained too much power and became, as I told the Boss, "untouchable."

Here is the thing that haunts me most about Fauci: If I had known then what I know now, I would have relished the opportunity to stand up at a press briefing with President Trump on my right shoulder and Fauci on my left. With the klieg lights a-blazing in the Brady Room, I would have hit Fauci right between the eyes with his Big Lie of Omission, and with that punch, Fauci would have been politically dead, buried, and gone by nightfall.

Now *that* would have been a hell of a day for President Trump and our republic. And the dethroning of Fauci alone might well have been enough to win the 2020 election.

Why do I say this? Because outing Fauci's role in the pandemic would have immediately shifted the blame for the whole blood-soaked catastrophe away from Donald Trump to both the Chinese Communist Party and Fauci himself. And that blame was the Boss's biggest political albatross in 2020.

Russia, Russia, Russia

A seventh strategic failure I want to give at least passing reference to was the abject failure of RINO attorney general Bill Barr to indict any number of co-conspirators in the infamous Russia Hoax. As Steve Bannon likes to say about such RINO behavior: "There are no conspiracies, but there are no coincidences."

As we have discussed, the Russia Hoax refers to the spurious claim that the 2016 Trump Campaign colluded with Russia to defeat Hillary Clinton and that Russia preferred Trump over Clinton because Russian intelligence operatives had damning evidence they could use to blackmail Trump once he ascended to the Oval Office. As Hoax maven Gregg Jarrett describes it:

> *It was an audacious plot put in motion by one of Clinton's foreign policy advisers and then sanctioned by the then-Democrat presidential candidate on July 26. But the genesis of the smear came from Clinton herself.*
>
> *For months, she had peppered her campaign speeches with increasingly venomous accusations that her opponent was a Kremlin asset and a "puppet of Putin." There was not a shred of plausible evidence.... But the lie didn't stop there. Through a conduit, her campaign commissioned an ex-British spy who composed an anti-Trump dossier of rumors and disinformation derived from a suspected Russian spy.*
>
> *These fabricated stories were then secretly and sedulously fed to James Comey's FBI and the gullible media, both of whom went after Trump with a vengeance.*
>
> *The result was the greatest mass delusion in American history and one of the dirtiest political tricks ever perpetrated.*[34]

We now know beyond any shadow of a doubt that the alleged "facts" of the Russia Hoax were indeed a cynical fiction ginned up by Democrat operatives paid by the Clinton campaign. These operatives, most prominently former British intelligence officer Christopher Steele, created a phony "Steele Dossier" that created the false Russia Hoax narrative.

Rogue Never-Trump elements within the FBI with names like Peter Strzok and Lisa Page would then use this dossier to bogusly obtain Foreign Intelligence Surveillance Act (FISA) warrants to spy on members of the Trump campaign. As events unfolded, the whole hoax itself would be given institutional credence by a series of false statements by top government officials and congressmen.

Those who have been implicated for allegedly helping to perpetuate this hoax include the former director of national intelligence James Clapper and CIA Director John Brennan under Obama, Congressman Adam "Shifty" Schiff, current Biden national security advisor Jake Sullivan, the aforementioned former FBI director James Comey, and, of course, a bevy of CNN and MSNBC reporters who set upon the Russia Hoax and Donald Trump like flies on buffalo chips.

I firmly believe here that if those who had been involved in perpetrating the Russia Hoax had been brought to justice—or even indicted before Election Day—this would have provided a *significant boost* to President Trump's reelection prospects. I say this because the Russia Hoax—hoax that it always was and always will be—still hangs like a cloud over President Trump. To this point, Gregg Jarrett notes:

> *For Hillary Clinton, inventing the lie was easy. Spreading the lie was even easier. For President Trump, uncovering the truth has been hard. The truth always has its enemies. This is the maxim—and chilling lesson—of the Russia hoax.*[35]

Of course, Strategic Failure #7 may be laid right at the doorstep of said Attorney General William Pelham Barr. Rather than take that investigation head on, this Georgie Bush RINO would job that investigation out to Connecticut's US Attorney John "Bull" Durham—knowing full well the delays that would entail.[36]

Predictably, all the Trump White House got out of Barr's gambit leading into Election Day was a lot of temporizing bull from Durham.

So, yet again, we have a clear case of Bad Personnel inexorably leading to Bad Politics.

But what I would give to see Tony Fauci in an orange jumpsuit sharing a cell along with alleged perpetrators of the Russia Hoax like Comey, Clapper, Brennan, Page, Strzok, and Schiff. Now that would be some long overdue justice.

First Use the Lawyers Before You Kill Them

Strategic Failure #8—the last but not least of a very bad bunch—was the catastrophic failure to learn the most basic lesson of the 2000 Bush v. Gore presidential race. To wit:

> *Every modern presidential campaign must have not only a large army of obligatory political shock-and-awe troops, a solid ground game, a sophisticated absentee ballot program, a multi-pronged small donor/large donor fundraising crusade, a sophisticated digital messaging capability, a rapid response ninja team, crisp communications capabilities, an army of surrogates hungry for earned media on cable TV and radio, clear-eyed and creative pollsters, and a video production arm cranking out hundreds of thirty-second ads.*
>
> *A truly modern presidential campaign must also recruit, maintain, and forward deploy large battalions of top shelf legal talent schooled, trained, and deeply experienced in the intricate details and minutia of election law.*

Remember here: Bush v. Gore was decided by a mere five hundred votes, and *it was decided not by the best candidate, but rather by the best lawyers*. In the mercurial weeks following the 2000 Election Day where the legal battle was won, those best lawyers happened to be mostly on the Republican side. In 2020, however, it would be the Democrats with the vastly superior legal edge.

So it was that in the wee hours of the morning after the November 3 election when it looked increasingly like Democrat operatives were indeed stealing the election from Donald Trump, the Trump campaign was caught with its lawyer pants down.

In the ensuing days and weeks of desperation and despair, and with virtually no help from the Trump campaign itself, a ragtag band of lawyers led by former New York mayor Rudy Giuliani—and misled by the kraken crackpot Sidney Powell—would be vastly outnumbered and out-lawyered in every single battleground state where the final election outcome would be contested—from Arizona, Georgia, and Michigan to Nevada, Pennsylvania, and Wisconsin.

Rudy, and his wingman Bernie Kerik, fought the good fight as they always do. But sending Rudy and Bernie into this breach was like sending in the Air Force to fight a land war.

Rudy and Bernie had no real experience in campaign law. They had been deserted by both the Republican National Committee and the Trump campaign itself. And it was just not going to work.

If, however, we had been as legally prepared in 2020 as we were in 2000, Donald Trump would likely still be sitting behind the Resolute Desk. And that was the tragedy of Strategic Failure #8: we did not stop the steal.

PART NINE

Taking It Back in 2024

THIRTY

Tearing Down the Pelosi House in 2022

The deal was years in the making, the culmination of forging contacts, hosting dinners, of flights to and from China. But on Aug. 2, 2017, signatures were quickly affixed, one from Hunter Biden, the other from a Chinese executive named Gongwen Dong. Within days, a new Cathay Bank account was created. Within a week, millions of dollars started to change hands.... [T]he new documents—which include a signed copy of a $1 million legal retainer, emails related to the wire transfers, and $3.8 million in consulting fees that are confirmed in new bank records and agreements signed by Hunter Biden—illustrate the ways in which his family profited from relationships built over Joe Biden's decades in public service.

—*The Washington Post*, March 30, 2022[1]

I began this book with a pair of admonitions drawn from the insights of Shakespeare and the American philosopher George Santayana:

- *We must not allow our 2020 past to become our 2024 prologue.*
- *If we do not remember the mistakes of the 2020 Trump campaign and first Trump term, we will indeed be condemned to repeat them.*

It is from the wisdom of these admonitions that I will now move forward with a chessboard look at how Donald John Trump can—indeed must!—be reelected president.

The 2024 rise of Trump must inevitably begin with the 2022 fall of a Democrat-controlled House of Representatives. Together, we must rip the People's House from the clutches of House Speaker Nancy Pelosi and her radical squad, and we must do so in a landslide not seen since the days of the Gingrich and Tea Party revolutions.

We must pursue this utter destruction of radical Democrat control of Capitol Hill for at least three reasons.

First, a Republican Congress will put a swift end to the cavalcade of fiscally irresponsible spending bills that have helped ignite a virulent stagflation. With the Speaker's gavel in Pelosi's misguided hands, we have borne witness to an orgy of misdirected spending that will only further bury Americans in debt while destroying the already precarious balance sheet of our increasingly rudderless Federal Reserve.

Second, a Republican Congress will stop Pelosi's radical Democrats in their woke tracks from further inflicting their far-left agenda on what is undeniably a center-right American public *and* republic.

Memo to Pelosi, AOC, the despicable Ilhan Omar, Shifty Adam Schiff, and others of their profligate ilk:

- America wants absolutely *nothing* to do with your higher taxes, punishing new regulations, a Green New Deal involving seven-dollars-a-gallon gas, and feckless energy policies that are leaving our nation and our families at the mercy of Russian oligarchs, Saudi Arabian princes, and a predatory OPEC cartel. Remember here: Under Donald Trump, America was energy independent—and we must be again!

- Nor do most Americans want critical race theory and gender-inclusive curricula taught in our schools, authoritarian mask and vaccine mandates imposed on our work force, the destruction of women's sports by transgender interlopers, a gutting of the First *and* Second Amendments, the defunding of our police, voting rights for felons, free health care for illegal aliens, and the obliteration of election integrity through an orgy of unrestricted absentee balloting.

Here, I must confess I am a bit conflicted. I am conflicted because the more stupid stuff Pelosi, AOC, and their minions do, the more their hubris and stupidity highlight the true genius of Donald Trump and further enhance the chances of Trump taking back the White House in 2024. It's not for nothing that "Trump Was Right"[2] is emerging as one of the most popular slogans of our time—and rightly so.

Of course, the third reason why we *must* take back the Speaker's gavel from Nancy Pelosi is that this will stop Pelosi's partisan, Never-Trump mob from continuing to weaponize the investigatory powers of Congress.

This is no small matter. The congressional assault on Donald Trump with two phony impeachment trials during the 2020 election cycle was very damaging politically to Donald Trump's reelection efforts—as Pelosi's two sham impeachment trials were intended to be.

Nor has Pelosi's weaponization of the House's investigatory powers been a "two impeachments and done" phenomenon. Now, well into the second year of the Biden regime, Pelosi's liars and leakers have continued their assault on Donald Trump—and top advisors like me and Dan Scavino—with numerous fake investigations. This includes most prominently a sham hyper-partisan, illegally formed kangaroo court otherwise known as "The U. S. House Select Committee to Investigate the January 6 Attack on the United States Capitol."

A Kangaroo Committee in King Biden's Time

Fully *seven* of the nine members of Pelosi's illegitimate committee are Democrats, and all seven of these Democrats have a more than five year long history of seeking to remove President Trump from office under one guise or another—impeachment, mentally unfit for office, yada, yada, and so it has gone.

As for Pelosi, she has admitted she wants to put President Trump "in prison"[3] while the Chair of this kangaroo court committee, Bennie Thompson, has described President Trump as "racist and unfit to serve."[4] For their parts, Democrats Adam Schiff and Jamie Raskin played key roles in the impeachment circuses while Schiff's lies and leaks were also at the center of the Russia Hoax.

Jamie Raskin himself sponsored legislation that would have removed Trump from office; Democrat Zoe Lofgren boycotted Trump's

2016 inauguration and Democrat Elaine Luria boycotted Trump's 2020 State of the Union address.

As for the two lone Republicans, Liz Cheney and Adam Kinzinger, they were among only a tiny handful of House Republicans who voted to impeach Trump. Each now hates Trump for the political whirlwind that followed, effectively ending their political careers.

Just how did this rabidly Never-Trump kangaroo committee metastasize? When it was first established, House Minority Leader Kevin McCarthy proposed fully *five* Republican members. When Speaker Pelosi rejected Ohio's Jim Jordan and Indiana's Jim Banks, McCarthy should have called a strike against the House until his selections were seated—or at least offered replacements along with a minority counsel. In either case, there would have been near partisan balance and ample opportunity for Republicans to keep Democrats in check.

Instead, McCarthy played right into Pelosi's hands by refusing to seat *any* Republicans. Pelosi countered by seating the RINOs Cheney and Kinzinger, and the Never-Trump game was on.

Unfettered by any Republican restraint, this kangaroo committee has decidedly *not* sought to get to the bottom of what happened on January 6. Instead, through the illegal and unconstitutional weaponization of Congress's investigatory powers, the committee's primary mission has been to shackle Donald Trump with criminal charges so as to keep Trump out of the White House and try to coerce and intimidate Trump advisers like me with threats of imprisonment.

Here, Pelosi knows full well that if her unruly mob can put Donald Trump in prison, he won't be out on the hustings campaigning any time soon. *Bye, bye, Trump 2024. Hello, civil war in America.*

Here's the overarching strategic political point:

If Pelosi stays in power as House majority leader through 2024, she and her minions will continue their all-out assault on Donald Trump in the days, weeks, and months leading up to both the presidential primary season as well as the general election, and it will be death by a thousand lies, leaks, and felonious innuendos.

To win back the Trump White House in 2024, we simply cannot have a Democrat Congress continually stirring up the political waters with their partisan abuse of Congress's investigatory powers. We must take that Pelosi abomination of a Congress back in the name of Trumpism, truth, and fairness.

Now, it is critical to emphasize here that this is not just a matter of Republicans seizing control of the House of Representatives. We must do everything in our powers to ensure that there are only *Trump Republicans* who are in full command of ALL of the major leadership positions.

These positions include House Speaker, whip, and conference chair along with the chairs of all of the major congressional committees—starting with the all-important Judiciary and Ways and Means Committees.

"No RINOs allowed" must be our Capitol Hill battle cry. As we have repeatedly discussed in this book, there continues to be a fierce battle within the Republican Party between Republican-in-name-only RINOs who derive their power from the globalist lucre of Wall Street, Silicon Valley, and multinational corporate interests versus Main Street Trumpists who embrace Populist Economic Nationalism and insist on secure borders, fair trade, and an end to endless wars.

Here, it is absolutely critical that we Deplorables—along with President Trump—firmly insist on the forced retirement of both Kevin McCarthy as Republican leader of the House and Mitch McConnell on the Senate side.

The only way these two leaders of the RINO pack have made their way up the greasy pole of congressional leadership has been by raising massive campaign contributions from the very same globalist corporate interests intent on taking down Donald Trump. McCarthy and McConnell have then these used this filthy lucre to help elect fellow RINO congressmen and senators who, in this Deep Swamp rite of passage, become beholden to McConnell and McCarthy and keep electing them as leaders.

This is a *systemic* failure; and it can only be addressed by taking out the current leadership trash. Remember here: every fish rots from the head down. So the heads of McCarthy and McConnell must roll. (By the way, my favorite replacement for McCarthy would be Ohio's Jim Jordan but there are others like Elise Stefanik who come readily to mind.)

The Tao of Trump

To make a Trump Republican House a reality in 2022, it all starts with Donald Trump. No one in political history has proven to be a more tireless and effective campaigner than the Boss, and he must go out and vigorously stump for every one of the candidates he endorses.

It follows that every candidate seeking Donald Trump's endorsement must first and foremost publicly embrace the Trump Populist Economic Nationalist and the Tough on China policy agendas laid out in this book. This means a firm candidate commitment to:

- The onshoring of American manufacturing jobs with the urgency of a Manhattan Project;
- Secure borders and the equally swift completion of a big, beautiful wall;
- The immediate deportation of all the illegal aliens entering the United States during the Biden regime;
- A swift return to strategic energy dominance;
- Cracking down on China's economic aggression through tough tariffs and by cutting off the flow of American capital and technology to Communist China; and
- An end to endless wars.

Each Trump-endorsed candidate must also provide an ironclad commitment to:

- A Trumpian, Teddy Roosevelt-style busting of the Big Tech Cancel Culture Not To Be Trusted likes of Google, YouTube, Facebook, and Twitter;
- Putting all those responsible for the Russia Hoax in jail; and
- Holding the Chinese Communist Party—along with Tony Fauci—both morally and financially accountable for unleashing a bioweapon and pandemic on America.

Of critical importance, every candidate seeking Trump's endorsement must likewise commit to getting to the bottom of both the stolen November 3 election and the January 6 violence.

Regarding that fateful January 6 day, a truly big remaining question is why House Speaker Pelosi allowed the Capitol to be so lightly guarded and why the Pentagon chose to keep National Guard troops at such a far distance despite repeated warnings from President Trump himself of possible violence. And yes, there is also that collateral disturbing question based on mounting evidence as to whether FBI informants and Antifa/BLM agitators played major roles in instigating the violence.[5]

There are other equally disturbing questions about Hunter Biden's "Laptop from Hell" that Trump-endorsed candidates must commit to thoroughly investigating. Here, the real scandal goes far beyond Hunter Biden's activities as an unregistered foreign lobbyist to cash in on his father's political celebrity. There also appears to have been numerous cover-ups of the Biden crime family scandal by federal law enforcement and America's national intelligence agencies seeking to insure a Biden victory in the November 3, 2020 election.[6] Moreover, this cover-up may well have started at the very top with Attorney General Bill Barr during the critical months leading up to that election.

While the Department of Justice may have had the laptop as early as December of 2019, the RINO Barr did nothing to authenticate its contents and advise the public accordingly.[7] As to why this matters, polls clearly indicate that if voters had been aware of the contents, Donald Trump would be president today.[8]

Use Your Human Agency

Down the grassroots chain, it is important that each of us donate either time or money to the slate of Trump candidates in the contestable districts and states where the House and Senate will be won or lost. To put this "contestable" point another way, please don't waste your time or money working for Trump candidates who are going to breeze to victory because of their popularity or the demographics of their district.

Instead, listen to shows like Steve Bannon's *WarRoom BattleGround* and find out *which* candidates are both worthy of your support and need your help to put them over the Trump top. Then, *please give these Trump-endorsed candidates whatever you can in time or money.*

With time, you can walk precincts, lick envelopes, or make phone calls. Alternatively, write a check for $5 or $5,000 *but* only for amounts you can reasonably afford.

Note that it is not just congressional races you should get involved in. If we are to win the White House back for Donald Trump in 2024, it is equally important you participate in down ballot races, particularly those races for secretary of state, and particularly in key 2024 battleground states like Arizona, Georgia, Michigan, Nevada, North Carolina, Pennsylvania, and Wisconsin.

In my *In Trump Time* book, I revealed how billionaires like George Soros and Mark Zuckerberg have used their megabucks to seize control of our election system and thereby contributed to the theft of the 2020 presidential race. Soros, in particular, was directly responsible for the election of secretaries of state in two key battlegrounds—Jocelyn Benson in Michigan and Kathy Boockvar in Pennsylvania. Soros-funded organizations also donated to Katie Hobbs in Arizona.[9]

Both Benson and Boockvar engaged in arguably illegal behavior to swing the election in favor of Joe Biden, teaching us once again that that "all politics is indeed local." Katie Hobbs was the single biggest impediment to getting a fair and legal count of the Arizona ballots.

So tune in to these secretary of state races particularly in 2022—and support Trump-endorsed candidates like Mark Finchem in Arizona, Jody Hice in Georgia, and Kristina Karamo in Michigan.[10] Trump-endorsed secretaries of state will be critical to stopping any attempt by the Democrats to steal the 2024 presidential election.

And if you are in Arizona, be sure to get behind Trump-endorsed Kari Lake, who is taking on the aforementioned Hobbs in the Arizona governor's race.

Finally, if you live in any of the battleground states where the 2020 election may well have been stolen, we also need to make sure that *every candidate for the state legislature supports a full canvas of the 2020 vote in their state.*

As I have said often, "It's the canvas, not the count." It is only through a thorough grassroots canvas of the vote that illegal absentee ballots can be fully identified. Remember here that it was only through such a canvas that it was ultimately determined that John F. Kennedy and the Democrats almost certainly stole the 1960 presidential election from Richard Nixon.

In the canon of Bannon, it must be Action, Action, Action, and we must all use our human agency to move the Trump needle up and down the ladder of the political offices that matter. Such action will be a key ingredient of the secret sauce for taking back the White House for Donald Trump in 2024.

THIRTY-ONE

No Facebook, No Fox, No Problem

Dominion Voting Systems on Friday morning filed a $1.6 billion defamation lawsuit against Fox News, alleging that the conservative network pushed false accusations that the voting company had rigged the 2020 election.... Dominion has...filed similar billion-dollar defamation suits against other Trump allies...including Rudy Giuliani, Trump's personal attorney... and Mike Lindell, the Trump-aligned pillow magnate.

—ABC News, March 26, 2021[11]

To return Trump to the White House in 2024, we must all kick the Facebook-Google-Twitter habit even as we endeavor to cut the Fox cable news cord.

I have made it abundantly clear here that Silicon Valley's social media oligarchs have become America's self-anointed censors and thought-control shifters. So every day you engage with Facebook and Twitter, limit your internet searches to Google, or view videos on Google's YouTube, you run the very real risk of being spoon-fed disinformation by woke leftists who have already revealed themselves to be virulently Never-Trump and who seek nothing less than to indoctrinate you and your children into the ways of their radical cancel culture, virtue signaling world.

Accordingly, we must begin this very day to wean ourselves from the worst of the worst of these woke organizations. So…

- As a substitute for Google's search engine, try DuckDuckGo;
- To kick the YouTube habit, give Rumble a spin; and
- On the Facebook/Twitter front, how about the Trump-backed Truth Social or my favorite "Twitter Killer" which I am helping to build—a social media app called GETTR.

More broadly, as the 2022 and 2024 election seasons approach, we in the Trump movement *must* work together to build alternative social media communities within which we can communicate directly and honestly with one another, without fear of censorship, shadow banning, or other tricks of the Facebook-Google-Twitter crowd.

Cutting the Fox News Cord

As we have also discussed extensively in this book, far too much of the so-called "mainstream media" spoon-feed us fake rather than real news. At the top of this pyramid of disinformation sits the overtly uber-liberal CNN, MSNBC, and PBS. Yet this problem also bleeds down to the broadcast news of ABC, CBS, and NBC, and this misinformation is particularly acute on Sunday shows like what the Boss likes to call Sleepy Chuck Todd's "Meet the Depressed" and Margaret Brennan's "Deface the Nation."

Yet, the biggest danger to a Trump 2024 presidential victory may not be any of these woke progressive news outlets who wear their Never-Trumpism on their teleprompters but rather a news organization that far too many in Trump Land still trust and still believe supports Donald Trump's return to the White House. I'm talking, of course, about the Fox Corporation with its Fox News and Fox Business flagships.

As we have discussed, in the golden era of Roger Ailes, Fox was a reliable conservative trumpet—and during the 2016 campaign, a fair and indefatigable Trump supporter. Today, however, Fox is at war with itself—to the point where a contentious battle between pro- and anti-Trump forces now ominously threatens both the rise of Donald Trump in 2024 and the taking of Congress by *Trump* Republicans in 2022.

The precipitating event for what effectively has been a Never-Trump coup at Fox was a multi-billion-dollar defamation suit filed by Dominion Voting Systems against Fox over its coverage of alleged voting machine fraud and irregularities in the November 3 election. In the face of that lawsuit, Fox fired the inimitable pro-Trump Lou Dobbs as a sacrificial lamb.

Fox's hope was that Dominion's lawyers would back off—or at least that is how much of the media reported the Dobbs de-platforming. Noted CNN Business:

> *Fox News' official reason for canceling Lou Dobbs' show—a post-election programing adjustment—doesn't quite add up. Dobbs was the highest-rated host on Fox Business. He often doubled his lead-in's ratings.*
>
> *Although Fox isn't saying, the timing of Dobbs' cancellation Friday appears to be no coincidence: It took place 24 hours after Dobbs and Fox were named in a $2.7 billion defamation lawsuit filed by voting technology company Smartmatic.*
>
> *Fox may see Dobbs as an acceptable sacrificial lamb. NPR media correspondent David Folkenflik said...that the network's decision... reminds him of the way Rupert Murdoch's news tabloids in London handled their phone-hacking scandals about a decade ago. "They would throw somebody over the side and see if that was enough."*[12]

Since the filing of the Dominion lawsuit, Fox has been a pale shadow of its former Roger Ailes self. On the one hand, Fox personalities like Tucker Carlson, Laura Ingraham, and Sean Hannity still seem to be at least mostly in sync with the Trump agenda. Each is, in fact, too big to be completely silenced by Fox management given their robust ratings.

On the other hand, Fox also has a key and influential member of its board of directors in former RINO congressman Paul Ryan who is as anti-Trump as it gets. Corporate governance may therefore be having a hand in guiding the Never-Trump movement inside Fox.

Talent-wise, there is also Fox's Karl Rove faction to contend with. Rove, as we have discussed in this book, is one of the biggest Trump haters on the planet, and Kingmaker Karl still hits very much above his weight when it comes to moving the on-air Fox Never-Trump agenda.

In fact, Rove is actively campaigning against Trump-endorsed candidates in key districts across the country, and Rove is in sync with other Never-Trumpers on Fox News, from Bret Baier and John Roberts to Brian Kilmeade and, before he left for CNN, the ever-acerbic Chris Wallace.

The not-so-stealth Never-Trump movement at Fox is further complicated by Fox's cancel culture executive team in charge of Fox programming and talent development. Both Suzanne Scott, the CEO of Fox News and Fox Business, and Lauren Petterson, president of Fox Business, have played key roles in keeping true Trump surrogates off the Fox airwaves like the aforementioned Rudy Giuliani and Mike Lindell along with, I might add, yours truly.

My case is particularly instructive as it draws a sharp contrast between former Trump officials like Larry Kudlow and Kayleigh McEnany who have bent the Never-Trump knee before Fox. They who are now flourishing with their on-air appearances—Kudlow with his own show and McEnany as a contributor.

In contrast, after leaving the White House, I was repeatedly invited by a large number of Fox News and Fox Business anchors and hosts to appear on their shows. This long list includes most prominently Judge Jeanine Pirro for her now cancelled eponymous Justice show—Jeanine initially invited me to be a weekly contributor to host a "five alarm fire" policy segment but that got nixed by Suzanne Scott.

In addition, I received repeated invites from other Fox pro-Trumpers like Rachel Campos-Duffy, Charles Payne, Mark Steyn, Gerard Baker, and Maria Bartiromo. Yet almost just as often, my requested appearances would be vetoed by "the second floor"—that's Fox code for Suzanne Scott, Lauren Petterson, and others in the executive suites.

On several occasions, even the seemingly untouchable Tucker Carlson was pressured to cancel long form interviews with me scheduled for his Fox Nation show. Fox producers have even killed pre-taped segments of mine that were scheduled to air—including a beauty on Fauci's role in funding bioweapons gain-of-function research at the Wuhan lab.

Here's the really broader point I'm trying to make: if we folks out here in Trump Land can't trust Fox to have the Boss's back when he will be fighting a huge woke and radical multimedia cartel leading into the 2024 cycle, then we must cut the Fox cable cord. To be abundantly clear and exact:

We must cut the Fox cable cord until Fox ceases its cancel culture, Never-Trump ways.

The Boss must lead the way on this. He should cease doing any and all interviews with Fox News and Fox Business unless and until the network both restores coverage of his rallies and ceases its cancellation of pro-Trump surrogates who hold different views than the Never-Trump producers, executives, and talent hiding behind the conservative Fox umbrella.

And Boss, this must be a highly disciplined and blanket ban. So no Tucker. No Sean. No Laura. No Maria. Not even a whiff of Mark Levin no matter how tempting.

While these folks have all shown strong sympatico with Trump and the Trump movement, each of these highly talented Fox hosts has been under tremendous pressure to reject many of the basic tenets of a Trump 2024 campaign, first and foremost of which is the issue of a stolen election.

No Cold Fox Turkey

In cutting the Fox cable cord, you, dear reader, will certainly not need to go cold turkey.

Today, for example, one of the very best sources of Trump and MAGA-related news is a pair of Steve Bannon shows—*War Room: Pandemic* and the aforementioned *WarRoom BattleGround*. Over the course of four hours a day, Bannon and his cadres of in-the-trenches journalists offer real news packaged in hard-edged analysis.

You may also want to consider as part of your daily news diet livestreaming Newsmax, One America News Network (OANN), Real America's Voice, Charlie Kirk's Turning Point USA featuring Jack Posobiec, and Mike Lindell's new Lindell-TV network.

On the written word front, I once again strongly recommend websites like the Hoft Brothers' Gateway Pundit, Just the News with John Solomon, Revolver News with Darren Beattie, Raheem Kassam's National Pulse, The Federalist featuring stars like Mollie Hemingway, and the hands-down best alternative national newspaper in the country, *The Epoch Times.*

And by the way, Boss, you may want to pursue a policy of détente with CNN leading up to the 2024 election. With Never-Trumpers Jeff

Zucker and Chris Cuomo gone in a cloud of sex scandals, with Zucker's replacement Chris Licht talking about a return to straight news, and with Liberty Media's John Malone publicly denouncing CNN for its woke content and bias—Liberty has a big stake in CNN—there may be an opportunity here.[13]

If hacks like John Berman, Alisyn Camerota, and Jake Tapper are put out to pasture, that may be your sign, Boss, to move in with an olive branch. In the meantime dear reader, please also consider this:

Even as you are cutting the Fox cable cord, do tune in on occasion to both CNN and MSNBC.

"Know thy enemy," is the concept here and there is no better way to understand the Never-Trump spin than to get it right from the horses' asses.

THIRTY-TWO

Good Personnel Is Good Policy Is Good Politics

You can tell a man by the company he keeps.

—Saki, *The Chronicles of Clovis*[14]

During his first term, Donald Trump became the greatest president in modern history *in spite* of Bad Personnel who regularly sought to disrupt, delay, or deter his Populist Economic Nationalist and Tough on China policy agendas.

During his second term, the Boss must succeed because of Good Personnel. There should be nothing left to chance.

Here is just one possible game plan to ensure that Good Personnel will end in Good Politics, both during the 2024 election season and once Donald John Trump reclaims the White House.

The VEEP Sweepstakes

The Boss should start by choosing a MAGA-sympatico VP as early as possible. Two who should lead the list include former secretary of state Mike Pompeo and Florida governor Ron DeSantis.

Pompeo weighs in with a heavy foreign policy advantage and clearly understands the existential threat that Communist China poses. DeSantis has shown courage *and* intelligence under pandemic fire. Of the two,

DeSantis clearly wins the popularity with voters contest, at least at this stage in the race.

In the VP discussion, there is also talk of South Dakota governor Kristi Noem. My guess is that she might be far better suited at this stage in her career for a high-ranking cabinet secretary position. With both Communist China and Russia on the revanchist move and both Iran and North Korea moving ever closer to a first strike nuclear capability on the United States, 2024 will no doubt be an election heavily weighted with foreign policy concerns. Like DeSantis, Noem simply does not yet have those foreign policy chops.

As for those who definitely should *not* be in the VEEP sweepstakes, the Boss has already and rightly ruled out Mike Pence—the *et tu Brute* traitor I memorialized in my *In Trump Time* book. At the top of the rest of this no-fly zone list, there is the ever-dangerous Lean and Hungry Look Nikki "Cassius" Haley along with Ted Cruz, who may be a good "conservative" in the narrow sense but simply does not have MAGA in his DNA.

Likewise on the *definitely not* list should be the rising star of Virginia governor Glenn Youngkin. While Youngkin may sound intriguing, one look at his globalist resume and ties to Wall Street offshoring predators like the Carlyle Group and McKinsey make Youngkin a non-starter.

In between the Big Yes possibilities and Certain Nos, we will also hear talk of candidates from the US Senate like Josh Hawley and Tom Cotton. Hawley likely took himself out of contention with his gratuitous, Mitch McConnell- and Karl Rove-coordinated hit on Missouri gubernatorial candidate Eric Greitens in March of 2022.[15]

Tom Cotton is as pure a China Hawk as they come and largely in tune with the Trump agenda. Here, Cotton's one big slam directed at Trump was a sniper shot at the Trump-sponsored First Step legislation, which has led to the early release of thousands of criminals in Federal prisons.[16]

Cotton ridiculed First Step as "soft on crime," but that attack may actually win Cotton points with the Boss since that legislation was a Made in Kushner fiasco—and the Boss knows it. Yet, I would far prefer Cotton as secretary of defense and designated Pentagon cleanser as he may lack the charisma and charm to campaign effectively as a vice president.

Last take: If DeSantis were to agree to the VP slot *prior* to the primary season, this single action would likely clear the entire Republican field. And by the way, Trump-DeSantis 2024 would likely be unstoppable.

DeSantis should see the wisdom of accepting such an offer from Trump as it would similarly clear the field for DeSantis in 2028 and usher in what would likely be the beginning of an eight-year run of DeSantis's own as president through 2036.

Memo to Ron: patience is as patience does.

Establishing a Trump Shadow Cabinet

In the spirit of "the best surprises are no surprises," and given the previous track record of less-than-stellar cabinet appointments as documented in this book, POTUS may also want to consider putting together an extensive deep bench "shadow cabinet." This brain trust should consist of some of the top people the Boss intends to appoint as cabinet secretaries and agency heads.

Here, the process should begin by putting some of the "old gang" back together again—at least those in the Trump administration who served with distinction and loyalty and deserve a second turn, either in their old post or a new one.

Some Trump "old gang" choices might include:

- Former Trump national security advisor Robert O'Brien moving to secretary of state;
- The ever-loyal and wise Ben Carson as secretary of Health and Human Services where he should have gone to begin with;
- Bob Lighthizer moving from his post as US trade representative to secretary of commerce with Nazak Nikakhtar as DepSec;
- Bob's old General Counsel Stephen Vaughn rising as the new USTR;
- Kash Patel coming out of the National Security Council shadows to serve as director of national intelligence;
- John Ratcliffe moving from DNI director to head the CIA;
- Ken Cuccinelli returning as head of Homeland Security and his co-pilot Mark Morgan once again leading Customs and Border Protection.

- Dan Brouillette in a second turn at Energy;
- Linda McMahon moving from the Small Business Administration to Housing and Urban Development;
- David Bernhardt in a second turn as secretary of interior; and
- Robert Wilkie returning at Veterans Affairs;

As for some "new gang" blood—with strong Trump loyalty ties—how about:

- Judge Jeanine Pirro at the Department of Justice as attorney general with my old staffer David Foley at the helm of the Office of Legal Counsel;
- Former Congressman Sean Duffy as secretary of transportation;
- A once falsely "me-too-ed" Andy Puzder finally as secretary of labor;
- Marcia Lee Kelly to run the Department of Education;
- Bill Gertz as another possibility for either DNI or CIA;
- Oracle CEO Safra Catz or Lara Trump as UN ambassador;
- Jim Fanell or Toshi Yoshihara as secretary of the navy; and
- Mike Pillsbury, Frank Gaffney, or Brian Kennedy as ambassador to China.

And for the health care and pandemic-related bureaucracies, how about:

- Doctor Robert Malone to run the National Institutes of Health;
- Dr. Harvey Risch as head of the FDA; and
- Either Dr. Steven Hatfill or Dr. Peter McCullough at the helm of the CDC?

This shadow cabinet could begin meeting regularly with the Boss at Mar-a-Lago and Bedminster to both critique Biden regime policies as well as to put forth initiatives to address the numerous crises this nation is facing.

As a "dominate the daily news cycle" bonus, these Trump shadow cabinet members could also begin appearing as Trump 2024 surrogates across the cable and broadcast news diaspora and out on the flyover country stump preaching the gospel of Trumpism. Of course, if any of these would-be cabinet secretaries were to stumble, Trump would be able to make a midcourse correction rather than be shackled with them once his second term begins.

A Rock Solid White House

Given the numerous Bad Personnel POTUS was saddled with *within the White House itself*, it would be equally useful to identify those who will likely serve in key senior staff positions.

Again, in the spirit of "getting the old gang back together again," John McEntee *must* be at the head of the list to return as director of personnel or in a possible turn as chief of staff. There is no one I trust more than Johnny Mac to have the Boss's back and pick the right Trump loyalists for the right jobs.

As first among "old gang" equals, there is also the Boss's old Tweet Meister and close personal friend Dan Scavino. He should be put in charge of the whole press shop and be given full authority to run the place—with Andy Surabian (the Ed Rollins of his time) handling the director of strategic communications post.

And of course Steve Bannon should serve as chief strategist.

Without question, I would also put the Boss's original "Body Man" during the 2016 campaign Keith Schiller back at the Boss's right shoulder as part of the operations side of the White House. Keith is gruff, tough, and no-nonsense—just my kind of guy.

Other "old gang" stars who bleed true Trump red, white, and blue include Jim Schultz, Bill McGinley, and Catherine Keller. Each is perfectly qualified for the positions of either staff secretary or White House legal counsel while McGinley could slip easily into the role of director of political affairs as well.

In this "old gang" vein, Rick Dearborn should finally be given the chance to run Legislative Affairs—although his past close affiliation with Senator Jeff Sessions may be a bump in the road for a Boss who rightly thinks Sessions was one of his worst cabinet picks.

Of course, Tyler Goodspeed should be given back the reins of the Council of Economic Advisers—or perhaps take the coveted treasury secretary spot.

As for Stephen Miller, he should direct his considerable energies to running the Domestic Policy Council and immigration policy and gracefully bow out from any speechwriting duties. He did a heck of a job in that post for five long years, from the campaign to the end of the Boss's first term. But this will be a new administration with new challenges, and the Boss will need a daily flood of fresh ideas.

As for "new gang" possibilities:

- Maria Bartiromo would make a heck of a press secretary;
- Dave Bossie *must* be chief of staff for operations;
- Dave's frequent co-author Corey Lewandowski *should always be at the Boss's side* as a senior counselor;
- Steve Cortes would be perfect as director of the National Economic Council;
- Jack Posobiec would be a brilliant young gun choice for national security advisor; and
- Martin Silverstein should be director of personnel if Johnny Mac moves to chief of staff—or at least get his long sought-after post as director of the US Agency for International Development.

As for yours truly, a Senate run by the Republican likes of Mitch McConnell, Mitt Romney, Chuck Grassley, Ben Sasse, and Lindsey Graham would never confirm me for any cabinet position—treasury would have been my choice.

In the White House, if I were chief of staff, I'd run it as a triumvirate with Bossie and Johnny Mac, while director of the National Economic Council would be a natural fit—as it would have been in the Boss's first term.

By the way, if I had been director of the National Economic Council from day one and Gary Cohn and Larry Kudlow had never darkened the door of the NEC, Donald Trump would have won in a landslide.

That said, I'd be just as happy to just see POTUS once again behind the Resolute Desk, but this time flanked by competent people he and the nation can trust. As the Buddha has said, "Desire is suffering," and the minute you want something in this life—especially anything in the Deep Swamp of Washington—somebody is going to have power over you.

A Bad Personnel Purge

Just as the Boss must surround himself with competent and loyal people, he would also be very well served by publicly cutting ties with all of the Bad Personnel he was associated with in his first term. Here, although this may stir up uncomfortable family issues, POTUS 47 must first and foremost signal a Jared Kushner-free administration.

Fortunately, Kushner has made the Boss's job easy in this regard. Kushner has already disqualified himself from future White House employment by cashing in on his White House connections to fund his entrepreneurial ventures. Jared is now simply too beholden to foreign nationals to get a top-level security clearance.

That said, the Clown Prince will still no doubt try to worm his way back into the White House or as an ambassador or special envoy. Please pull a Nancy Reagan here, Boss, and just say no.

Even after you read this book, Boss, you will still have no idea just how much damage the Kushner Rasputin did to you and your agenda during his four years at 1600 Pennsylvania Avenue, and that work of fiction Jared has published about his time in the White House is just self-serving manure to obscure such damage.

As for the rest of the not-so best, the Boss would likewise do well to purge forever all those on the Trump 2020 campaign who failed so miserably both to prosecute the campaign itself and seek remedies for a stolen election. Besides Kushner, those who should never darken the Trump 2024 campaign door include Brad Parscale, Bill Stepien, Justin Clark, and Alex Cannon.

Kindhearted though he is, POTUS may also want to avoid like the plague any rapprochement with any of those Bad Personnel who worked behind his back and did so much to harm his administration. As I fully document in this book, this far-too-lengthy roster includes scoundrels and fools ranging from Steve Mnuchin, Larry Kudlow, Gary Cohn, Derek Lyons, and Mick Mulvaney to Chris Liddell, Joe Hagin, H. R. McMaster, Rob Porter, and Mark Meadows.

Remember here, Boss: Both Kudlow and Mulvaney publicly abandoned you after January 6 while Meadows ignored your direction to assert executive privilege and failed to bring home the economic stimulus bacon. In the meantime, like Kushner, Mnuchin is cashing in all his chits from Wall Street to Beijing for selling your trade and tariff policies out to the Chinese Communists, European Union burghers, and other foreign governments.

And, Boss: How about establishing a Lindsey Graham-free zone at Mar-a-Lago, Bedminster, and all Trump golf courses. This poodle of a politician is pure Trump kryptonite who repeatedly failed in his duties to investigate the Russia Hoax—to the point of never EVER following through on his tough talk promises as chair of the Senate Judiciary Committee to subpoena witnesses and hold hearings.

Even more to the point, Lindsey Graham's instincts on key policy issues, including his penchant for amnesty for illegals and open borders, are anathema to the Trump Deplorables base. So please, Boss: no phone calls from Lindsey, no golf games, no visits to Mar-a-Lago, and no rally appearances for the not-so-great senator from the truly great state of South Carolina.

In this same out-with-the-scoundrels vein, you may want to put Liz Harrington or Susie Wiles in charge of immediately cleaning up the roster of what has been billed as your "think tank."

This America First Policy Institute *should* have been the fountainhead of your Trump 2024 policy initiatives. Instead, it has turned out to be a gravy train employing all manner of mediocrity and Never-Trump grifters, including many like Larry Kudlow, Chad Wolf, and Cliff Sims who opposed your policies or did you damage during your first term.

Indeed, other than a few high caliber members like Keith Kellogg, David Bernhardt, and Andy Puzder, these grifters need to get off the Boss's dole and be replaced by true Trumpers of the highest intellectual caliber.

Roll Heads at the RNC

Finally, there is the festering matter of a RINO-infested Republican National Committee. Here, one of the worst choices the Boss made after the 2020 election was to allow Ronna McDaniel to continue as RNC Chair.

McDaniel did an absolutely horrendous job during the 2020 election cycle. She both captained the titanic loss of the White House and Senate even as Pelosi consolidated her power in the House.

In the aftermath of that November 3 debacle—and with both Mitch McConnell and McDaniel's uncle Mitt Romney cheering her on—Ronna Romney McDaniel also master-minded the stealth opposition of the RNC to legally contest the results of the 2020 election.

Yes, when Rudy Giuliani and Bernie Kerik desperately needed money, staff, and lawyers to fight the good fight to "stop the steal," Ronna and the RNC were nowhere to be found. As Bannon loves to say, there are no conspiracies, but there are no coincidences.

So how about either the aforementioned Liz Harrington or Marcia Lee Kelly as RNC head? Harrington did yeoman's work as a Trump surrogate at the RNC and is pure nails. Marcia Kelly was an absolute force at the White House, has served as director of operations for the RNC so she knows the terrain, and ably staffed the First Lady.

Replacing McDaniel with either of these dynamic Republican women would turn this critical cog in the 2024 Trump victory machine from a stuck in the mud vintage Ford Falcon into a Shelby Cobra.

So as the Boss does indeed love to say: Let's Go!

Let's go take the House and White House back under the banner of Trumpism and make some history!

Endnotes

PART ONE

1 Matthew Boesler and Emily Graffeo, *Bloomberg*, "Why Stagflation Is Back on Some Traders' Radars," *Washington Post*, February 27, 2022, https://www.washingtonpost.com/business/energy/why-stagflation-is-back-on-some-traders-radars/2022/02/2 5/8e93e83c-95f8-11ec-bb31-74fc06c0a3a5_story.html.
   See also: Greg Ritchie and Liz McCormick, "Investors Seek Refuge From Surging Costs, Stagflation Threat," *Bloomberg*, February 24, 2022, https://www.bloomberg.com/news/articles/2022-02-24/investors-scramble-for-inflation-protection-after-russia-attack.

2 Jeff Cox, "Inflation has taken away all the wage gains for workers and then some," CNBC, November 10, 2021, https://www.cnbc.com/2021/11/10/inflation-has-taken-away-all-the-wage-gains-for-workers-and-then-some.html.

3 Callie Patteson, "New photos reveal disturbing conditions at US-Mexico border facilities." *New York Post*, January 11, 2022, https://nypost.com/2022/01/11/new-photos-show-disturbing-conditions-at-us-mexico-border-facilities/.

4 Charlotte Cuthbertson and Steve Lance, "Cartels Have Operational Control of US Border, Are 'Terrorizing' the US, Rep. Chip Roy Says," *The Epoch Times*, January 30, 2022, https://www.theepochtimes.com/cartels-have-operational-control-of-us-border-are-terrorizing-the-us-says-rep-chip-roy_4245522.html.

5 "Illegal immigrants bring disease into the U.S.," Times-News, August 31, 2018, https://www.thetimesnews.com/story/opinion/columns/2018/08/31/column-illegal-immigrants-bring-disease-into-us/10881450007/ get more data for other diseases.

6 Rebecca Camber, "Afghanistan is becoming a breeding ground for jihadis again just months after the West's withdrawal in the face of Taliban advancements and they will pose a threat to the UK, MI5 chief warns," *Daily Mail*, February 20, 2022, https://www.dailymail.co.uk/news/article-10533393/Afghanistan-breeding-ground-jihadis-months-Wests-withdrawal-MI5-chief-warns.html.

7 Dominic Giannini, "Putin 'determined to rebuild' Soviet Union," 7News.com.au, February 24, 2022, https://7news.com.au/politics/ukraines-top-diplomat-calls-for-help-c-5832524.

8   Darragh Roche, "Biden Admin Turning to Venezuela for Oil Sparks Bipartisan Backlash," *Newsweek*, March 8, 2022, https://www.newsweek.com/biden-admin-venezuela-oil-sparks-bipartisan-backlash-nicolas-maduro-1685866.

9   Gustaf Kilander, "Covid death toll under Biden will soon overtake number of lives lost under Trump," Independent, January 14, 2022, https://www.independent. co.uk/news/world/americas/us-politics/covid-omicron-death-rates-biden-latest-b1993234.html.

10 Tal Axelrod, "More voters would pick Trump over Biden if election were held today: poll," *The Hill*, December 6, 2021, https://thehill.com/homenews/campaign/584585-more-voters-would-pick-trump-over-biden-if-election-were-held-today-poll.

11 Jenni Fink, "A Third of Voters Think 2020 Election Should Be Overturned, but Fewer Think It Will Be," *Newsweek*, October 27, 2021, https://www.newsweek.com/third-voters-think-2020-election-should-overturned-fewer-think-it-will-1643093.

12 Kristen Palamara, "15 Quotes From West Wing That Will Stick With Us Forever," Screenrant.com, November 23, 2020, https://screenrant.com/west-wing-quotes/. https://screenrant.com/west-wing-quotes/

13 Dave Boyer, "White House not a 'dump' for Trump but others disagree," *Washington Times*, August 2, 2017, https://www.washingtontimes.com/news/2017/aug/2/white-house-a-dump-for-trump/.

14 Boyer.

15 Jason Horowitz et al., "Breaking down the Situation Room," *Washington Post*, May 5, 2011, https://www.washingtonpost.com/wp-srv/lifestyle/style/situation-room.html.

16 Allan Smith, "This White House staffer might have the most important behind-the-scenes job in the administration – controlling what gets to Trump," *Business Insider*, September 7, 2017, https://www.businessinsider.com/rob-porter-trump-white-house-staff-secretary-2017-8.

17 Angela Fritz, "What's behind the intense 2017 Atlantic hurricane season," *Washington Post*, September 23, 2017, https://www.washingtonpost.com/news/capital-weather-gang/wp/2017/09/23/harvey-irma-maria-why-is-this-hurricane-season-so-bad/.

18 Jonathan Cheng, "Contradicting Trump, McMaster says U.S. will pay for South Korean Thaad deployment," MarketWatch.com, April 30, 2017, https://www.marketwatch.com/story/contradicting-trump-mcmaster-says-us-will-pay-for-south-korean-thaad-deployment-2017-04-30.

19 "National Security Act of 1947," Govinfo.gov, https://www.govinfo.gov/content/pkg/COMPS-1493/pdf/COMPS-1493.pdf.

20 "National Security Council," Obama White House Archives.gov, https://obamawhitehouse.archives.gov/administration/eop/nsc/.

21 Mark F. Cancian, "Limiting Size of NSC Staff," Center for Strategic and International Studies, July 1, 2016, https://www.csis.org/analysis/limiting-size-nsc-staff.

22 Rosie Gray, "H.R. McMaster Cleans House at the National Security Council," *The Atlantic*, August 2, 2017, https://www.theatlantic.com/politics/archive/2017/08/hr-mcmaster-cleans-house-at-the-national-security-council/535767/.

23 "Citizens United v. Federal Election Commission 558 U.S. 310 (2010)," Justia, US Supreme Court, January 21, 2010, https://supreme.justia.com/cases/federal/us/558/310/.

Endnotes

24 Jon Schwarz, "Donald Trump's White House Counsel is Proud 'Architect' of America's Corrupt Big Money Politics," *The Intercept*, December 4, 2016, https://theintercept.com/2016/12/04/donald-trumps-general-counsel-is-proud-architect-of-americas-corrupt-big-money-politics/.

25 Schwarz.

26 Michael D. Shear et al., "Judge Blocks Trump Order on Refugees Amid Chaos and Outcry Worldwide," *New York Times,* January 28, 2017, https://www.nytimes.com/2017/01/28/us/refugees-detained-at-us-airports-prompting-legal-challenges-to-trumps-immigration-order.html%20/.

27 Andrew Restuccia et al., "White House bracing for another staff shakeup," *Politico*, November 10, 2017, https://www.politico.com/story/2017/11/10/white-house-staff-shake-ups-244779.

PART TWO

1 "Donald Trump's Jobs Speech Full Transcript," Live Index.org, June 29, 2016, https://liveindex.org/24324/2016/06/donald-trumps-jobs-speech-full-transcript/.

2 Peter Navarro, "The Economics of the 'China Price'," *China Perspectives*, November–December 2006, https://journals.openedition.org/chinaperspectives/3063.

3 "Donald Trump's Jobs Speech Full Transcript," Live Index.org.

4 "Donald Trump's Jobs Speech Full Transcript."

5 "Donald Trump's Jobs Speech Full Transcript."

6 Ben Popken, "Why Trump Killed TPP – And Why It Matters To You," NBC News, January 23, 2017, https://www.nbcnews.com/business/economy/why-trump-killed-tpp-why-it-matters-you-n710781.

7 Avalon Zoppo et al., "Here's the Full List of Donald Trump's Executive Orders," NBC News, February 14, 2017, https://www.nbcnews.com/politics/white-house/here-s-full-list-donald-trump-s-executive-orders-n720796.

8 Joseph S. Pete, "Trump nominee Wilbur Ross a divisive figure in steel industry," NWI Times.com, December 4, 2016, https://www.nwitimes.com/business/steel/trump-nominee-wilbur-ross-a-divisive-figure-in-steel-industry/article_6ff2b253-45be-576c-99c9-91837c710a06.html.

9 John Bowden, "Trump pressured Mnuchin on labeling China a currency manipulator: report," *The Hill*, August 15, 2019, https://thehill.com/policy/finance/457603-trump-pressured-mnuchin-to-label-china-a-currency-manipulator-report.

10 Jacob Pramuk, "Trump spent about half of what Clinton did on his way to the presidency," CNBC, November 9, 2016, https://www.cnbc.com/2016/11/09/trump-spent-about-half-of-what-clinton-did-on-his-way-to-the-presidency.html.

11 "Oprah Winfrey Interviews Donald Trump in 1988," YouTube video, uploaded by user Andrew Philbrick on July 30, 2015, https://www.youtube.com/watch?v=GZpMJeynBeg.

12 "Speech: Donald Trump Delivers a Speech at the New York Economics Club, September 15, 2016," YouTube video, uploaded by Factbase Videos on September 2, 2019, https://www.youtube.com/watch?v=nrJSttssNZI.

13 Alexander B. Gray and Peter Navarro, "Donald Trump's Peace Through Strength Vision for the Asia-Pacific," *Foreign Policy*, November 7, 2016, https://foreignpolicy.com/2016/11/07/donald-trumps-peace-through-strength-vision-for-the-asia-pacific/.

14 Jason Silverstein, "Lawsuit says Trump 2016 campaign staffer was punished after supervisor got her pregnant," CBS, December 24, 2019, https://www.cbsnews.com/news/trump-2016-campaign-staffer-says-she-was-punished-after-supervisor-got-her-pregnant-lawsuit/.

15 Igor Bobic, "Trump Spokesman Jason Miller Says He Won't Take Top White House Job," *Huffington Post*, December 24, 2016, https://www.huffpost.com/entry/jason-miller-trump-white-house_n_585f18d3e4b0de3a08f58df4.

16 Eric Levitz, "White House (Falsely) Declares Trump's Inauguration Crowd the Largest in History," *New York Magazine*, January 21, 2017, https://nymag.com/intelligencer/2017/01/the-trump-white-house-is-already-disseminating-propaganda.html#:~:text=The%20White%20House%20press%20secretary%20further%20bolstered%20his,Metro%20Authority's%20initial%20estimates%20tell%20a%20different%20story.

17 Brian Stelter, "In their own words: The story of covering Election Night 2016," CNN Business, January 5, 2017, https://money.cnn.com/2017/01/05/media/election-night-news-coverage-oral-history/index.html.

18 "Peter Navarro: Dow 25,000 Within Donald Trump's First Term | Squawk Box | CNBC," YouTube video, uploaded by CNBC on November 9, 2016, https://www.youtube.com/watch?v=zWDlMq9mjRk.

19 Dan McCue, "Dow Jones Industrial Average Tops 25,000 for First Time," Courthouse News Service, January 4, 2018, https://www.courthousenews.com/dow-jones-industrial-average-tops-25000-for-first-time/.

20 Moving to 25,000 from 18,859—that's where the Dow was the day after Election Day—represented a 33 percent gain, to be exact.

21 Damian Paletta, "Border adjustment tax plan splits White House officials," *Washington Post*, March 3, 2017, https://www.heraldnet.com/business/border-adjustment-tax-plan-splits-white-house-officials/.

22 "Biographical Data, Mark Green," *The Hill*, https://thehill.com/people/mark-green.

23 Toshi Yoshihara and James R. Holmes, *Red Star Over the Pacific*, US Naval Institute Press, 2010.

24 Jamey Keaten, "Postal union accepts reform, quashes US walkout threat," Associated Press, September 25, 2019, https://apnews.com/article/europe-international-news-peter-navarro-china-united-states-462275bdffed4f60b43a47799c93312d.

25 Keaten.

26 Damian Palette and Nick Timiraos, "Trump Names Goldman President Gary Cohn Director of National Economic Council," *Wall Street Journal*, December 12, 2016, https://www.wsj.com/articles/trump-names-goldman-president-gary-cohn-as-director-of-national-economic-council-1481573082

27 "Press Release - President-Elect Donald J. Trump Appoints Dr. Peter Navarro to Head the White House National Trade Council," December 21, 2016, https://www.presidency.ucsb.edu/documents/press-release-president-elect-donald-j-trump-appoints-dr-peter-navarro-head-the-white.

Endnotes

PART THREE

1 "'This American carnage': Trump's inauguration speech, January 20, 2017," *Sydney Morning Herald*, January 20, 2021, https://www.smh.com.au/world/north-america/this-american-carnage-trump-s-inauguration-speech-january-20-2017-20210120-p56vkm.html.

2 Michael D. Shear, "Chief of Staff Orders an Overhaul for Security Clearances," *New York Times*, February 16, 2018, https://www.nytimes.com/2018/02/16/us/politics/john-kelly-rob-porter-clearance.html.

3 Melissa Chan, "It Started Raining the Moment Donald Trump Was Inaugurated President," *Time*, January 20, 2017, https://time.com/4641165/donald-trump-inauguration-rain/.

4 May Bulman, "Rain starts as Donald Trump begins first speech as President and people interpret it as a prophetic sign," *Independent*, January 21, 2017, https://www.independent.co.uk/news/world/americas/donald-trump-rain-speech-inauguration-president-us-sign-prophecy-a7538686.html.

5 "The Inaugural Address," White House Archives, January 20, 2017, https://trump-whitehouse.archives.gov/briefings-statements/the-inaugural-address/.

6 "Acosta confirmed as Secretary of Labor," National Association of Letter Carriers, April 27, 2017, https://www.nalc.org/government-affairs/legislative-updates/alex-acosta-confirmed-as-secretary-of-labor.

7 National Association of Letter Carriers.

8 CNN, "Miami Herald: Trump cabinet member accused of giving wealthy alleged pedophile 'deal of a lifetime,'" WCPO Cincinnati, November 29, 2018, https://www.wcpo.com/news/national/miami-herald-trump-cabinet-member-accused-of-giving-wealthy-alleged-pedophile-deal-of-a-lifetime.

9 "Ag and Food Sectors and the Economy," Economic Research Service, U.S. Department of Agriculture, updated February 24, 2022, https://www.ers.usda.gov/data-products/ag-and-food-statistics-charting-the-essentials/ag-and-food-sectors-and-the-economy/#:~:text=Agriculture%20and%20its%20related%20industries%20provide%2010.9%20percent,and%20food%20sectors—10.9%20percent%20of%20total%20U.S.%20employment.

10 Kimberly Amadeo, "US Manufacturing Statistics and Outlook," The Balance, May 6, 2021, https://www.thebalance.com/u-s-manufacturing-what-it-is-statistics-and-outlook-3305575.

11 Thomas Madison, "BOMBSHELL VIDEO! White House leaker has been discovered!" Powdered Whig Society, February 21, 2017. [URL Inactive]

12 Louis Nelson, "Paul Ryan" We're 'extremely close' to having the votes to pass Obamacare repeal," *Politico*, May 3, 2017, https://www.politico.com/story/2017/05/03/paul-ryan-obamacare-repeal-votes-237923.

13 Bryan Bender and Maggie Severns, "'I loved John McCain': Inside Arizona's GOP movement to defeat Donald Trump," *Politico*, November 8, 2020, https://www.politico.com/news/2020/11/08/john-mccain-arizonas-gop-defeat-donald-trump-434913.

14 Kyung Lah, "Arizona GOP censures Flake, Ducey and McCain, signaling a fractured party in a key swing state," CNN Politics, January 24, 2021, https://www.cnn.com/2021/01/23/politics/arizona-gop-censure-mccain-flake-ducey/index.html. Biden appointed McCain Permanent Representative of the U.S. Mission to the UN Agencies.

15 Andrew Desiderio, "Did Republicans Lose Orange County for Good?" *Politico*, September29,2019,https://www.politico.com/magazine/story/2019/09/29/republicans-orange-county-california-228110/.

16 Allyson Chiu, "Bill Stepien was ousted over Bridgegate. Now he's in charge of Trump's reelection campaign," *Washington Post*, July 16, 2020, https://www.washingtonpost.com/nation/2020/07/16/trump-campaign-stepien-bridgegate/.

17 Paul A. Eisenstein, "Trump's new limo cost $1.5M and comes with a fridge full of his blood type," NBC News, September 25, 2018, https://www.nbcnews.com/business/autos/trump-s-new-limo-cost-16m-comes-fridge-his-blood-n912841.

18 "How Much Does a Pickup Truck Weigh?" RoadSumo, https://roadsumo.com/how-much-does-a-pickup-truck-weigh/.

19 Ryan Bort, "10 Key Ways House Democrats Plan to Investigate the Trump Administration," Yahoo Entertainment, December 28, 2018, https://www.yahoo.com/entertainment/10-key-ways-house-democrats-191455971.html.

20 Megan McCluskey, "The Significance of Bran Stark's Cryptic Conversation with Littlefinger on *Game of Thrones*," *Time*, August 6, 2017, https://time.com/4889240/game-of-thrones-bran-stark-littlefinger-chaos-conversation/.

21 "By delegation from the Attorney General, the Assistant Attorney General in charge of the Office of Legal Counsel (OLC) provides legal advice to the President and all executive branch agencies…. All executive orders and substantive proclamations proposed to be issued by the President are reviewed by OLC for form and legality, as are various other matters that require the President's formal approval. Office of Legal Counsel, United States Department of Justice." "About the Office," The United States Department of Justice, https://www.justice.gov/legal-careers/job/attorney-adviser-13.

22 "Presidential Memorandum Regarding Withdrawal of the United States from the Trans-Pacific Partnership Negotiations and Agreement," Trump White House Archives, January 23, 2017, https://trumpwhitehouse.archives.gov/presidential-actions/presidential-memorandum-regarding-withdrawal-united-states-trans-pacific-partnership-negotiations-agreement/.

23 Peter Coy, "Peter Navarro, Trade Warrior," Bloomberg Businessweek, May 8–14, 2017, https://www.magzter.com/stories/Business/Bloomberg-Businessweek/Peter-Navarro-Trade-Warrior.

24 Shawn Donnan and Demetri Sevastopulo, "White House civil war breaks out over trade," *Financial Times*, March 10, 2017, https://www.ft.com/content/badd42ce-05b8-11e7-ace0-1ce02ef0def9.

25 Donnan and Sevastopulo.

26 The formal list of Executive Orders (EO) and Presidential Memoranda (PM) included:
EO 13785: Establishing the Enhanced Collection and Enforcement of Antidumping and Countervailing Duties and Violations of Trade and Customs Laws. March 31, 2017.
EO 13786: Regarding the Omnibus Report on Significant Trade Deficits. March 31, 2017.
EO 13788: Buy American and Hire American. April 18, 2017.
EO 13796: Addressing Trade Agreement Violations and Abuses. April 29, 2017.
EO 13797: Establishment of the Office of Trade and Manufacturing Policy. April 29, 2017.

PM 17: Steel Imports and Threats to National Security. April 20, 2017.

PM 21: Aluminum Imports and Threats to National Security under the Trade Expansion Act of 1962. April 27, 2017.

See "List of executive orders by Donald Trump," Wikipedia, https://en.wikipedia.org/wiki/List_of_executive_orders_by_Donald_Trump.

See also, "Memorandum on Steel Imports and Threats to National Security," Gov-Info.com, April 20, 2017, https://www.govinfo.gov/content/pkg/DCPD-201700259/pdf/DCPD-201700259.pdf.

See also, "Presidential Memorandum for the Secretary of Commerce," White-House.gov, April 27, 2017, https://web.archive.org/web/20170428001350/https://www.whitehouse.gov/the-press-office/2017/04/27/presidential-memorandum-secretary-commerce.

27   Alexandra Petri, "Opinion: Reince Priebus and Stephen Bannon: A love story," *Washington Post*, February 23, 2017, https://www.washingtonpost.com/blogs/compost/wp/2017/02/23/reince-preibus-and-stephen-bannon-a-love-story/.

28   Patrick J. Buchanan, Nixon's White House Wars, (New York: Crown Forum, May 2017), p. 57.

29   For a thoughtful analysis, see, for example, Barry Popik, "Personnel is Policy," Barrypopik.com, March 13, 2013, https://www.barrypopik.com/index.php/new_york_city/entry/personnel_is_policy#:~:text='Personnel%20is%20policy"%20is%20a%20saying%20used%20to,victory%20and%20during%20his%20first%20year%20in%20office.

30   "Clete R. Willems," biography, Akin Gump, https://www.akingump.com/en/law-yers-advisors/clete-r-willems.html.

31   Dan Friedman, "The Trump Administration Orders an Al Jazeera Affiliate to Register as a Foreign Agent," Mother Jones, September 15, 2020, https://www.motherjones.com/politics/2020/09/trump-doj-al-jazeera-fara-uae-qatar/.

32   "Lobbyist Profile: Kelly Ann Shaw," Open Secrets, https://www.opensecrets.org/federal-lobbying/lobbyists/summary?id=Y0000057457L&cycle=2020.

33   "Hogan Lovells," Wikipedia, https://en.wikipedia.org/wiki/Hogan_Lovells.

34   "Kelly Ann Shaw" biography, Hogan Lovells, https://www.hoganlovells.com/en/shaw-kelly-ann.

35   Tina Nguyen, "'Idiots,' 'Anarchists,' and 'Assholes': John Boehner Unloads on Republicans in Post-Retirement Interview," *Vanity Fair*, October 30, 2017, https://www.vanityfair.com/news/2017/10/john-boehner-on-republican-party.

36   Pittsburgh Post-Gazette post, Facebook, July 12, 2019, https://www.facebook.com/pittsburghpostgazette/posts/madeleine-westerhout-then-a-republican-national-committee-aide-broke-down-crying/10157464976719826/.

37   Allan Smith, "Priebus reportedly told Trump he would 'lose by the biggest landslide in American political history' after the 'Access Hollywood' tape," *Business Insider*, September 8, 2017, https://www.businessinsider.com/bannon-priebus-trump-access-hollywood-tape-2017-9.

38   Portia Crowe, "Goldman Sachs' No. 2 exec will get a big payout now that he's joining Trump's administration," *Business Insider*, December 12, 2016, https://www.businessinsider.com/goldman-sachs-gary-cohn-to-defer-capital-gains-tax-on-shares-sold-2016-12.

PART FOUR

1 A. W. Geiger, "16 striking finding from 2016," Pew Research, December 21, 2016, https://www.pewresearch.org/fact-tank/2016/12/21/16-striking-findings-from-2016/.

2 Laura Silver et al, "Americans Fault China for Its Role in the Spread of COVID-19," Pew Research, July 30, 2020, https://www.pewresearch.org/global/2020/07/30/americans-fault-china-for-its-role-in-the-spread-of-covid-19/.

3 Kat Devlin et al., "U.S. Views of China Increasingly Negative Amid Coronavirus Outbreak," Pew Research, April 21, 2020, https://www.pewresearch.org/global/2020/04/21/u-s-views-of-china-increasingly-negative-amid-coronavirus-outbreak/. "About nine-in-ten U.S. adults see China's power and influence as a threat – including 62% who say it is a *major* threat."

4 Devlin et al.

5 "Full Text of Clinton's Speech on China Trade Bill," Federal News Service, March 9, 2000, https://www.iatp.org/sites/default/files/Full_Text_of_Clintons_Speech_on_China_Trade_Bi.htm.

6 Lauren Carroll, "Trump: Since China joined WTO, U.S. has lost 60,000 factories," "Politifact, March 24, 2017, https://www.politifact.com/factchecks/2017/mar/24/donald-trump/trump-china-joined-wto-us-has-lost-60000-factories/.
See also: "[T]he Census Bureau's Business Dynamics Statistics series [tallied a loss of] 73,757 manufacturing establishments from 2001 to 2014. There were 348,513 manufacturing establishments in 2001 and 274,756 in 2014." Emily Larsen, "Fact Check: Did the US Lose 70,000 Factories Under Bush and Obama?" CheckYourFact.com, April 12, 2018, https://checkyourfact.com/2018/04/12/fact-check-did-the-us-lose-70000-factories-under-bush-and-obama/.

7 "Tracing Trump's Aggressive Tariff Strategy Back to the 1980s | Trump's Trade War | Frontline," YouTube video, Frontline PBS, May 6, 2019, https://www.bing.com/videos/search?q=president+trump+talked+about+china+since+1990s&view=detail&mid=E3F38ADE9D58BC967B78E3F38ADE9D58BC967B78&FORM=VIRE.

8 The sanctions prohibit travel to mainland China, Hong Kong and Macao or doing business with China. "Foreign Ministry Spokesperson Announces Sanctions on Pompeo and Others," Ministry of Foreign Affairs of the People's Republic of China, January 20, 2021, https://www.fmprc.gov.cn/mfa_eng/xwfw_665399/s2510_665401/2535_665405/202101/t20210120_697094.html.

9 Ministry of Foreign Affairs.

10 Eli Yokley, "As Trump and Biden Spar Over China, Neither Has a Clear Edge With Voters on the Subject," Morning Consult, May 20, 2020, https://morningconsult.com/2020/05/20/trump-biden-trust-china-coronavirus-polling/.
See also: Josh Lederman, "Battleground voters not buying Trump's tough talk on China, new poll shows," NBC News, September 28, 2020, https://www.nbcnews.com/politics/2020-election/battleground-voters-not-buying-trump-s-tough-talk-china-new-n1241215.

11 Peter Schweizer, "How five members of Joe Biden's family got rich through his connections," *New York Post*, January 18, 2020, https://nypost.com/2020/01/18/how-five-members-of-joe-bidens-family-got-rich-through-his-connections/.

12 See, for example, Alexandra Ma, "Trump praises 'my good friend, Xi Jinping for 'great help' with historic Kim Jong Un peace talks," *Business Insider*, April 27, 2018,

https://www.businessinsider.com/north-korea-summit-peace-talks-trump-praise-xi-jinping-2018-4.

13 Donna Borak, "Wilbur Ross: US exploring other remedies for ZTE ban," CNN Business, May 15, 2018, https://money.cnn.com/2018/05/14/news/companies/us-china-zte-penalties/index.html.

14 Kyle Daly and Margaret Harding McGill, "Team Trump's 5G Misfires," Axios, February 7, 2020, https://www.axios.com/team-trumps-5g-misfires-barr-kudlow-20f5ad01-97db-4a66-b7df-6f5d67e659cb.html.

15 Reuters Staff, "White House's Kushner says Oracle's TikTok deal being reviewed," Reuters, September 15, 2020, https://www.reuters.com/article/us-china-bytedance-tiktok-oracle-whiteho/white-houses-kushner-says-oracles-tiktok-deal-being-re-viewed-idUSKBN2661WW.

16 Yeshi Dorje, "Tibetan Re-Education Camp Journal Tells of China's Tactics Now Used on Uighurs," Voice of America, May 25, 2019, https://www.voanews.com/a/tibetan-re-education-camp-journal-tells-of-china-s-tactics-now-used-on-uighurs/4932153.html.

17 Derek Grossman, "Military Build Up in the South China Sea*," Rand Corporation, https://www.rand.org/content/dam/rand/pubs/external_publications/EP60000/EP68058/RAND_EP68058.pdf.

18 Zachary Keck, "The CCP Didn't Fight Imperial Japan; the KMT Did," *The Diplomat*, September 4, 2014, https://thediplomat.com/2014/09/the-ccp-didnt-fight-imperial-japan-the-kmt-did/.

19 Myah Ward, "15 times Trump praised China as coronavirus was spreading across the globe," *Politico*, April 15, 2020, https://www.politico.com/news/2020/04/15/trump-china-coronavirus-188736.

20 Zachary Evans, "Trump Praises Xi for Handling of Coronavirus Outbreak as Death Toll Passes 600," *National Review*, February 7, 2020, https://www.nationalreview.com/news/trump-praises-xi-for-handling-of-coronavirus-outbreak-as-death-toll-passes-600/.

21 Andrew Restuccia and Doug Palmer, "Ross losing sway with Trump on China," *Politico*, May 14, 2018, https://www.politico.com/story/2018/05/14/ross-trump-china-trade-commerce-539279.

22 Pan Kwan Yuk, "US hits China's ZTE with denial of export privileges," *Financial Times*, April 16, 2018, https://www.ft.com/content/77bc02d4-4174-11e8-803a-295c97e6fd0b.

23 Jennifer Read, "Secretary Ross Announces Activatin Of ZTE Denial Order In Response To Repeated False Statements To The U.S. Government," EMSNow, April 16, 2018, https://www.emsnow.com/secretary-ross-announces-activation-zte-denial-order-response-repeated-false-statements-u-s-government/.

24 Yuk, "US hits China's ZTE with denial of export privileges."

25 Donna Borak, "ZTE pays $1 billion find to US over sanctions violations," CNN Business, June 22, 2018, https://money.cnn.com/2018/06/22/news/companies/zte-us-fine-trade-case/index.html.

26 Jacob Pramuk, "Republican Sen. Marco Rubio warns: Trump's reversal on China's ZTE is a national security risk," CNBC, May 14, 2018, https://www.cnbc.com/2018/05/14/marco-rubio-slams-trump-reversal-on-chinese-company-zte.html.

27 Pramuk.

28 Jackie Wattles and Sherisse Pham, "President Trump says he's working with China to save ZTE," CNN Business, May 14, 2018, https://money.cnn.com/2018/05/13/technology/business/trump-zte-corporation-china-commerce/index.html.

29 Kate O'Keeffe et al., "Mnuchin Said to Advise U.S. Firms to Seek Huawei Exemptions," *Wall Street Journal*, July 10, 2019, https://www.wsj.com/articles/mnuchin-urges-u-s-firms-to-seek-huawei-exemptions-11562798183.

30 By the way, the tip of the lobbying spear for wireless companies in support of Huawei was the Cellular Telecommunications Industry Association, known now simply as CTIA. Not only did its deep-pocketed members not give one whit about national security. The organization itself was—and is—a cesspool of revolving door politics. A prime example: CTIA's CEO from 1992 to the 2004 wound up as an Obama-Biden-appointed chairman of the Federal Communications Commission "henhouse."

31 As Gheorge Rider notes: "The value of Pork Chop Hill is that it ha[d] no value. It was important as a contest of wills." "Why was the Battle of Pork Chop Hill so important?" *Quora*, 2021, https://www.quora.com/Why-was-the-Battle-of-Pork-Chop-Hill-so-important.

32 Christian Datoc, "EXCLUSIVE: Trump Was Furious With Mnuchin Over TikTok Global Deal, Current And Former Admin Officials Say," *Daily Caller,* September 23, 2020, https://dailycaller.com/2020/09/23/exclusive-donald-trump-furious-steve-mnuchin-treasury-tiktok-global-deal/.

33 Gurmeet Kanwal and Monika Chansoria, "China Preparing Tibet as Future War Zone," *Deccan Herald*, June 2, 2011, accessed January 8, 2015, http://www.deccan-herald.com/content/165996/china-preparing-tibet-future-war.html.

34 Henry Holloway, "BORDER HELL: Chinese 'death squads' hunted and slaughtered Indian troops as 500 soldiers fought gruesome Medieval hand-to-hand battle," *The Sun*, June 19, 2020, https://www.thesun.co.uk/news/11902650/china-death-squads-india-troops-medieval/.

35 Article 7 of Communist China's National Intelligence Law requires any company that has operations on the Chinese mainland to provide its data directly to the Chinese government. See, for example, "Keynote Remarks as Prepared for Delivery," NCSC Director William Evanina to the International Legal Technology Association, June 4, 2019, https://www.dni.gov/files/NCSC/documents/news/20190606-NCSC-Remarks-ILTA-Summit_2019.pdf#:~:text=Article%207%20of%20China's%20National%20Intelligence%20Law%20states,,in%20accordance%20with%20the%20law,%20and%20maintain%20the.

36 Madhumita Murgia et al., "Microsoft worked with Chinese military university on artificial intelligence," *Financial Times*, April 10, 2019, https://www.ft.com/content/9378e7ee-5ae6-11e9-9dde-7aedca0a081a.

37 Karl Evers-Hillstrom, "TikTok deploys lobbyists tied to Trump, top Democrats as US considers ban," OpenSecrets.org, July 13, 2020, https://www.opensecrets.org/news/2020/07/tiktok-deploys-lobbyists/.

38 "US Navy ship to be named after Harrisburg at Capitol ceremony," CBS21 News, October 10, 2019, https://local21news.com/news/local/us-navy-ship-to-be-named-after-harrisburg-at-capitol-ceremony.

39 Ellen Nakashima et al, "TikTok's fate was shaped by a 'knockdown, drag-out' Oval Office brawl," *Washington Post*, August 10, 2020, https://www.washingtonpost.com/technology/2020/08/08/trump-tiktok-mnuchin-navarro/.

40 Erin Griffith and David McCabe, "'There's No There There': What the TikTok Deal Achieved," *New York Times*, September 20, 2020, https://www.nytimes.com/2020/09/20/technology/tiktok-trump-victory.html.

41 Asawin Suebsaeng, "Trump Adviser Peter Navarro Slams Steve Mnuchin as 'Neville Chamberlain,'" *Daily Beast*, May 24, 2018, https://www.thedailybeast.com/trump-adviser-peter-navarro-slams-steve-mnuchin-as-neville-chamberlain.

42 See, for example, Chris Buckley and Austin Ramzy, "China's Detention Camps for Muslims Turn to Forced Labor," *New York Times*, December 16, 2018, https://www.nytimes.com/2018/12/16/world/asia/xinjiang-china-forced-labor-camps-uighurs.html.
See also, "Forced Labor in China's Xinjiang Region," U.S. Department of State, July 1, 2021, https://www.state.gov/forced-labor-in-chinas-xinjiang-region/.

43 See, for example David Stavrou, "China's 'XXX Files': '25 Thousand People Disappear Each Year, Their Organs Are Harvested,'" *Haaretz*, December 4, 2020, https://www.haaretz.com/world-news/MAGAZINE-china-s-xinjiang-xxx-files-thousands-uighur-disappear-organs-harvested-1.9340106.
See also, Will Martin, "China is harvesting thousands of human organs from its Uighur Muslim minority, UN human-rights body hears," *Business Insider*, September 25, 2019, https://www.businessinsider.com/china-harvesting-organs-of-uighur-muslims-china-tribunal-tells-un-2019-9.

44 "DHS Cracks Down on Goods Produced by China's State-Sponsored Forced Labor," U.S. Customs and Border Protection, September 14, 2020, https://www.cbp.gov/newsroom/national-media-release/dhs-cracks-down-goods-produced-china-s-state-sponsored-forced-labor

PART FIVE

1 Alexis Levinson and Tim Alberta, "Trump Bulldozes Blue Wall, Wins White House," *National Review*, November 9, 2016, https://www.nationalreview.com/2016/11/2016-election-donald-trump-wins-white-house-historic-upset/.

2 The Electoral College results for 2020 had 306 votes for Joe Biden and 232 for Donald Trump. If Trump had carried the Blue Wall states of Michigan, Pennsylvania, and Wisconsin, he would have won comfortably by a vote of 278 to 260.

3 "Death by China: How America Lost Its Manufacturing Base (Official Version)," YouTube video, DeathByChina, uploaded April 10, 2016, https://www.youtube.com/watch?v=mMlmjXtnIXI.

4 Katie Reilly, "Read Hillary Clinton's 'Basket of Deplorables' Remarks About Donald Trump Supporters," *Time*, September 10, 2016, https://time.com/4486502/hillary-clinton-basket-of-deplorables-transcript/.

5 "Full Rush Transcript Hillary Clinton Part//CNN TV One Democratic Presidential Town Hall," CNN, March 13, 2016, https://cnnpressroom.blogs.cnn.com/2016/03/13/full-rush-transcript-hillary-clinton-partcnn-tv-one-democratic-presidential-town-hall/.

6 David Roberts, "Hillary Clinton's 'coal gaffe' is a microcosm of her twisted treatment by the media," *Vox*, September 20, 2017, https://www.vox.com/energy-and-environment/2017/9/15/16306158/hillary-clinton-hall-of-mirrors.

7 Roberts.

8 Damian Paletta, "Internal White House documents allege manufacturing decline increases abortions, infertility, and spousal abuse," *Washington Post*, October 17, 2017, https://www.washingtonpost.com/news/business/wp/2017/10/17/internal-white-house-documents-allege-manufacturing-decline-increases-abortions-infertility-and-spousal-abuse/?arc404=true.

9 See, for example, David Autor et al., "When Work Disappears: Manufacturing Decline and the Falling Marriage-Market Value of Young Men," National Bureau of Economic Research, December, 2018, https://www.nber.org/papers/w23173. See also more generally, https://chinashock.info/.

10 "Death by China: How America Lost Its Manufacturing Base (Official Version)."

11 Peter Navarro, "The Causes and Costs of Illegal Immigration through the United States' Southwest Border," February 2020, https://peternavarro.com/the-navarro-report/.

12 Keith Collins et al., "Hispanic Voters Deliver a Texas Win for Trump," *New York Times*, November 10, 2020, https://www.nytimes.com/interactive/2020/11/05/us/texas-election-results.html.

13 "The Inaugural Address," White House Archives.

14 This includes payroll taxes, profit taxes, and sales taxes associated with the Buy American, Hire American activity.

15 Paul Mozur et al., "Popular Chinese-Made Drone Is Found to Have Security Weakness," *New York Times*, July 23, 2020, https://www.nytimes.com/2020/07/23/us/politics/dji-drones-security-vulnerability.html.

16 "Secretary Bernhardt Signs Order Grounding Interior's Drone Fleet for Non-Emergency Operations," U.S. Department of the Interior, January 29, 2020, https://www.doi.gov/pressreleases/secretary-bernhardt-signs-order-grounding-interiors-drone-fleet-non-emergency.

17 Troutman Pepper, "President Biden Suspends Bulk Power System Executive Order; Directs Agencies to Address Public Health- and Climate- Related Rules," JD Supra, February 10, 2021, https://www.jdsupra.com/legalnews/president-biden-suspends-bulk-power-9493584/.

18 "Trump's First One Hundred Days: Federal Contracting With Corporate Offshorers Continues," Good Jobs Nation and Public Citizen's Global Trade Watch, https://www.citizen.org/wp-content/uploads/gjn-gtw-report-federal-contracting-with-corporate-offshorers-continues-final.pdf.

19 Good Jobs Nation and Public Citizen's Global Trade Watch.

20 Good Jobs Nation and Public Citizen's Global Trade Watch.

21 "United States of America and the WTO," World Trade Organization, https://www.wto.org/english/thewto_e/countries_e/usa_e.htm#:~:text=The%20United%20States%20of%20America%20has%20been%20a,a%20member%20of%20GATT%20since%201%20January%201948.

22 "WTO Agreement on Government Procurement (GPA)," International Trade Administration, https://legacy.trade.gov/mas/ian/tradeagreements/multilateral/wto/tg_ian_002072.asp.

23 Matt Groch, "Buy American Order A Good First Step: Enacting EO's Goals Requires President Biden to End 60 Nations' Trade-Pact Buy American Waivers," Public Citizen, January 25, 2021, https://www.citizen.org/news/buy-american-order-a-good-first-step-enacting-eos-goals-requires-president-biden-to-end-60-nations-trade-pact-buy-american-waivers/.

24 "Donald Trump Speech Transcript August 6: Whirlpool Manufacturing Plant," Rev. com, August 6, 2020, https://www.rev.com/blog/transcripts/donald-trump-speech-transcript-august-6-whirlpool-manufacturing-plant.

25 "Whirlpool Corporation Free and Fair Trade," Whirlpool Corporation, 2018, http://assets.whirlpoolcorp.com/files/Free-and-Fair-Trade-Fact-Sheet-Jan2018.pdf#:~:text=Whirlpool%20Corporation%20filed%20a%20safeguard%20petition%20with%20the,Samsung%20and%20LG%20to%20evade%20U.S.%20trade%20laws.

26 Whirlpool Corporation.

27 Whirlpool Corporation.

28 Whirlpool Corporation.

29 Whirlpool Corporation.

30 Nicole Cornett, "CMC Steel to Build $300M Micro Steel Mill in Mesa, Arizona," *Expansion Solutions Magazine*, August 17, 2020, https://www.expansionsolutions-magazine.com/steel-micro-mill-mesa-arizona/.

PART SIX

1 S.V. Date, "Win Or Lose, Trump's Top Campaign Aides Are Raking In The Cash," *HuffPost*, May 7, 2020, https://www.huffpost.com/entry/trump-consultants-rich-reelection-money_n_5eb1dae5c5b62b850f93abb3.

2 Shane Goldmacher and Maggie Haberman, "How Trump's Billion-Dollar Campaign Lost Its Cash Advantage," *New York Times*, September 7, 2020, https://www.nytimes.com/2020/09/07/us/politics/trump-election-campaign-fundraising.html?referringSource=articleShare.

3 "Who is Brad Parscale?" *60 Minutes*, CBS, February 27, 2018, https://www.cbs.com/shows/60_minutes/video/elHhrLFmOS2ZYFqRG68KQPAu0_aUKPKC/who-is-brad-parscale-/.

4 Natalie Winters, "REPORT: Zuckerberg Spent Half a Billion Dollard Coercing States To Adopt Pro-Dem Turnout Measures," National Pulse, December 16, 2020, https://thenationalpulse.com/2020/12/16/zuckerberg-election-influence/.

5 Ben Ashford, "EXCLUSIVE: Donald Trump's demoted campaign manager Brad Parscale starts work on his new digital strategy role with beer in hand at his $2.4 million Florida home's pool," *Daily Mail*, July 20, 2020, https://www.dailymail.co.uk/news/article-8541057/Shirtless-Brad-Parscale-sips-beer-poolside-2-4M-Florida-home-demoted.html.

6 S.V. Date, "Win Or Lose, Trump's Top Campaign Aides Are Raking In The Cash."

7 Associated Press, "How Trump plowed through $1 billion, losing his campaign's cash advantage." *Los Angeles Times*, October 19, 2020, https://www.latimes.com/world-nation/story/2020-10-20/how-trump-plowed-through-1-billion-losing-cash-advantage.

8   "Joe Biden aims to outspend Donald Trump on TV ads ahead of US election," *Financial Times,* August 5, 2020, https://www.ft.com/content/012896c0-71ee-4081 -a3a5-8b1ca864b214.

9   Amy Ta, "Gone in 60 seconds: Super Bowl ads cost candidates $10 million per minute," KCRW, January 31, 2020, https://www.kcrw.com/news/shows/kcrw-features/ gone-in-60-seconds-super-bowl-ads-cost-candidates-10-million-per-minute.

10   Brian Schwartz, "Silicon Valley billionaire Peter Thiel makes a big midterm splash with $250,000 donation to Trump fund," CNBC, October 15, 2018, https://www. cnbc.com/2018/10/15/silicon-valley-billionaire-peter-thiel-donates-250000-to-trump-fund.html?dlbk.

11   Associated Press, "How Trump plowed through $1 billion, losing his campaign's cash advantage."

12   Brett Samuels, "Kushner predicts much of the country will be 'back to normal' in June," *The Hill,* April 29, 2020, https://thehill.com/homenews/administration/495212-kushner-predicts-much-of-the-country-will-be-back-to-normal-in-june.

13   While the protesting crowds during the Vietnam War were far larger than BLM-Antifa militias putting the White House under siege, the Vietnam War protesters were far more peaceful. Nixon, for example, never had to flee to an underground bunker. At least to my knowledge, no Vietnam War protester ever lit fire to a church across the street from the White House.

14   Igor Derysh, "Robert and Rebekah Mercer bail on Trump campaign – they spent $49 million in 2016," *Salon,* June 18, 2019, https://www.salon.com/2019/06/18/robert-and-rebekah-mercer-bail-on-trump-campaign-they-spent-49-million-in-2016/.

PART SEVEN

1   White House Archives of Peter Navarro.

2   Peter Navarro and Aron Spencer, "September 11, 2001: Assessing the Costs of Terrorism," (Santa Monica, CA: Milken Institute, 2001).

3   Steve Brown, "U.S. office market will take years to recover from pandemic," *Dallas Morning News,* September 28, 2020, https://www.dallasnews.com/ business/real-estate/2020/09/28/us-office-market-will-take-years-to-recover-from-pandemic/.

4   Wolf Richter, "Most Distorted Labor Market Ever: Charts by Sector," Wolf Street, September 8, 2021, https://wolfstreet.com/2021/09/08/most-distorted-labor-market-ever-job-openings-charts-by-sector/.

5   Jack Brewster, "GOP Suddenly Expresses Urgency On Stimulus: 'Congress Needs To Act In July'," *Forbes,* July 2, 2020, https://www.forbes.com/sites/jackbrewster/ 2020/07/02/gop-suddenly-expresses-urgency-on-stimulus-congress-needs-to-act-in-july/?sh=4b0f1adb72b5.

6   Abacus Payroll, "2021 Federal Payroll Tax Rates," Abacus Payroll Inc., December 15, 2020, https://abacuspay.com/2021-federal-payroll-tax-rates/#:~:text=2021%20 Federal%20Payroll%20Tax%20Rates%20%20%20,No%20limit%20%20%20 $18,240.00%20No%20limit. The FICA/OASDI employee rate is 6.2% and the Medicare rate is another 1.45%.

7   Summer Concepcion, "Mnuchin Blames Dems For No Payroll Tax Cut In COVID Bill Despite GOP's Rejection Of It," Talking Points Memo, July 26, 2020, https:// talkingpointsmemo.com/news/mnuchin-covid-bill-payroll-tax-cut.

8 "Cost of Living Index by State 2022," World Population Review, https://worldpopulationreview.com/state-rankings/cost-of-living-index-by-state.

9 "Japan to Fund Firms to Shift Production Out of China," *Bloomberg*, https://www.bloomberg.com/news/articles/2020-04-08/japan-to-fund-firms-to-shift-production-out-of-china.

10 Brian T. Kennedy, "Facing Up to the China Threat," The Patriot Post, October 24, 2020, https://patriotpost.us/opinion/74397-facing-up-to-the-china-threat-2020-10-24.

11 Talia Kaplan, "Kudlow claims US is in 'a strong V-shaped recovery'despite Wall Street selloff," Fox Business, September 21, 2020, https://www.foxbusiness.com/economy/kudlow-economy-v-shaped-recovery-market-selloff.

12 Larry Kudlow, "Fed Right, Trump Wrong," *National Review*, August 19, 2015, https://www.nationalreview.com/corner/federal-reserve-donald-trump/.

13 Larry Kudlow, "The Housing Bears Are Wrong Again," *National Review*, June 20, 2005, https://www.nationalreview.com/2005/06/housing-bears-are-wrong-again-larry-kudlow/.

14 Larry Kudlow, "Bush Boom Continues," *National Review*, December 7, 2007, https://www.nationalreview.com/kudlows-money-politics/bush-boom-continues-larry-kudlow/.

15 Larry Kudlow, "Lay Off the Panic Button," *National Review*, February 5, 2008, https://www.nationalreview.com/kudlows-money-politics/lay-panic-button-larry-kudlow/.

16 Ryan Koronowski, "Trump's new economic adviser is really bad at economics. Here are the receipts," Think Progress, March 14, 2018, https://archive.thinkprogress.org/larry-kudlow-bad-economic-predictions-f02ebf47c918/.

17 Elizabeth Leary, "Bad Media Calls of 08: Did They Really Say That?," *Kiplinger*, January 6, 2009, https://www.kiplinger.com/article/investing/t031-c000-s001-bad-media-calls-of-08-did-they-really-say-that.html#:~:text=Larry%20Kudlow%2C%20economist%20and%20syndicated%20columnist.%20What%20He,business.%22%20-%20August%2028%2C2008%20CNBC's%20Kudlow%20%26%20Company.

18 Alexander Panetta, "Trump's new economic advisor says leaving NAFTA his greatest fear," *Design Engineering*, March 15, 2018, https://www.design-engineering.com/nafta-kudlow-1004029530-1004029530/.

19 Scott Horsley, "Yellen Urges Congress To 'Act Big' To Prop Up Pandemic-Scarred Economy," NPR, January 21, 2021, https://www.wwno.org/2021-01-19yellen-urges-congress-to-act-big-to-prop-up-pandemic-scarred-economy.

20 Lauren French and Jake Sherman, "House conservative seeks Boehner's ouster," *Politico*, July 29, 2015, https://www.politico.com/story/2015/07/house-conservative-john-boehner-ouster-120742.

21 "Congressional Job Approval," Real Clear Politics, https://www.realclearpolitics.com/epolls/other/congressional_job_approval-903.html.

PART EIGHT

1 John F. Steward, The Reaper (New York: Greenberg, 1931), 239; "origin of the expression 'never argue with someone who buys ink by the barrel," Stack Exchange, https://english.stackexchange.com/questions/67527/origin-of-the-expression-never-argue-with-someone-who-buys-ink-by-the-barrel.

2 Mark Levin, "February 17, 2021," *The Mark Levin Show*, February 17, 2021, https://www.marklevinshow.com/2021/02/17/february-17-2021/.

3 *Oxford University Press,* s.v., "propaganda," https://www.lexico.com/en/definition/propaganda.

4 Bruce Lannes Smith, *Encyclopaedia Britannica Online,* s.v. "propaganda," https://www.britannica.com/topic/propaganda.

5 *Merriam-Webster,* s.v. "propaganda," https://www.merriam-webster.com/dictionary/propaganda.

6 *Oxford Reference,* s.v. "propaganda," https://www.oxfordreference.com/view/10.1093/oi/authority.20110803100349558#:~:text=%5BLatin%2'propagation'%5D,corporation%20(compare%20agenda%20setting).

7 Darren K. Carlson, "How Americans Get Their News," *Gallup,* December 31, 2002, https://news.gallup.com/poll/7495/How-Americans-Get-Their-News.aspx.

8 Doublas A. McIntyre, "Over 2000 American Newspapers Have Closed in Past 15 Years," 24/7 Wall Street, July 23, 2019, https://247wallst.com/media/2019/07/23/over-2000-american-newspapers-have-closed-in-past-15-years/.

9 Jaime Cone, "Gannett Layoffs Hit Ithaca Journal Hard," Ithaca.com, November 2, 2016, https://www.ithaca.com/news/ithaca/gannett-layoffs-hit-ithaca-journal-hard/article_ed3da7ba-a10c-11e6-bf2d-9f3a703b3746.html.

10 Adam Rosenberg, "Amazon delivers a killing blow to the pro-Trump social network, Parler," *Mashable,* January 10, 2021, https://mashable.com/article/parler-amazon-web-hosting-suspended.

11 Avery Hartmans, "Jeff Bezos used Instagram to take an apparent swipe at a senior Trump official who accused him of ducking an important meeting," *Business Insider,* February 6, 2020, https://www.businessinsider.com/amazon-jeff-bezos-shades-white-house-adviser-instagram-post-2020-2.

12 Peter Navarro, "Anthony Fauci has been wrong about everything I have interacted with him on: Peter Navarro," USA Today, July 14, 2020, https://www.usatoday.com/story/opinion/todaysdebate/2020/07/14/anthony-fauci-wrong-with-me-peter-navarro-editorials-debates/5439374002/.

13 The Editorial Board, "A Navarro Recession?" *Wall Street Journal,* August 11, 2019, https://www.wsj.com/articles/a-navarro-recession-11565216137.

14 Gabriel Sherman, "The Loudest Voice in the Room," Random House, January 14, 2014.

15 "#CNNTapes Reveal Network's Bias Against President Trump, Tucker Carlson ... 'He [Trump] is Acting Erratically, and I Think We Need to Lean into That' ... 'You Have to Talk About The Naked Racism of Tucker Carlson ... White Supremacy Hour They Have on Fox News,'" Project Veritas, December 1, 2020, https://www.projectveritas.com/news/cnntapes-reveal-networks-bias-against-president-trump-tucker-carlson-he/.

16 The Editorial Board, "A Debate That Can't Be Ignored," *New York Times,* September 30, 2020, https://www.nytimes.com/2020/09/30/opinion/trump-biden-debate-2020.html?action=click&module=RelatedLinks&pgtype=Article.

17 The Editorial Board, "Elect Joe Biden. Reject Donald Trump," *USA Today,* October 20, 2020, https://www.usatoday.com/in-depth/opinion/todaysdebate/2020/10/20/elect-joe-biden-reject-donald-trump-editorials-debates/5919435002/.

Endnotes

18 The Editorial Board, "Joe Biden for president," *Washington Post,* September 28, 2020, https://www.washingtonpost.com/opinions/2020/09/28/editorial-board-endorsement-joe-biden/.

19 "Trump Approval Index History," *Rasmussen Reports,* https://www.rasmussen reports.com/public_content/politics/trump_administration/trump_approval_index_history.

20 Jeffrey M. Jones, "Trump Job Rating Steady; Other Mood Indicators Tick Up," *Gallup,* October 21, 2020, https://news.gallup.com/poll/322310/trump-job-rating-steady-mood-indicators-tick.aspx.

21 Megan Brenan, "Biden's Favorability Rises to 55%, Trump's Dips to 42%," *Gallup,* November 30, 2020, https://news.gallup.com/poll/326885/biden-favorability-rises-trump-dips.aspx?utm_source=alert&utm_medium=email&utm_content=morelink&utm_campaign=syndication.

22 Brenan.

23 "NEW POLL: Overwhelming Majority of Americans Support Protections for People With Pre-Existing Conditions," Protect Our Care, July 30, 2018, https://www.protectourcare.org/new-poll-overwhelming-majority-of-americans-support-protections-for-people-with-pre-existing-conditions/.

24 See, for example, Sheera Frenkel and Annie Karni, "Proud Boys celebrate Trump's 'stand by' remark about them at the debate," *New York Times,* September 29, 2020, https://www.nytimes.com/2020/09/29/us/trump-proud-boys-biden.html.

25 Yaron Steinbuch, "Black Lives Matter co-founder describes herself as 'trained Marxist," *New York Post,* June 25, 2020, https://nypost.com/2020/06/25/blm-co-founder-describes-herself-as-trained-marxist/.

26 "The Bentsen-Quayle Vice Presidential Debate," The Commission on Presidential Debates, October 5, 1988, https://debates.org/voter-education/debate-transcripts/october-5-1988-debate-transcripts/.

27 Chris Whipple, "Opinion: Mark Meadows has earned his title of worst chief of staff in history," *Washington Post,* January 15, 2021, https://www.washingtonpost.com/opinions/2021/01/18/mark-meadows-worst-chief-staff-ever-trump/.

28 Dr. Robert Malone and Peter Navarro, "Vaccine inventor questions mandatory shot push, Biden's Covid-19 strategy," *Washington Times,* August 5, 2021, https://www.washingtontimes.com/news/2021/aug/5/biden-teams-misguided-and-deadly-covid-19-vaccine-/.

29 See for example, Dr. Robert Malone and Peter Navarro, "Just say no to Biden and Fauci's universal vaccination nation," *Washington Times,* January 12, 2022, https://www.washingtontimes.com/news/2022/jan/12/just-say-no-to-biden-and-faucis-universal-vaccinat/.

30 This Task Force as an entity would become official the next day, January 29, 2020.

31 Kyle Smith, "Anthony Fauci's Misadventures in Fortune Telling," *National Review,* April 20, 2022, https://www.nationalreview.com/2021/04/anthony-faucis-misadventures-in-fortune-telling/.

32 In effect, Fauci's grant money was used to transfer gain-of-function technologies and techniques to the Chinese. Armed with such intellectual capital, Chinese scientists were then able to turn harmless bat viruses into human killers.

33 Jeff Carlson and Hans Mahncke, "Scientists Who Were Instrumental to COVID-19 'Natural Origin' Narrative Received Over $50 Million in NIAID Funding

in 2020-21," Epoch Times, January 25, 2022, https://www.theepochtimes.com/scientists-who-were-instrumental-to-covid-19-natural-origins-narrative-received-over-50-million-in-niaid-funding-in-2020-2021_4220769.html?utm_source=partner&utm_campaign=imctgm01.

34 Carlson and Mahncke.

35 Gregg Jarrett, "'Russia hoax' was lie created by Hillary Clinton and one of the dirtiest political tricks ever," Fox News, October 7, 2020, https://www.foxnews.com/opinion/russia-hoax-lie-hillary-clinton-gregg-jarrett.

36 "Barr The Door, Here Comes Bull Durham," Only In Bridgeport, May 13, 2019, http://onlyinbridgeport.com/wordpress/barr-the-door-here-comes-bull-durham/.

PART NINE

1 Matt Viser et al., "Inside Hunter Biden's multimillion-dollar deals with a Chinese energy company," Washington Post, March 30, 2022, https://www.washingtonpost.com/politics/2022/03/30/hunter-biden-china-laptop/.

2 See for example, Jenny Beth Martin, "Trump was right; so were we," Washington Times, June 18, 2021, https://www.washingtontimes.com/news/2021/jun/18/trump-was-right-so-were-we/.
See also, Rod Liddle, "So Trump was right: the election was rigged. And our next one will be too," The Times, September 26, 2021, https://www.thetimes.co.uk/article/so-trump-was-right-the-election-was-rigged-and-our-next-one-will-be-too-n0x3lv7fv.
Timothy B Lee, "Donald Trump was right about TikTok," Full Stack Economics, March 25, 2022, https://fullstackeconomics.com/donald-trump-was-right-about-tiktok/.
Sean O'Grady, "Voices: Trump was right, Merkel was wrong – and it's made it harder to save Ukraine," Independent, March 22, 2022, https://www.independent.co.uk/voices/donald-trump-merkel-germany-ukraine-war-b2041226.html.

3 Eli Watkins, "Politico: Pelosi told Dems she wants Trump 'in prison,'" CNN Politics, June 6, 2019, https://www.cnn.com/2019/06/06/politics/nancy-pelosi-trump-in-prison-house-democrats/index.html.

4 Harold Gater, "Bennie Thompson calls Trump racist for lynching comment," Clarion Ledger, October 22, 2019, https://www.clarionledger.com/story/news/politics/2019/10/22/bennie-thompson-calls-trump-racist-lynching-comment/4066640002/.

5 See for example, "Meet Ray Epps, Part 2: Damning New Details Emerge Exposing Massive Web Of Unindicted Operators At The Heart Of January 6," Revolver News, December 18, 2021, https://www.revolver.news/2021/12/damning-new-details-massive-web-unindicted-operators-january-6/.

6 David Harsanyi, "How the media covered up the Hunter Biden story – until after the election," New York Post, December 10, 2020, https://nypost.com/2020/12/10/how-media-covered-up-the-hunter-biden-story-until-after-the-election/.

7 "What We Know and Don't About Hunter Biden and a Laptop," New York Times, September 13, 2021, https://www.nytimes.com/2020/10/22/us/politics/hunter-biden-laptop.html.

8 Jordan Boyd, "Poll: One In Six Biden Voters Would Have Changed Their Vote If They Had Known About Scandals Suppressed By Media," The Federalist, November 24, 2020, https://thefederalist.com/2020/11/24/poll-one-in-six-biden-voters-

would-have-changed-their-vote-if-they-had-known-about-scandals-suppressed-by-media/.

9 "AZ Sec. of State Katie Hobbs takes money from foreign governments and George Soros," Patriots for Truth, November 16, 2020, https://patriots4truth.org/2020/11/16/az-sec-of-state-katie-hobbs-takes-money-from-foreign-governments-and-george-soros/.

10 Joan E. Greve, "'Arsonists with keys to the firehouse': once-obscure state races fuel fears for US democracy," *The Guardian*, March 12, 2022, https://www.theguardian.com/us-news/2022/mar/12/us-elections-secretary-of-state-democracy-brad-raffensperger.

11 Olivia Rubin, "Dominion files $1.6 billion lawsuit against Fox News over false election fraud claims," ABC News, March 26, 2021, https://abcnews.go.com/US/dominion-files-16-billion-lawsuit-fox-news-false/story?id=76699634.

12 Alexis Benveniste, "Why Fox canceled Lou Dobbs," CNN Business, February 8, 2021, https://www.cnn.com/2021/02/07/media/lou-dobbs-fox-reliable/index.html.

13 Brian Stieglitz, "Chris Licht says his directive as new CNN boss is to make sure it 'remains the global leader in NEWS' in hint network will move away from heavy opinion-based content reviled by Discovery's biggest shareholder," *Daily Mail*, February 28, 2022, https://www.dailymail.co.uk/news/article-10561149/Chris-Licht-appointed-new-CNN-chief-replace-Zucker.html.

14 In 1591, this quote surfaces as, "If a man can be known as nothing else, then he may be known by his companions." H.H. Munro – "Sake" – repurposed it in 1912 in its present form, https://www.answers.com/Q/Who_said_a_man_is_known_by_the_company_he_keeps. There is also the view that this originated in an Aesop's Fable. See https://grammarist.com/proverb/a-man-is-known-by-the-company-he-keeps/.

15 See, for example, Kelsey Carolan, "Hawley says Greitens should drop out of Senate race amid abuse allegations," *The Hill*, March 21, 2022, https://thehill.com/homenews/campaign/599088-hawley-says-eric-greitens-should-drop-out-amid-abuse-allegations/. See also Grace Panetta, "McConnell privately said that the GOP 'caught a break' when new abuse allegations against Missouri Senate candidate Eric Greitens surfaced, report says," *Business Insider*, March 25, 2022, https://www.businessinsider.com/mcconnell-said-gop-caught-a-break-with-greitens-allegations-report-2022-3.

16 Mola Lenghi, "More than 3,000 prisoners released under First Step Act, CBS Evening News, July 19, 2019, https://www.cbsnews.com/news/first-step-act-thousands-released-from-prisons-halfway-houses-today-2019-07-19/.